Dedicated to J. Stanley Brown, C. E. Spicer, Dr. William Rainey Harper, the 1900-1901 Joliet Township High School Board of Trustees, and early JJC faculty members for pioneering the community college movement in Joliet, Illinois. Their commitment to a quality experience for students, their perseverance during challenging times, and their dedication to democratizing higher education opened the doors to affordable and accessible college education and the priceless opportunity for lifelong learning. These pioneer educators in Joliet, Illinois, transformed higher education in America, and people everywhere are forever in their debt.

PUBLICATION STAFF:

Author: Robert E. Sterling

Text Editors: Patrick Asher,
    Patrick McGuire, Sharon Peck

Project Editor: Robert E. Sterling

Book Design: Diane Kramer

Photo Editor: Michael Bruner

Publisher: G. Bradley Publishing

Sponsor: Joliet Junior College

ISBN-0-943963-81-8
PRINTED IN THE UNITED STATES OF AMERICA

JOLIET Junior College

1901 TO 2001:

A PICTORIAL HISTORY OF AMERICA'S OLDEST PUBLIC COMMUNITY COLLEGE

Robert E. Sterling

Joliet Junior College, Illinois Community College District 525

Table of Contents

Foreword

One hundred years have passed since J. Stanley Brown started a post-secondary educational program at Joliet Township High School that was the based on a concept developed and nurtured by Dr. William Rainey Harper, then President of the University of Chicago. While it is doubtful that either man fully understood the magnitude of this new creation we now call the community college, it has evolved into a truly unique segment of American education. With some 1200 community and technical colleges scattered across the country, millions of students use them as their points of access to higher education and to career and technical programs.

We at Joliet Junior College are proud that our college is the nation's oldest continuously operating community college. I am pleased that Dr. Robert Sterling, a retired Joliet Junior College historian, department chair, and the superb author of several other pictorial history works, agreed to write *Joliet Junior College, 1901 to 2001: A Pictorial History of America's Oldest*

Public Community College. The book captures the essence of the college as it grew from just six students into an institution that now serves close to eleven thousand credit students each year.

Dr. Sterling possesses a wonderful ability to weave narration around pictures in a manner that you feel as though you are experiencing the event or the examined time period first hand. Anyone who has ever been affiliated with the college will be particularly pleased with his work and will enjoy the book for many years to come as it is shared with family and friends. I extend my compliments to Dr. Sterling for an exceptional job of writing and illustration.

J. D. Ross, President
Joliet Junior College

Board of Trustees, 2001. **Seated:** Student Trustee Rosa Salazar, Chair Eleanor McGuan-Boza. **Standing:** Robert J. Wunderlich, Vice Chair Richard Dystrup, Secretary Jeffrey A. May. Not Pictured: Susan Block, David R. Cryer, Marilyn Hertko.

CHAPTER 1

The Founding and Formative Years
1893 to 1919

Joliet Junior College, the oldest public community college in the United States, is celebrating its centennial in 2001. The two individuals most instrumental in the formation of the college in Joliet and the beginning of the community college movement were J. Stanley Brown and Dr. William Rainey Harper. Brown was the superintendent of Joliet Township High School in 1901, and Harper was president of the University of Chicago. The setting was a spacious, new township high school building completed in 1901 and touted as one of the nation's most exemplary secondary schools with a superior faculty, modern equipment, and ample space to accommodate students enrolled in college-level classes. Beginning with six "postgraduate" students in the arts and sciences and twenty-five students enrolled in a two-year normal academic program for elementary teachers, the junior college remained affiliated with the high school until 1967, when it became a separate Class I community college.

J. Stanley Brown came to Joliet in 1893 to serve as principal of Joliet High School.[1] When he arrived, the nation's economy was temporarily suffering the sluggish effects of the Depression of 1893. The new principal found that many of his students came from working class families and, if they finished high school, they probably would not go on to college. However, Brown understood the value of a college education and encouraged students to continue beyond their high school diploma. In a public speech, he stated that "since September, 1894, some continuous effort has been made to inspire pupils to continue their work in some higher institutions after graduating here."[4] Unfortunately, the expense of leaving home and attending college was beyond the financial reach of many students. Brown placed so much value on college education, however, that he occasionally made personal loans to students to enable them to pursue a college degree.[5]

Under the leadership and influence of its new administrator, Joliet High School experienced a dramatic growth in enrollment, as well as a significant improvement in the quality of instruction. The number of students attending the school nearly tripled between 1893 and 1901, increasing from 208 to 600.[6] Soon after his arrival, Brown began upgrading the curriculum, perhaps as early as 1894, to include courses with college-level content. He also encouraged universities to award college credit or advanced standing to Joliet students who had taken these more rigorous courses in such subjects as physics, chemistry, and mathematics.[7] Responding to a letter from Brown, Professor Francis W. Kelsey of the University of Michigan wrote the following on June 2, 1896:

I am much pleased to learn that you have taken your students over more than the required preparatory work. If you will kindly give to those who come to the University of Michigan a certificate to the effect that the extra work has been well done, I will see that advanced credit is given for it.[8]

Two years later, Professor Joseph H. Drake visited Joliet and later wrote to Brown that he was favorably impressed with the high school curriculum and confirmed that the University of Michigan was "glad to give some advanced credit for work done in this way."[9] In 1901, J. Stanley Brown also stated that "our own great University of Illinois . . . admits our recommended graduates into the sophomore class without conditions and enables them to complete a four years' course in three years."[10] It is abundantly clear that shortly after Brown became principal, students were able to earn college credit by taking "postgraduate" courses at Joliet High School. Thus, Brown not only encouraged his students to go on to college, but he made it possible for them to gain advanced standing in certain universities with which he had negotiated transfer agreements.

Another Joliet educator who was partially responsible for initiating college-level coursework in the local high school was the head of the Science Department, Chauncey E. Spicer. He not only taught some of the advanced science classes, but also served as Brown's assistant. Spicer and Brown were different in many ways, but their administrative styles seemed to complement each other. Miss Elizabeth Barns, a longtime faculty member under Spicer and Brown, observed:

Dr. Brown had the widest vision on educational matters. He was not afraid of trying things. He had a vision of the future. With C. E. Spicer, they made a perfect team. Mr. Spicer was a person who had a perfect genius for detail and he would take Dr. Brown's vision and work it into a program. The two of them worked together very well.[11]

Although Brown deserves considerable credit for starting the community college in Joliet, he sought no plaudits for the accomplishment, but deferred to his friend at the University of Chicago, President William Rainey Harper, as the true visionary and architect of the junior college. At the National Conference of Junior Colleges in 1920, in a presentation on "The Growth and Development of Junior Colleges in the United States," Brown modestly stated that "Joliet takes no credit for it, but concedes it to the man of vision, Dr. William R. Harper, the first president of the University of Chicago."[12]

From its beginning in 1892, Harper divided his own university into the Academic College (freshmen and sophomores) and the University College (juniors and seniors). Four years later, the lower level Academic College was given a new name: "Junior College."[13] It appears that Harper was actually prepared to drop the freshman and sophomore years altogether from the University of Chicago and to rely on small colleges and public high schools to cover the first two years of college. Harper believed that "the work of the freshman and sophomore years is only a continuation of the academy or high school work. It is a continuation, not only of the subject-matter studied, but of the methods employed. It is not until the end of the sophomore year that university methods of instruction may be employed to advantage."[14]

Although Harper is often considered the "father of the junior college," he was not the first educator to embrace the idea of separating freshman and sophomore-level college work from the university experience; he was, however, in the unique position as the founder of a university to refine and implement the idea. Since the middle of the nineteenth century, American educators had been comparing unfavorably the educational system in the United States with that of other countries, especially Germany. In 1851, Henry P. Tappan, who would become president of the University of Michigan the following year, suggested that American secondary schools should become more like the Gymnasia in Germany by preparing students for the university's true work of specialization and research. Likewise, in his 1869 inaugural address as president of the University of Minnesota, William Watts Folwell advocated the transfer to secondary schools of "those studies which now form the body of work for the first two years in our ordinary American colleges." Folwell believed that freshman and sophomore college students were not mature enough to do university work. He further articulated this idea in a presentation at the 1875 meeting of the National Education Association: "The work of the first two years of the college is the work of the secondary school, and there it can be done most efficiently and economically. Turn this work over to the high school, and that institution has at once its function, and the whole of it."[15]

The ideas of Tappan and Folwell and other early educators foreshadowed the work of William Rainey Harper at the University of Chicago. Harper was not only a man of vision but a person of action. Having differentiated between "junior college" and "senior college" work at his own institution, Harper began bringing high schools into the discussion of educational reorganization. In order to promote dialogue and coordinated programming between his university and regional high schools, in November 1892 Harper began holding regular conferences in Chicago to which selected secondary schools were invited. These meetings eventually became known as "Conferences of the Affiliated and Cooperating Schools." After his arrival in Joliet in 1893, Brown became an active participant in these meetings. In 1899, the University of Chicago approved Joliet High School as a cooperating school and began awarding students credit for advanced work that was certified by their high school teachers.[16]

Brown and Harper had a lot in common and enjoyed a personal friendship. Both had been born in Ohio and had an association with the Baptist-based Denison University, Brown as a student and graduate in 1889 and Harper as a faculty member from 1876 to 1879. Both were men of faith who were active in the Baptist denomination; they often met at Baptist conventions where they discussed education as well as religion. In fact, Brown's son, Dr. Grant Brown, recalled that his father and Harper roomed together at a National Baptist Convention and talked long into the night about how to make the first two years of college available to promising high school students with limited financial resources.[17]

As important as J. Stanley Brown, William Rainey Harper, and C. E. Spicer were to the origin of Joliet Junior College, there would have been no college in Joliet at the turn of the century if a new high school building had not been built. A recently enacted state law permitted the establishing of township high school districts, and on April 4, 1899, local voters approved the creation of the Joliet Township High School District by a vote of 2,725 to 329. Two months later in a special election, voters overwhelmingly approved (1,446 to 1) a proposition to select and purchase a site and to erect a new township high school. These important decisions made possible the expansion of the high school's existing postgraduate courses into a six-year high school program which included the first two years of college. The creation of the new township district in 1899 broadened the tax base sufficiently to fund the junior college in its infancy, and the building of a new high school in 1901 provided modern classrooms and laboratories for teaching freshman and sophomore-level college classes. The new Joliet Township High School Board of Trustees named J. Stanley Brown superintendent and supported his efforts to use the new building to expand the postgraduate courses into well-defined one and two-year programs, which eventually became known as Joliet Junior College.[19]

It is impossible to pinpoint the precise date when Joliet Junior College actually began. There was neither a legal charter filed nor an official resolution passed to mark the beginning of the formal two-year college program in Joliet. Although 1901 has been commonly accepted by many researchers as the year of the college's founding, others suggest 1902 as a more accurate date.[22] A few have even suggested that Joliet Junior College was not founded or established, but rather evolved from early postgraduate courses. Dr. Roosevelt Basler, for example, who served as superintendent of Joliet Township High School and Junior College from 1943 to 1945, stated:

> Such expressions as 'established,' 'formed,' and 'came into existence' convey a wholly erroneous impression concerning the conditions at Joliet. . . . The early beginnings of the Joliet Junior College were characterized by a slow, gradual, and evolutionary growth. In truth the college evolved – it was not 'established,' 'formed,' or begun at any particular date.[23]

A 1919 survey of junior colleges conducted by President Monroe Stowe of the University of Toledo in cooperation with the U. S. Bureau of Education similarly concluded that "Joliet Junior College seems to resemble Topsy, in that it has just grown."[24]

It is true that students at the high school had been taking advanced classes for college credit since the mid-1890s and that the number of classes accepted for advanced standing had been steadily growing. In fact, when the new township high school was dedicated, J. Stanley Brown informed his listeners that students had been successfully entering the University of Illinois as sophomores by taking appropriate freshman-level courses at the high school.[25] It appears, however, that Brown both expanded and organized these postgraduate classes into a coherent two-year program by the beginning of the second semester in January 1901. On December 4, 1900, Brown reported to the School Board that "five postgraduate students had been entered." He revised this a month later on January 7, 1901, when he reported "the enrollment of one additional post-graduate student" who would enter on February 1.[26]

These references to "entering" postgraduate students appear to suggest that the students were entering a specific program of study, not simply taking a variety of loosely related postgraduate classes as had been the case in the past. Students at the high school had been taking advanced classes for college credit for several years, but this is the first such announcement by Superintendent Brown to the School Board regarding the enrollment of postgraduate students. Something had apparently changed; namely, a small group of high school graduates had enrolled in a two-year, college-level arts and science program. Some twenty years later at a meeting of the National Conference of Junior Colleges, J. Stanley Brown stated that "a junior college was started at Joliet with five or six students. . . . The development at Joliet was slow at first, but it was continuous, and it did not stop for a moment."[27] This comment by Brown suggests, first, that he believed the college had, indeed, been "started" and, second, that it began with the six postgraduate students who entered in the spring semester of 1901.

Another two-year program, a normal course for training elementary teachers, was started eight months later in the fall semester of 1901. Superintendent Brown outlined the course requirements at a July Board meeting and in September informed the Board that twenty-five students were enrolled in the program.[28] Brown had long been interested in teacher training and had served as president of a normal school in Oregon before coming to Joliet. Also, when he left Joliet, Brown assumed the presidency of Northern Illinois Normal School, now known as Northern Illinois University. Prior to the introduction of the normal course in 1901, teachers could become certified to teach simply by passing a county examination, even without a high school diploma. Joliet grade schools, however, were becoming more selective, and people who had both a diploma and normal school training were more likely to find teaching positions than those without.

By the fall of 1902, the two postgraduate programs were growing; school records indicate that twenty-two students were enrolled in the postgraduate arts and science program alone. As a matter of clarification as well as a statement of school policy, the Board of Trustees passed a resolution on December 3, 1902, stating that "graduates of the High School may take Post Graduate Work without any additional cost." Township taxpayers were, thus, fully funding the first two years of college for a growing number of Joliet Township High School graduates. This decision was made quietly by Brown and his Board without any public fanfare or front page stories in the local press.[29]

J. Stanley Brown's stature as a respected educator continued to grow when he was appointed by William Rainey Harper in the fall of 1902 to chair an important committee established at the annual Conference of Affiliated and Cooperating Schools. The general theme of the conference was educational reorganization. Harper framed the subject in the form of four propositions, the second of which was "to extend the work of the secondary school to include the first two years of college work." He then appointed three committees of seven members each to study the matter of school reorganization from the perspective of the elementary school, the secondary school, and the college, respectively. The members of these three committees were known collectively as the Committee of Twenty-One. Not surprisingly, Harper appointed his friend J. Stanley Brown, superintendent of a nearby high school with an extended six-year program already in place, to chair the committee examining reorganization from the viewpoint of the secondary school.[30]

The three committees presented their reports the following year at the general conference in November 1903 where the subject of school reorganization was thoroughly discussed. Brown submitted a very favorable report from his committee, heartily endorsing Harper's ideas. He mentioned that in the past five years, high schools had been improving their curricula and that some had "increased the work to five or six years." Although he made no direct reference to his own high school in Joliet, he did state that "these movements have gone on, are going on, without any blare of trumpet." Brown made it clear that despite the reservations and dissenting opinions voiced by a few committee members, the conference attendees were not debating some futuristic idea, but rather an educational plan already in existence. In fact, the suggested program of required and elective coursework for the extended fifth and sixth years of high school presented by Brown to the conference almost mirrored the program then in place at Joliet Township High School. In his report, Brown also discussed some of the practical benefits of adding the first two years of college to secondary schools, arguments still made today, one hundred years later, in support of community college education. Some high school graduates cannot go away to college for financial reasons, said Brown, and others should not go away because they need "close magisterial and parental supervision."[31]

Although William Rainey Harper influenced—and perhaps inspired—J. Stanley Brown, there is no evidence that Harper played a direct role in establishing America's oldest community college in Joliet. Harper and his staff certainly did not use a "'hard-sell' approach" in persuading the local School Board to establish a junior college, as one educator has suggested.[33] Rather, Brown and his assistant, C. E. Spicer, appear to have been the prime movers in the creation of the college. Although Harper lived less than fifty miles away, he neither visited Joliet nor offered any personal assistance in shaping Board policy or public opinion with respect to the high school's postgraduate program. In fact, Harper's correspondence files contain no indication that he directly assisted or personally advised Brown during the critical years of the college's infancy.

C. E. Spicer enjoyed an excellent vantage point for commenting on William Rainey Harper's role in founding Joliet Junior College. Spicer came to Joliet in 1891, two years before Brown arrived, and remained until 1937, eighteen years after Brown's departure. He developed and taught the earliest postgraduate courses in physics and chemistry, chaired the Science Department, and served as Brown's assistant at both the old school and the new Joliet Township High School. Spicer was so highly regarded by the Board of Trustees that he was twice offered the position of superintendent. He refused both times, preferring instead to remain in the classroom during the school year and to spend the summer months in northern Michigan at the family cottage in the resort town of Frankfort.[35] As to the origin and early development of the junior college, it was Spicer's view that

> *Dr. Harper's contribution to the establishment of our junior college came after, and not before, the fundamental courses therein had been functioning. What we then needed was recognition from established colleges, without which we could not have survived. He and members of his faculty heartily endorsed our efforts. . ... Many other colleges also granted us such credits, but none perhaps so willingly as did the University of Chicago. Some seemed to think that we were trespassing on their territory. . . . Probably our effort would have failed of success had we not received his 'recognition,' and, too, we would have failed, had not our efforts successfully responded to an economic community need.*[36]

In commenting on the origin of the junior college in Joliet, Spicer underscored the importance from the very beginning of the college meeting the community's economic needs. He recognized that not all postgraduate students would transfer to a university to complete their college degrees. Some students lacked the ability, interest, resources, or parental support to continue beyond the lower-level college courses offered at the high school. For them, however, there were jobs available in the ranks of middle management in the many businesses and smokestack industries in and around Joliet. Although the early one- and two-year college programs were steeped in the arts and sciences and included no technical training, there were, nonetheless, mid-level employment opportunities available in the local economy for people with some college education.

Postgraduate courses in physics, chemistry, and surveying were sometimes taken selectively by employees or prospective employees of local business and industry. Spicer considered these courses to be the "nucleus from which the junior college grew. They were the ones that could be made immediately remunerative to students . . .. Of the three, chemistry was the one that furnished the largest amount of employment."[37] Although Spicer believed that the college's early success was due, in part, to its ability to meet an economic need in the Joliet community, it is clear that the predominant purpose of the college program in these early years was to meet the needs of students transferring into baccalaureate programs at senior institutions. However, the school did meet the vocational needs of Joliet's industrial society through a variety of lower-level courses taught in the high school evening program, which began in 1912.[38] Although Superintendent Brown spent countless hours negotiating transfer credits for college-bound students, there is no evidence that he ever met with local business leaders to determine whether postgraduate courses were providing students with skills appropriate for the workplace. All such efforts to tailor college courses to meet the needs of the business community would happen later in the school's history.

During its formative years, the college-level program enjoyed the full support of the High School Board of Trustees, five respected community leaders with progressive views on the importance of quality education. They seemed willing to follow Superintendent Brown's lead both in erecting a state-of-the-art school building and in extending the high school program to include the first two years of college. Like Brown, they quietly made momentous decisions without seeking headlines or public acclaim. In fact, Board minutes reflect very little mention of the postgraduate program, except for an occasional reference by Brown to enrollment data.

Although J. Stanley Brown often spoke at professional conferences out of town and wrote articles in educational journals about the junior college in Joliet, neither he nor his Board of Trustees publicized the college in the local media. One searches Joliet newspapers in vain for either college advertising or feature stories on early college activities. There appears to have been a conscious effort by school officials to permit the college program to develop slowly, unaided—or perhaps unhindered—by local public promotion.

Brown was well aware of the potential adverse reaction by taxpayers to the use of local high school unds to support college-level education. At a 1903 conference where Brown was a presenter, a professor from the University of Michigan asserted, "I do not believe there is a board of education in Michigan that would incur such a risk."[39] A 1906 editorial in the *School Review* sounded a similar note, suggesting that "public high schools are likely to encounter considerable difficulty in doing this because of the increased cost involved for necessary equipment and teaching staff."[40] Ira D. Yaggy, a contemporary observer who served on Brown's first postgraduate advisory committee and later became the first dean of the junior college, affirmed that the low-keyed approach was purposely taken because "Dr. Brown was very much afraid that the taxpayers might object to using high school funds for college work if it were publicized too much."[41]

Sometimes overlooked by historians and researchers in their analyses of Joliet Junior College and the reasons why it survived to become the nation's oldest public community college are the success stories of the early postgraduate students. Many of them not only went on to earn college degrees, but they returned to Joliet and made significant contributions to the community. They became successful teachers, doctors, business people, and community leaders, bearing daily witness to the quality of the institution and the importance of supporting it.

Superintendent Brown took a special interest in his postgraduate students and for several years served as their personal advisor. He spent many hours articulating the postgraduate courses with colleges and universities and developing a list of classes approved for transfer credit by these senior institutions. Brown addressed the problem in his report, "Present Development of Secondary Schools According to the Proposed Plan," presented at the fall 1904 conference at the University of Chicago. He said that students taking advanced work in high school were "continually asking: 'How much credit shall I receive for this when I enter college?'" Noting the perplexity of the problem, Brown advocated the development of a common standard. Citing his own experience in Joliet, he stated that various colleges and universities were awarding credit for postgraduate courses in history, literature, science, mathematics, and foreign language, "but at no institution of the higher order have all these subjects been accredited."[42] The task of advising students to ensure a smooth transfer with no loss of credit was, indeed, time-consuming. In 1912, Brown appointed a committee of three faculty members to advise postgraduate students. Four years later the advisors became known as the Junior College Committee.[43]

Although few records exist from the early phase of the formative years, it appears that the postgraduate students of the early twentieth century were similar, in many ways, to college students today. Outside the classroom, they enjoyed a variety of physical, social, and cultural activities and established meaningful and memorable traditions. In an article on the "Evolution of the Joliet Junior College," Thomas M. Deam, Assistant Superintendent of Joliet Township High School, remarked that until 1914 the "'postgraduate' department of the high school was establishing itself and building up traditions necessary to crystallize itself into a recognized unit."[44]

An early issue of the *Joliet Township High School Bulletin,* devoted exclusively to the history of the junior college, observed that the postgraduates of 1905-1906 already possessed a "group conscious[ness]" as they "presented plays, participated in athletics, held banquets, and recorded their 'deeds' in the high school annual." The publication went on to note that "these extra-curricular activities were without question a factor of considerable importance in the growth of the junior college." A Joliet high school teacher, who had been a postgraduate student in 1909, wrote in the same *Bulletin* that the early postgraduate students "enjoyed much of the spirit of the present J.J.C."[45]

Athletic activities were also important in developing a cohesiveness among postgraduate students, both men and women. Some of the earliest pictures in the brief postgraduate section of the high school yearbooks are photographs of athletic teams. Competition was limited, at first, to other teams within the high school and postgraduate program. In 1916, however, the "Little Six" basketball conference was organized, and in January 1917 the Joliet squad began playing teams from Crane, De Paul, Lane, Lewis, and Wheaton. This is apparently when the school colors purple and white were selected. Under "Junior College Notes" in the 1917 issue of *The J,* the writer expressed confidence that "at the end of the season the boys wearing purple and white will emerge victorious."[47]

In 1916, postgraduate students at Joliet Township High School shed the image and aura of being advanced high school students; they came to be known thereafter as "collegians" and their school as "Joliet Junior College." Superintendent Brown and members of the advisory committee met with the postgraduate students at the beginning of the 1916 school year and "nearly every remark that was made emphasized the fact the students present were . . . Collegians."[48] In the fall issue of *The J,* under the subheading "The Passing of the P. G.," Edna O. Knowlton noted the change:

The scientific world has been lately electrified by the sudden disappearance of a species long familiar, and the appearance, in the stead thereof, of an entirely new type. I refer to the case of the P. G. . . . Its place has been taken by the Collegian, a new form, possessed of all the traits necessary for a successful animal . . . .[49]

The transformation from postgraduate to collegian occurred just after the college program had survived its only real threat during the formative period. The president of the School Board announced in 1915 that increasing high school and college enrollments had created a pressing need for more classrooms. One of the suggestions offered by a Board member to resolve the problem of space was "the non-admission of postgraduates."[50] If austere measures were necessary, the college program was apparently one of the frills that might be cut. Fortunately, however, the Board decided instead to rent space temporarily in nearby churches and to support a building program. Voters approved the expansion plan in 1916, and when the new addition was finished in 1917, it was known as the junior college division. Not only had the PGs (postgraduates) become collegians, but they now had a section of the building designated primarily for their use. They had their own entrance, their own classrooms, and their own assembly room; they were also permitted to move throughout the new college addition without securing hall passes. This "new era of independence" made the junior college even more attractive to graduating high school seniors.[51]

During the latter stage of the college's formative period, several other significant developments occurred. In 1917, Brown worked with the North Central Association of Colleges and Secondary Schools to secure accreditation for Joliet Junior College.[52] In the same year, the State Examining Board approved JJC's normal school credits for certification without examination; this meant that stu-

dents who completed the college's two-year teacher training program would receive teaching certificate without taking the county exam. Then, after success fully teaching for one year, they could upgrade their certificate with the approval of the county superin tendent.[53] The following year, in 1918, Joliet Junior College held its first formal graduation ceremony with Superintendent J. Stanley Brown proudly awarding diplomas to twenty-one students.

These landmark developments of 1917-1918 were tempered, however, by World War I and its impact on the college. In the "Junior College Notes" of *The J* in October 1918, it was pointed out that almost all of the male students had "heeded the patriotic call" by enrolling in the S.A.T.C. (Student Army Training Corps) and would soon be leaving for training camps at several different colleges and universities. Five female students also responded to the wartime need by entering nurses' training hospitals. Those who remained in "Dr. Brown's Seminary for Young Women," it was noted, would have more time for "intensive work." However they, too, got involved in the war effort by selling War Savings Stamps, volunteering with the Red Cross, and assisting at the registration board.[54]

The end of an era came in 1919 when J. Stanley Brown submitted his resignation. There had been growing criticism regarding the cost of operating the high school, especially administrative costs. The local newspaper carried a front-page story by columnist Jack Thorne questioning the school's comparatively high tax rate. Interestingly, there was no mention made of the junior college and its free tuition for all graduates of Joliet Township High School. Four days later, the same newspaper informed its readers that the School Board had granted Brown a month's leave to undertake an assignment in Washington, D. C.[55] Then, a few days later at the May 20 Board meeting, J. Stanley Brown presented his "conditional resignation," to take effect August 1.[56] Although it was rumored that he had been offered the presidency of Northern Illinois Normal School in DeKalb, Brown went to the nation's capital to direct the Treasury Department's Thrift and Savings Campaign. While in Washington, Brown sent his official resignation to the Board, which was accepted on July 11. Following a short stint in Washington, Brown did indeed accept the presidency at Northern, where he remained from 1919 to 1927.[57]

Although J. Stanley Brown departed Joliet Junior

College under a cloud of criticism, he left behind an impressive record of achievement. Under his leadership, an imposing new township high school had been built that rivaled many small colleges in size and amenities. Today, 100 years later, the building still serves Joliet students as one of two high school campuses, an enduring testament to the quality and durability of the structure. One can only wonder how many other high schools built at the turn of the century have crumbled in disrepair or disappeared from the cityscape. Brown's most significant legacy, however, was the role he played in introducing postgraduate courses at the high school in the mid-1890s, expanding and organizing them into a two-year program in 1901, quietly nurturing and shaping this educational innovation during its formative period, and working with North Central Association to achieve accreditation for Joliet Junior College in 1917. When Brown left Joliet in 1919, few, if any, paid tribute to his accomplishments or celebrated his tremendous achievement in giving form and substance to William Rainey Harper's educational vision. Joliet Junior College served as a model to educators and legislators throughout the nation as they began developing community colleges.

J. Stanley Brown retired in 1927, after serving eight years as president of Northern Illinois Normal School. He now had more time for his family and enjoyed long visits with his three sons, including Grant, who lived in Joliet. He also looked forward to relaxing at Grant's summer home in Frankfort, Michigan. This visionary educator died in September 1939 while vacationing there; he was brought back to Joliet for burial in Oakwood Cemetery.[58] Once again, local leaders failed to pay tribute to Brown's significant and historic role in launching the community college movement in the United States. Today, in 2001, J. Stanley Brown casts a much longer shadow over the sweep of educational history than he did at his passing in 1939. From the vantage point of one hundred years, especially looking back over the dramatic growth of community colleges in recent decades, educators and historians are perhaps in a much better position today to recognize and appreciate the pioneer work of J. Stanley Brown.

J. Stanley Brown was originally from Ohio, where he had graduated from Denison University in 1889 at the age of twenty-six with an A.B. degree in classical languages. Prior to his appointment in Joliet, he had been a department chair and instructor of Latin and Greek at Blandville College in Kentucky and president of Arlington College in the same state. His career path then took him to the Northwest, where he served for one year as president of a state normal school in Oregon. During his early years as both a student and an educator, Brown developed an understanding of the plight of students who possessed the ability but lacked the resources to attend college. Following his own graduation from high school, Brown had to work for three years as a rural school teacher in order to save enough money to attend Denison.[2]

The College Community—Joliet in 1893

Located forty miles southwest of Chicago, Joliet was an important transportation and industrial center in northern Illinois. Both the Des Plaines River and the Illinois and Michigan Canal provided the city with the means of transporting people and products by water. In the 1880s, however, the river and cana were eclipsed by rails and steam. Joliet's railroad network extended in all directions and included th Rock Island, Chicago and Alton, Santa Fe, Michiga Central, and Elgin, Joliet and Eastern Railroads.

Looking north on Chicago Street from the Jefferson Street intersection in 1895, this is how the business district looked when J. Stanley Brown began his administrative duties at Joliet High School. The principal modes of transportation were bicycles, horse-drawn carriages, and the streetcar. The high curbs, rough roads sprinkled with horse pollution, and unsightly rows of utility poles are visual reminders of the late nineteenth century cityscape.

This view of the Des Plaines River in 1895 shows the old stone bridge at Jefferson Street. The Illinois and Michigan Canal ran through Joliet on the west side of the river. The upper gate of the guard lock on the I & M Canal can be seen at the west end (right side) of the bridge. Hidden behind the clump of trees are the locktender's house and the lower basin.

From a town of about 2,500 people in 1850, Joliet had grown into a city of some 23,000 in 1890 and 30,000 in 1900. Not only had the city's population increased substantially by the turn of the century, but it also had become more ethnically diverse. Newcomers to the region were attracted primarily by job opportunities in Joliet's limestone quarries, its steel mill and related industries, and the EJ&E Railroad.[3]

With Van Buren Street in the foreground and Jefferson Street beyond, this rooftop photograph provides an expansive view of the maze of railroad tracks in the downtown area. Indeed, several major carriers provided Joliet with freight and passenger service. With so many rail lines converging and crossing city streets, it is not surprising that local leaders pressed the railroads to relocate and elevate their tracks, an immense project undertaken in 1908.

Often called the "City of Stone," Joliet rests on a thick bed of limestone, which gave rise to a thriving quarry industry in the latter part of the nineteenth century. By 1890, twenty-five stone companies, including the one pictured here, employed some 1,500 people and did $1.5 million in business annually. Joliet limestone was used to build local houses, churches, schools, stores, factories, and the state prison. It was also shipped by water and rail throughout the Middle West for use in building such structures as the state capitol buildings in Illinois and Michigan, the Lincoln Monument in Springfield, the Rock Island Arsenal, and numerous county jails and courthouses.

Also known as the "City of Steel," Joliet was a major steel-producing center for many years. The original plant had two blast furnaces for reducing iron ore into pig iron, often called crude iron. In the mid-1870s, Bessemer converters were installed to produce high quality steel. The Joliet plant was a primary supplier of steel rails for companies extending railroad service into western states and territories. When J. Stanley Brown came to Joliet in 1893, the steel mill was the community's largest employer, boasting a payroll of some 2,000 people.

The Elgin, Joliet and Eastern Railway (EJ&E) ran from Waukegan, Illinois to northern Indiana in a 130-mile arc around the city of Chicago at a distance of about 40 miles from the downtown area. The railroad provided freight service for industrial customers in the area, but it also offered other lines an interchanging or bridging service to avoid the traffic and congestion of Chicago. "Around Chicago – Not Through It" was an advertising slogan of the EJ&E Railway. Here a group of employees gathered to pose for a picture on Engine 589. In many ways, the labor force at both the steel mill and the EJ&E Railway resembled an ethnic "salad bowl," a mix of various nationalities that came to the Joliet area looking for economic well-being and social acceptance. J. Stanley Brown found that many of his students at Joliet High School were first or second-generation Americans.

Old Joliet High School

By 1899, the old Joliet High School had become so crowded that hallways and closets were being used for classrooms. When a representative from the University of Michigan visited Joliet in 1898 to evaluate post-graduate courses for transfer credit, he remarked on these conditions in a follow-up letter to Brown: "The school as a whole made a favorable impression on both Dr. Reed and myself, tho' we both felt you were carrying a heavy handicap in having to work in such an unsuitable building."[18]

Dr. William Rainey Harper

Born in Ohio in 1856 of Scotch-Irish parents, William Rainey Harper entered Muskingum College at age ten. He graduated at fourteen years of age and presented a speech in Hebrew as part of the graduation ceremony. Too young by his parent's standards to be sent off to graduate school, he worked in his father's store, taught a college course in Hebrew, and organized a community band during the next few years. At age seventeen he entered Yale as a graduate student and received his Ph.D. before his nineteenth birthday.

During the next several years, Harper pursued a career in teaching that took him to colleges in Tennessee, Ohio, and Illinois. He became known as a gifted scholar, teacher, and administrator, and in 1886 Yale offered the thirty-year-old Harper an endowed professorship. Five years later, he was lured away from Yale by the offer of the presidency of the University of Chicago. With the financial backing of John D. Rockefeller, Harper had nearly a free hand in building this new university.

As president of the University of Chicago, Dr. Harper began implementing and promoting an educational plan that included the concept that the primary responsibilities of a university are specialization and research and that the first two years of college are essentially preparatory. Other college educators had earlier espoused this view, but Harper was in the ideal position to implement it. The idea that high schools could offer their graduating seniors lower-level college work eventually found acceptance among secondary school educators like J. Stanley Brown in Joliet.

Joliet Township High School, 1901 – "The Pride of Joliet"

At the dedication of the new Joliet Township High School building on April 4, 1901, each speaker lavishly praised the design and durability of the structure. Board member Henry Leach described the imposing new structure as a "lasting monument to the progressive spirit of a wide-awake community." He went on to prophetically suggest that the building would be "standing in excellent condition one hundred years hence." The architect who designed the school, F. S. Allen, characterized its general style as Gothic but with a flat roof. At a total cost of $220,382 for both the property and fur-

nished building, the School Board had spared no expense in providing Joliet Township students with the most modern high school imaginable. Edward S. Draper, President of the University of Illinois, was applauded heartily when he described the structure as "the finest high school building in America."[20]

Built of Joliet limestone with Bedford trim, the new building had eighty-seven rooms. The hallway floors and wainscoting, as well as the stair treads, were made of Vermont marble accented with darker Tennessee marble. The classroom floors were con-

Facing Jefferson Street to the south and bounded by Eastern Avenue on the west and Herkimer Street on the east, Joliet Township High School (pictured below) was one of the finest school buildings in America at the turn of the century. In this view of the school from the southwest, the Eastern Avenue Baptist Church can be seen on the left, beyond the utility pole and the Porter Brewery delivery wagon. The new building was frequently visited by architects, school board members, and college representatives looking for ideas in school design and construction.

The outer office pictured in the photo on the left served as both a faculty room and administrative reception area. Just outside Superintendent J. Stanley Brown's office was a small switchboard that operated the school telephones; the city telephone can be seen nearby hanging on the wall. Also, located here in the outer office was the master clock that controlled all of the clocks and bells in the school.

structed of maple, while the doors and entrances were crafted of oak by a Swiss wood carver. Special care had been taken to install the most modern heating and ventilation systems. The switchboard in the central office provided telephone contact between the superintendent and teachers in forty different rooms. A master clock regulated all the secondary clocks throughout the building and also could be programmed to ring bells that signaled the end of class periods. C. E. Spicer, head of the Science Department, was especially proud of the science laboratories, the quality of which surpassed labs found in most small colleges across America. The new high school even had an assembly hall that seated fifteen hundred people, nearly three times more than the school's enrollment in 1901. Judge A. O. Marshall, President of the School Board, captured the feeling of those at the dedication ceremony when he described the new township high school as "the pride of Joliet and a monument to the liberality and enterprise of its people."[21]

The physiography laboratory contained the latest maps, globes, charts, and other materials necessary for the study of physical geography. The demonstration table in the front of the room was equipped with gas, water, electricity, steam, and compressed air.

Four rooms, including the lab pictured here, were devoted to the study of physics. At each of the eight heavy oak tables were four student workstations furnished with lockers, adjustable supports, gas, and electric current. The teacher's fully-equipped demonstration table was positioned at the front of the room. Along some of the walls were stone shelves supported by the exterior walls of the building; these provided a stable support for the lab's delicate instruments. Also, permanently installed on the walls were adjustable pendulum supports. Another feature of the room was an arc light in a brass case with adjustable focusing lenses that could be used in experiments with light. C. E. Spicer taught some of the earliest college-level courses in this laboratory.

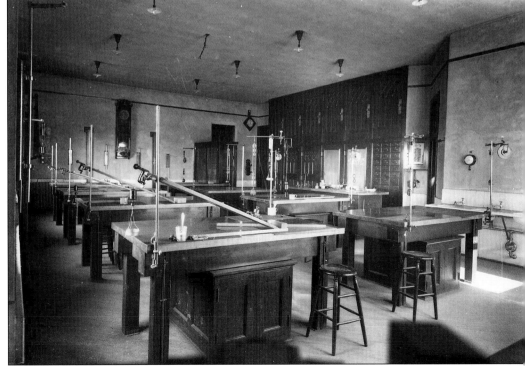

The chemistry department had three rooms, namely a lecture room, classroom, and the laboratory pictured here. This lab could accommodate thirty-two students, eight at each of the four tables. Built of oak with plate glass tops, the tables provided students with pneumatic troughs, hoods, bottle racks, gas, water, electricity, and drawers and lockers for personal storage. The chemistry lab was the envy of visiting science teachers who toured the new building.

Students were exposed to a variety of artwork throughout the building, including the piece seen here. The high school class of 1901 donated as a memorial this copy of the well-known statue "The Wrestlers." Located on the landing near the main stairway, the art piece attracted the attention of students and visitors alike. Following the example of the building's first graduating class, other classes likewise raised money and presented their own memorials to the school which included such gifts as paintings of old Joliet, a stage curtain, a copy of the Parthenon frieze, and statues or busts of Washington, Lincoln, and Louis Jolliet.

Many future teachers in the normal course did their student teaching at the smallest public school in Joliet, Irving School on South Richards Street. The principal was the only full-time employee in this two-room building, which housed only the first and second grades. Under the principal's supervision, eight students did their practice teaching at the school each semester, four in the morning and four in the afternoon, with two student teachers assigned to each grade. The children who attended Irving School came primarily from the Salem Orphan's Home.

A FIVE-YEAR COURSE

First Year – Latin, Algebra, Greek and Roman History or Physiography, English.

Second Year – Latin, Plane Geometry, Mediaeval and Modern History or Botony, English.

Third Year – Latin, Advanced Algebra and Solid Geometry, English History, Physics, Literature.

Fourth Year – Latin, American History, Literature, Chemistry or Plane Trigonometry and College Algebra.

Fifth Year – Latin, German or French, Literature, Advanced Physics, Geology and Astronomy.

A SIX-YEAR COURSE

First Year – Latin, Physiography, Arithmetic, Greek and Roman History, English, Algebra.

Second Year – Latin, Botany, Mediaeval and Modern History, Drawing, English, Plane Geometry.

Third Year – Latin, Advanced Algebra, Solid Geometry, German, French or Spanish, English History, Literature, Physics.

Fourth Year – Latin, Plane Trigonometry and College Algebra, German, French or Spanish, American History, Literature, Chemistry.

Fifth Year – Latin, Literature, German, French or Spanish, Analytic Chemistry, Spherical Trigonometry and Advanced Botany, Zoology and Physiology.

Sixth Year – Latin or Literature, Analytic Geometry and Advanced Physics, Geology and Astronomy, Political Economy, Science of Government and Psychology, German, French or Spanish.[32]

C. E. Spicer played a key role in the founding and early development of Joliet Junior College. As Superintendent J. Stanley Brown's assistant, Spicer was heavily involved in the day-to-day operation of the school. In addition to teaching courses in physics and chemistry, he assisted Brown in implementing the postgraduate courses, which became the nucleus of the two-year college program. Spicer could be very stern when disciplining students and was known, on occasion, to lean over close to an unruly male and reprimand him while squeezing the boy's thigh with his vise-like grip. A combination of Spicer's demeanor and his powerful grip caused even the most disobedient culprit to leave the office with a vow of good behavior.[34]

Two of the best-known early students whose postgraduate credits permitted them to finish their university degrees in three years were Elizabeth Barns and Harry J. Atkinson. Both graduated from Joliet Township High School in 1902 and later returned to teach in the high school and junior college. Upon her graduation from Northwestern University in 1905, Barns began a 43-year teaching career in Joliet. She was chair of the Social Science Department when she retired in 1948. Atkinson graduated from the University of Illinois and in 1907 joined the faculty of Joliet Township High School. He was one of three faculty members who left Joliet during World War I to serve in the military. Atkinson returned to teach a variety of high school and college math classes; at his retirement in 1948 he was assistant superintendent.

In the center photo Harry Atkinson and Elizabeth Barns were honored in 1976 at a Joliet Junior College alumni banquet.

In 1912, J. Stanley Brown appointed Ira D. Yaggy, Virgil C. Lohr, and Celia Drew to serve on the first postgraduate advisory committee. The three advisors became known as the Junior College Committee in 1916. Yaggy remained on the committee until 1926, when he became the first dean of the junior college, a position he held until his retirement in 1947.

In 1907, the play *David Garrick* was presented by the high school Alumni Association to help raise money for a bust of Louis Jolliet to be placed over the south entrance of the new high school building. The cast was composed largely of postgraduate students who were enthusiastically applauded by a packed house. Most notably, "the appearance of Squire Chivy, when intoxicated, took the house by storm." The production was also a financial success with enough money being raised to complete the statue project. Postgraduates could point with pride to the likeness of the city's namesake over the school's main entrance, knowing they had played a significant role in funding the project.[46]

| Helen Schroeder | | Palma Gross | Lafayette Stocker | | William Miller | | Leonard Fredricks |
| Hugh Carson | | Robert Laraway | Lucille Norton | | | Russell Bigelow | | George Wel |

"David Garrick" Given by the Post-Graduates in 1907

The gymnasium was located in a separate building a block-and-a-half south of the high school on Richards Street. Physical training classes for both men and women were held during nine periods of the day, while afternoons and evenings were devoted to team practices and games. The gym's balcony could seat about four hundred spectators. Nearby there were two tennis courts and an athletic field for the outdoor sports of football, baseball, and track.

The 1909 women's postgraduate basketball team won the school championship by defeating the high school seniors 12 to 5. The PGs practiced for weeks in preparation for the contest and proudly wore their white uniforms as pictured here. Some members of the team had been playing together since their freshman year in high school. **Front Row:** Wilcox and Cowing. **Back Row:** Sackett, Mason, and Kelly.

23

Original Building

The 1917 addition to the high school increased the size of the building by about one-half. Added to the north side of the building along Herkimer Street, the new section was known as the "college division." The two photographs show the appearance of the east side of the building before and after the addition. On June 17, 1918, an open house was held with students conducting special demonstrations in classrooms and laboratories throughout the building. Guides were available to point out the new addition's distinctive features, which included paintings and statuary in corridors and rooms.

The new addition to the building in 1917 made it possible for the junior college to have its own assembly room pictured here. The shelves on the left wall held several hundred books, the nucleus of a collection that would soon become a separate college library. Although having their own space was an important step in creating a college atmosphere, students wanted even more of a college environment. For example, some wondered why their assembly room was furnished with long rows of fixed desks instead of tables and chairs.

1917 Addition

Custodians took special pride in keeping the building looking new. They are pictured here posing with feather dusters and brooms.

When J. Stanley Brown resigned in 1919, he left behind an impressive legacy of accomplishments. The new township high school was a tangible testament to his leadership as a builder, and the junior college program was an educational innovation that forever changed the character of higher education in America. For twenty-six years, Brown had been a familiar sight, working in his office at a rolltop desk.

During World War I, female students at JJC volunteered in a number of war-related organizations and activities including the Red Cross. Pictured here in a patriotic parade in September 1917 are Red Cross workers collecting money. Bystanders can be seen tossing money onto an outstretched bed sheet carried by volunteers in long white dresses with bright red sashes.

CHAPTER 2

Establishing a College Identity
1919 to 1939

C. E. Spicer was vacationing at his summer home in Frankfort, Michigan, when he learned that J. Stanley Brown had resigned as superintendent of Joliet Township High School and Junior College. The School Board offered the position to Spicer, who had ably served as Brown's assistant for the past twenty-six years. Even though a substantial salary increase accompanied the offer, Spicer declined. He was unwilling to give up teaching his science classes, chairing the Science Department, and spending his summer months in northern Michigan. Assistant Principal Ralph Bush also refused the superintendent's position. He, too, remained at the school as an administrator and history teacher until 1927 when he left to become a junior college dean in Long Beach, California.[1]

By the time Brown's resignation became effective on August 1, 1919, Dr. L. W. Smith was hired to fill the vacancy. Smith's experience as an undergraduate student was strikingly similar to that of his predecessor. Like Brown, Smith was from Ohio with a bachelor's degree from Denison University. And like Brown, he had found it necessary to work his way through college, thereby gaining an appreciation of affordable college education. Smith later continued his studies at the University of Chicago where he earned both a master's degree and a doctorate. Prior to accepting the Joliet position, he had been a teacher in three states, a school principal in Kankakee, Illinois, and most recently had served for eleven years as superintendent of Thornton Township High School in nearby Harvey, Illinois. While at Thornton, Smith gained notice for introducing vocational shop programs and agriculture into the school curriculum. Indeed, he was recognized throughout the state as an outstanding educator and was selected to serve as the first president of the Illinois High School Principals' Association. He was also an active member of the North Central Association of Secondary Schools and Colleges.[2]

Dr. L.W. Smith's administrative responsibilities in Joliet uniquely included a traditional high school program, a continuation school, vocational school, Americanization school, and night school, as well as

the nation's oldest junior college. When Smith arrived in 1919, he was surprised to learn that Joliet Junior College was better known in the educational community outside Joliet than it was in the district that financially supported it. Indeed, during the founding and early formative years, neither Superintendent Brown nor the School Board had publicized the junior college locally, presumably out of concern that township taxpayers might resist the added expense of freely providing the first two years of college to students in the high school district. By 1920, however, things were changing. The 1917 addition to the building was commonly known as the college division, and enrollments were on the increase, attributed, in part, to the return of World War I veterans. Besides, Joliet Junior College was no longer an educational experiment or novelty; the junior college movement was gaining momentum and acceptance across the nation.

During Smith's tenure as the chief administrator from 1919 to 1928, he expanded the college curriculum and actively promoted a separate and distinct identity for JJC even though the college continued to share facilities with the much larger township high school. By the end of his first year, Smith had authorized the printing of the first college catalog, the creation of a separate college library with a full-time librarian, the planning of a three-phase building expansion program, and the establishment of an office for the three-member Junior College Committee that registered and advised all college students.

The new catalog in 1920 outlined six college programs: literature and arts, science, engineering, pre-legal, pre-medical, and a special program for training teachers. Although they were patterned after the University of Illinois, the courses of study were broad enough to permit students to successfully transfer into almost any college or university. However, only students with an overall scholastic average of at least 80 percent were recommended for transfer. This first catalog reflected the early "feeder" and "weeder" functions of the college. JJC offered primarily parallel programs designed to feed transfer students into four-year coleges and universities while weeding out weaker students with an academic average under 80 percent.[3]

The creation of a separate college library in 1920 provided students a "pleasant, well-lighted room" where they could engage in "real study" as they pursued one of four degrees then being conferred: associate in arts, associate in science, associate in engineering, and associate in education.[4] Like other high school-based junior colleges, JJC's identity as a separate institution was slow to take shape. The new library, however, significantly enhanced the college atmosphere on campus. Also, the awarding of associate degrees at formal commencement exercises, which began in 1918, was an important reminder each year that students, indeed, were pursuing nationally-recognized college degrees and not simply taking advanced classes in a two-year high school extension program.

Under Smith's leadership during the 1920s, there were significant changes in the college curriculum as the institution's identity and purpose began evolving from "junior college" to "community college." During the formative years prior to World War I, J. Stanley Brown, Smith's predecessor, had concentrated on developing courses of study that paralleled the first two years of university work. Few other junior colleges existed, and it was important that students attending JJC receive full credit when transferring to four-year schools. Except for the two-year teacher-training program known as the normal course, the early emphasis clearly was on the transferability of JJC classes, especially in math and science. During this early period, the curriculum included pre-professional courses of study designed to prepare students to enter legal, medical, and engineering programs. In short, Joliet Junior College had been established primarily as a two-year upward extension of Joliet Township High School to prepare students to enter a university or professional school with junior class standing.

After World War I, junior colleges increased in number and gained greater acceptance among educators and the community at large. Post-war changes in the curriculum reflected a growing interest in the social sciences, new teaching methods, and the realization that the junior college should offer the local community more than college transfer courses. At JJC, for example, a modern European history class was introduced much like the one offered at the University of Illinois. The course at the junior college, however, was taught largely by students under the guidance of instructor Ralph Bush. A similar student-based teaching strategy was also used in sociology classes.[6] Furthermore, the school *Bulletin* and college catalogs of the mid-1920s marketed certain college programs as both transfer and terminal in nature. A new pre-commerce curriculum, as well as several variations of the engineering curriculum, was intended to prepare students either to enter the local job market or to continue studying for an advanced degree.[7] By 1931, the college curriculum had been expanded to include occupational courses specifically designed for non-transfer students. The school *Bulletin* announced that now there was "special emphasis also upon terminal courses, designed to train the many young people of Joliet whose school life is going to end when they leave Junior College."[8]

School publications underscored the college's success in attracting local high school graduates and preparing them to transfer to senior institutions or to find mid-level jobs in the Joliet area. Of the 348 graduates of Joliet Township High School in 1930, more than one hundred enrolled in the junior college; only thirty-three seniors chose some other college or university.[9] Joliet Junior College was becoming the kind of institution advocated in 1931 by Walter Crosby Eells in his highly regarded book, *The Junior College,* namely a "people's college." Eells encouraged junior colleges to become schools that "provide collegiate opportunity for the mass of high school graduates who can't, won't or shouldn't become university students."[10] The school *Bulletin* offered the following reasons for students to attend Joliet Junior College: its inexpensive cost, small class size, excellent teachers, the desire of parents to keep children in the home environment, and the college's new vocational courses.[11]

Follow-up studies of JJC students in the 1920s showed that increasing numbers of graduates were terminating their formal studies and looking for employment. For example, of the forty-five members of the graduating class of 1927, eighteen transferred to senior institutions, while twenty-one immediately went to work.[12] The college truly was in a period of transition from narrowly serving academically gifted students to more broadly training students for semi-professional jobs as well. A few college-level courses were even offered in the evening from 7:20 to 9:30 p.m. The only charge was an enrollment fee of $1, which was refunded if the student attended four-fifths of the class sessions.[13] Though JJC was not yet a comprehensive community college, it was moving steadily in that direction. Not only was it accessible, but the college was becoming adaptable and more relevant to students' diverse needs.

Soon after he arrived in Joliet, Superintendent Smith realized that an extensive building expansion program was necessary. Classrooms and laboratories were inadequate and crowded, enrollments were steadily climbing, and new programs were needed, especially in vocational training. The school was renting space in nearby churches and commercial buildings. The lunchroom was inconveniently located across the street, and the gymnasium was a block and a half away. A school traffic officer patrolled the busiest intersections, keeping an eye on students hurrying to off-campus buildings. Despite the comparatively small size of the junior college in relation to the school's other programs, Smith publicly announced that new college science labs and specially-equipped pre-engineering classrooms were needed. Without questioning the added expense of funding two years of college work, township voters approved the sale of $750,000 worth of bonds to fund phase one of the expansion plan.

Within five years of Dr. Smith's arrival, college enrollment had more than doubled. Unlike his predecessor, Smith boldly publicized the economic and academic advantages of attending the junior college. The message reached even students outside the district who enrolled in ever-increasing numbers. In fact, in the 1921-22 academic year, one-fifth of the freshman class was composed of non-resident students who paid a modest out-of-district tuition fee. Furthermore, a few Joliet students transferred back from the University of Illinois when they realized that the same courses could be taken free of charge at the junior college. The building expansion program was also an important factor in the growth of the college; it provided additional space to expand the curriculum, especially in the area of vocational training.[15]

Despite the college's positive image portrayed by Smith and other school officials, occasional rumors surfaced that some students had difficulty transferring junior college credits into senior institutions. Smith grew impatient with those who questioned the transferability of JJC courses. At a meeting of the School Board on November 15, 1926, the superintendent read letters from both the University of Illinois

and the University of Chicago certifying the validity and acceptability of JJC credits. The Board passed a motion to have the two letters published on the front page of the Joliet *Herald-News* in an effort to end the rumors of transfer problems.[16]

Superintendent Smith was very active in state and national organizations and knew how highly regarded Joliet Junior College was among the nation's educational leaders. He was anxious that Joliet residents understand the role of JJC in the junior college movement and that they share his pride in the institution's reputation. Smith informed district residents that the college was often studied by national educators and prominently mentioned in reports on the role of junior colleges in higher education. He stated that "since Joliet Junior College has thus established a precedent for other institutions of its kind and is a vigorous exponent of the junior college idea, it should not be without honor in its own country, and in its own house, and among its own kindred." At the time, few Joliet residents fully understood and appreciated JJC's historic role in the junior college movement. Indeed, by the late 1920s, some ninety other junior colleges were patterned, to a large extent, after the pioneer institution in Joliet.[17]

Dr. L. W. Smith supported students in their effort to establish a college atmosphere even though the campus was devoted primarily to educating some 3,000 high school students. Despite their circumstances in the 1920s, the few hundred JJC students did make considerable progress in developing a separate identity and cohesiveness, largely through a variety of extracurricular activities. Both intercollegiate and intramural athletics provided men and women opportunities to compete in sports. Men's basketball and baseball teams vied for conference championships against five other schools in the Northern Illinois Junior College Conference. JJC sometimes fielded track, tennis, and golf teams as well. Initially, women participated in intramural contests in a few sports, such as basketball, baseball, and field hockey. The formation of the Women's Athletic Association (W.A.A.) in the fall of 1925, however, greatly expanded athletic and social opportunities for female students. Under the guidance of faculty sponsor Phoebe Henderson Kirby, women's activities eventually included track, tennis, horseback riding, swimming, rifle-shooting, folk dancing, interpretive and tap dancing, shuffleboard, volleyball, badninton, golf, bowling, a Christmas Tea, and a Mother and Daughter Banquet.

A number of clubs and organizations were formed by students with special academic and social interests. Language clubs were formed for students interested in French and German, drama and music clubs for those interested in the performing arts, the Scalpel Club for pre-medical students, and a social and literary club called the Growlers. A Student Council was organized in 1928 with Charles McKeown, later a lawyer and civic leader in Joliet, serving as the first president. The following year, the college newspaper, *The Blazer,* made its appearance, and a few years later the college published its own yearbook. In 1931, the *Joliet Township High School Bulletin* noted the significance of these clubs and activities: [21]

> *These extra-curricular activities were without question a factor of considerable importance in the growth of the junior college. Not only did they help crystallize the junior college into an institution, but they went far in arousing a desire or a willingness among high-school seniors to do their first years of beginning work in Joliet.* [21]

The numerous social and academic clubs provided leadership training and promoted individual student development. Conversely, freshman and sophomore students at large colleges and universities had far fewer leadership opportunities available to them.

During his nine years in Joliet, Superintendent Smith was active professionally in state and national organizations. He published articles, participated in educational conferences, and during the summer months taught classes at such schools as the University of Chicago, the University of California, and the University of Michigan. At Michigan, he taught a summer course on "The Origin and Administration of Junior Colleges." At Smith's request, the School Board sent him to California in October of 1927 to study that state's best junior colleges. Seven months later, Smith resigned to accept the position of superintendent of schools in Berkeley, California. Although his decision to leave Joliet was unexpected, it was not surprising that his name appeared on a short list of candidates for the Berkeley position. When the Joliet Board accepted Smith's resignation on June 7, 1928, the Board again asked Assistant Superintendent C. E. Spicer to take the district's top job. Once again Spicer declined. [22]

Educators from across the nation applied for the highly desirable position of Superintendent of Joliet Township High School and Junior College. At a special meeting on July 30, 1928, the Board announced that W. W. Haggard had been selected to fill the vacancy. Haggard was currently serving as principal of Rockford Senior High School in Rockford, Illinois. He held a master's degree from the University of Michigan and a bachelor's degree from Maryville College in his native Tennessee. He had also administered high schools in Petoskey and Saginaw, Michigan. When he applied for the job in Joliet, Haggard was serving as secretary-treasurer of the Illinois Principals' Association and vice president of the Big Seven High School Conference. [23]

Haggard began his administrative responsibilities in Joliet at a time when the high school and junior college were enjoying unprecedented growth and success. A year later, however, the stock market crash and ensuing depression seriously tested the mettle and leadership of the new superintendent. By the time of his departure in 1939, the economy was showing some signs of improvement, but war clouds were gathering over Europe and the Far East. Indeed, the decade of the 1930s was an interesting and challenging period in the history of the college.

Beginning with Haggard's administration, the day-to-day operation of the junior college shifted from the high school superintendent to the college dean, a position created in 1926 with the appointment of Ira D. Yaggy. Since he registered and advised all college students and supervised their social activities, Dean Yaggy was generally regarded as the person who made decisions and "ran the college." [24]

During the 1930s, there were few major additions or changes in the college curriculum. The most significant changes reflected the national trend in junior colleges of providing occupational education for non-transfer students. For example, a two-year electrical engineering program was introduced in 1930 for students interested in acquiring jobs in local industry. The program was discontinued two years later, however, as an economy measure necessitated by the depression. An agreement with Silver Cross Hospital to provide academic courses for nurses in training proved to be much more successful. [25] In fact, the college continued to offer such classes as chemistry, anatomy and physiology, psychology, and bacteriology until 1969 when the hospital closed its training program and supported JJC's new associate degree program in nursing. On the other hand, the two-year normal course for training elementary teachers had been primarily a terminal program since its inception in 1901, but in the late thirties, it became a pre-professional transfer program. The Illinois General Assembly passed a law effective in 1943 that required elementary teachers to hold a bachelor's degree.[26]

Junior college transfer courses and programs continued to mirror those at the University of Illinois. Whenever the U of I changed course content, prerequisites, or program requirements, similar revisions were soon made at JJC. Administrators and faculty regularly visited the university campus and corresponded with the registrar to keep abreast of any changes. These articulation efforts with the U of I and other colleges minimized transfer problems and maximized student success in junior and senior-level classes. Studies of junior college transfer students were conducted by both JJC administrators and outside agencies and, without exception, showed that Joliet transfer students performed better in the last two years of college than those students who spent all four years at the same college or university. In fact, similar studies throughout the years have consistently yielded the same results, a point often emphasized in college advertising and marketing.[27]

The Great Depression of the 1930s stretched the district financially and prompted significant changes in managing the school's resources. Thousands of dollars in district funds were tied up in bank closings, and real estate taxes were slow to be paid. The Board of Trustees resorted to paying school bills with warrants and school employees with 6 percent orders and locally-issued scrip. Beginning in 1932, employee contracts contained a provision granting the School Board the right to cancel pay periods. For the next several years, teachers and other employees annually lost up to 25 percent of their salaries through payless paydays. Between 1932 and 1938, canceled pay periods cost employees the equivalent of a year's wages. Other economy measures included a reduction in faculty and a corresponding increase in teaching load and class size.

With an uncertain future and few jobs available, young men and women in the Joliet area took advantage of the free college education at JJC. The combination of a sharp increase in college enrollment and an acute shortage of funds prompted the School Board on February 8, 1932, to adopt a resolution requiring resident students to pay tuition until the financial crisis passed. Initially the fee was set at $25 per semester, but was raised to $35 the following year. Non-resident students were charged a rate of $100 per semester. The $35 tuition charge for district residents remained in place until 1949. Although school officials anticipated a dramatic drop in college enrollment, perhaps by as much as one-third, the decline was hardly noticeable. Furthermore, students were now required to buy their own examination booklets and to pay a $1.50 graduation fee. Although the new costs certainly created a hardship for students, *The Blazer* sounded a positive note in the fall of 1932:

> *The biggest effect the depression has had on the college is that students have made up their minds really to do things in their studies. After paying all the necessary money and realizing how scarce the money is, the students are applying themselves with added determination to get their money's worth out of the school.*[30]

Fortunately, new sources of revenue were found in the form of grants, scholarships, and loans. A $6,000 grant from the Carnegie Corporation was used to expand and remodel the library and add four thousand books to the college collection. New Deal programs were tapped to help students pay their tuition and fees. A grant of $4,500 enabled fifty-five students to work as aides in the library, laboratories, and various offices. The National Youth Act (NYA) also provided jobs for students who were looking for ways to meet college expenses. The School Board awarded scholarships to the top male and female students in surrounding high schools. Service clubs and private donors also established scholarships for worthy students with financial need. Finally, the College Loan Fund was available for students to borrow money to pay their college bills.[31]

Despite economic hard times, students enjoyed extracurricular activities and continued to develop a college identity and collegiate atmosphere on campus. Surprisingly, the first college yearbook was published during the depression in 1933 when two students convinced Dean Yaggy that it could be financed solely through student sales. The Student Council sponsored a contest in 1935 for a new, livelier college song. The winner was Stanley Johnson, who wrote a song more suitable for arousing school spirit at pep rallies. New student clubs were formed in the 1930s, including a

Current Events Club that met at noon and discussed timely topics in the news. Like other college campuses in the mid-1930s, JJC was caught up in the peace movement and held an anti-war day on April 22, 1936.

Sporting events and athletic competition provided students a welcome diversion from academic stress and economic concerns. Aubrey A. "Fizz" Wills joined the athletic department in 1928 and enjoyed considerable success coaching college basketball and baseball teams. Beginning in 1931, the basketball team won eleven consecutive conference titles; the team also won three consecutive state championships during the mid-1930s. The baseball, tennis, and golf teams also won conference titles and proudly squeezed their trophies into the crowded case.

Although the Northern Illinois Junior College Conference was devoted primarily to intercollegiate sports, it broadened its scope in 1934 to include other student activities. With Dean Yaggy then serving as president of NIJCC, Joliet Junior College hosted the first annual student conference. Following a general meeting, student representatives from eight junior colleges adjourned to breakout sessions where they exchanged information and ideas about publications, clubs, and campus concerns.[33] Delegates raised such issues as the 11:30 p.m. curfew for college parties to learn whether students at other colleges had similar social restrictions. Since the vast majority of junior colleges were located on high school campuses, the creation of an appropriate college environment was often a matter of disagreement between students and administrative staff.

Although the public junior college movement started in Illinois, the state lagged behind others in developing new institutions. Of the nation's ninety-two public junior colleges in 1929, only six were located in Illinois. Since these colleges were supported by high school tax levies and were not legally part of the state's higher education system, their very existence could have been jeopardized if challenged by taxpaying citizens. Even more disturbing to supporters of public junior colleges was a 1927 opinion rendered by the Illinois Attorney General stating that "a board of education has no authority under the laws of the State to establish or maintain a junior college." This meant that Joliet Junior College had existed "extra-legally" since its beginning in 1901.[34]

Even though Joliet taxpayers had never questioned the legality of JJC, Superintendent Haggard believed that it was time to legitimatize existing junior colleges and provide a process for creating additional two-year colleges throughout the state. With Haggard taking the lead, a committee representing suburban junior colleges attempted, with limited success, to enlist the support of university leaders and the state Department of Education. Superintendent of Public Instruction John Wieland agreed to offer assistance but was clearly reluctant to provide leadership; there were other more pressing problems on his agenda. Dean Thomas Benner and President Willard of the University of Illinois were evasive and reluctant to support the plan proposed by Haggard's committee. They were not sure how the university would be impacted financially if junior colleges began competing for the state's limited educational resources. They also thought that clearer guidelines were needed for creating new junior college districts. A state law passed in 1931 authorized the public school system of Chicago to establish one junior college, but no provision was made for the rest of the state. JJC and the other Illinois junior colleges continued to exist without express legal sanction.[35]

It was apparent to Haggard and other junior college leaders that they would have to move ahead on their own. With the support of the newly organized Illinois Association of Junior Colleges, Haggard drafted a bill that Senator Richard Barr of Joliet agreed to support. The measure was enacted into law in May 1937. The statute established the legality of existing junior colleges and provided general guidelines for creating new two-year colleges. Although the IAJC was pleased that member institutions now had legal status, President Willard of the U of I believed the measure left too many unanswered questions. There was no systematic plan for creating new junior colleges, and there was no clear provision for supporting these institutions financially. Despite its shortcomings, the law was an important first step in validating junior college education in Illinois. Additional steps would be taken later but not with the leadership of W. W. Haggard. He resigned in 1939 to accept a position in the far Northwest as president of Western Washington College of Education.[36]

During Haggard's eleven years as superintendent of Joliet Township High School and Junior College, he had been active professionally at the state and national levels. In 1937 he earned a doctorate from the University of Chicago, while at the same time, serving as president of the American Association of Junior Colleges. When he left Joliet, Dr. Haggard was secretary of the North Central Association and president of the Northwestern Division of the Illinois Education Association.[37]

The year 1939 also marked the end of C. E. Spicer's long career at the high school and junior college. He retired and moved to his summer home in Frankfort, Michigan. At his final commencement exercises, three generations of students paid tribute to the man they admired and respected. He had taught them science, counseled them, befriended them, and disciplined them when necessary. He

remarked that it was time to leave before "I meet no the grandchildren, but the great-grandchildren of m first pupils." The departure of Haggard and Spice marked the end of an era, a period characterized b stable leadership during uncertain and challengin times. The new era beginning in 1939 would brin far less stability to the superintendent's office Indeed, four men held the school's top job during th next eight years and faced the perplexities of Worl War II and its impact on higher education.[38]

Dr. L. W. Smith, Superintendent, 1919 – 1928

W. W. Haggard, Superintendent, 1928 - 1939

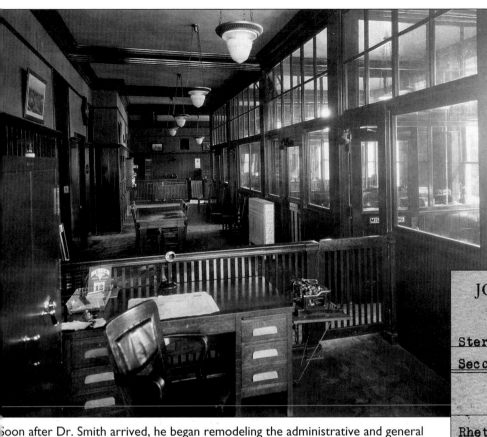

Soon after Dr. Smith arrived, he began remodeling the administrative and general office space. Pictured here in 1922 is the expanded office area with the registrar's desk in the foreground and the reception area beyond. Set off by glass partitions on the right are the offices of the assistant superintendent, assistant principal, supervisor of vocational education, and personnel director. The clerical space at the far end was adjacent to the superintendent's office and was staffed by five secretaries engaged in general office work.

JOLIET JUNIOR COLLEGE

Record of

Sterling, Everett

Second Semester, 1925-26

Subject	Semester Hours	Grade
Rhetoric	3	92
Math. 3	3	89
Zoology 2	5	82
Geology	2	86
Inorg. & Qual.	4	88
Gym.	1	85
Math. 2	2	96
Previous Credits		
Total Credits		

Passing Grade 75. For the significance of other grades and of abbreviations, see other side.

KEEP THIS CARD FOR REFERENCE

Junior College Committee

Pictured here is the report card or grade record of Everett Sterling, a freshman in 1925-26. At semester's end, instructors assigned numerical grades to each person enrolled in class. Only students with a cumulative average of 80 percent or higher were recommended for transfer to senior institutions.

The typewriter, duplicating machine, wicker wastebasket, wall cases, and storage drawers are reminiscent of school offices seventy-five years ago.

High School Library shared by college students before 1920

When Dr. L. W. Smith became superintendent in 1919, a top priority of his administration was the creation of a separate college library. Although a small collection of books had been kept in the college assembly room, JJC students usually resorted to using the larger high school library. A "long-suffering janitor" also hauled books back and forth from the public library. Within a year, however, Smith's goal was achieved. A college library was established, and a full-time librarian, Pauline Dillman, was appointed to catalog and oversee the college's growing collection of 1,400 books. Within a decade the library boasted 5,500 bound volumes, 800 pamphlets, and 65 periodicals. Students added their own touches to the room by hanging inspirational pictures and designing a special college emblem for the wall. Not only was the new library an important academic resource for students, but it was also a significant development in fostering a college atmosphere and identity on campus.[5]

College Library after 1920 with Librarian Pauline Dillman

One of the most interesting and unusual instructional settings was the combined lecture room, biology laboratory, and museum pictured here in 1927. The wide ends of the trapezoidal tables faced the windows to permit all students to receive the maximum amount of natural light. The instructor's desk was used for scientific demonstrations and was equipped with hot and cold water, steam, compressed air, and electricity. The wall cases with glass fronts contained specimens of plants, mounted birds and small mammals, and a variety of other related materials. The cases also contained microscopes, lantern slides, and numerous pictures and diagrams of plant and animal life. The living plants on the tables were grown in the school greenhouse. Representatives from other colleges and high schools who toured the building were especially interested in visiting this unique science room.

The high school and junior college boasted one of the finest school-based greenhouses in the state. Located near the biology labs, the greenhouse enabled science instructors to demonstrate the various phases of germination and plant development. In addition to ordinary seed plants and ferns, the greenhouse supported living specimens of unusual and rare plant life indigenous to other climates and regions of the world. Besides its educational value, the greenhouse served the practical purpose of providing decorative plants and flower arrangements for special events at the school.

During the 1920s, an increasing number of classes were offered that doubled as both transfer courses and terminal occupational courses, such as the surveying class pictured here in 1928.

Until this photograph was taken in 1923 for *The J,* school publications did not distinguish between high school and college teachers. Gathered here in front of the school's distinctive doors are members of the junior college faculty. Board policy at this time provided that the minimum standards for teaching at the high school and junior college were a master's degree and two years of teaching

experience. During the 1920s, faculty members occasionally asked the School Board to re-evaluate their level of pay. There appears to have been a significant disparity between the salaries of teachers and administrators. In 1928, for example, the superintendent's salary was $11,000, while male teachers earned an average of $2,706 and female faculty members were paid an average of $2,572 per year.

Building for the Future

Rapid growth of the district's comprehensive program, namely the high school, continuation school, vocational school, Americanization school, night school, and junior college, prompted the School Board in the early 1920s to begin planning for an extensive three-phase building program. The school *Bulletin* explained to parents and the public alike the dire need for additional space:

At present we are using as classrooms two wash rooms, three storage rooms, three rooms lighted only by artificial light, [and] the women's rest room. Besides utilizing every available foot of space in the high school, no matter how unsuitable, we are occupying six outside buildings, all but one of them being on the opposite side of the street from the high school. [14]

Since expansion was blocked by the Eastern Avenue Baptist Church on the northwest side of the original building, architect D. H. Burnham developed a plan that literally surrounded the church on three sides. Meanwhile, the School Board continued its protracted negotiations with church leaders for the purchase of their building.

Township voters approved phase one of the expansion program on August 31, 1920. Completed in 1922, the addition fully extended the east side of the building along Herkimer Street. On the west side along Eastern Avenue, however, the church property prevented a continuous expansion of the original build-

| Dr. F.W. Werner | Mr. Clarence Sterling | Mr. J.A. Olhaver | Mr. L.A. Sherwood | Mr. Arthur Montzheimer |
| President | Secretary | Vice President | | |

The men pictured here were members of the School Board in the early 1920s when a three-phase expansion plan was envisioned and designed. By 1925, the first two additions to the building were completed.

At the School Board's request, the City of Joliet vacated Van Buren Street between Eastern Avenue and Herkimer Street in order to permit the expansion of the building. Pictured here with Herkimer Street in the foreground is phase one of the building program nearing completion in 1922. The section known as the "bridge" in the center of the photograph joined the 1917 addition (the "college division") on the left to the new 1922 addition on the right.

ing. The new addition gave the school an unusual shape: it was a block wide at the two ends and about half as wide in the center section, with the church property cutting into the middle of the building on Eastern Avenue. The 1922 addition included a new boys' gym with an elevated running track, a large lunchroom with separate facilities for teachers, and several new rooms for shops and occupational classes.

With the assistance of arbitrators, an acceptable price was finally established for the Eastern Avenue Baptist Church. The church was razed in 1923 for phase two of the expansion plan. Completed in 1925, the centerpiece of the new addition was a large auditorium. In 1930, voters approved the last major addition to the north end of the building, a girls' gym. Designed as an extension to the existing gym, a folding partition could divide the space for separate activities or open it for events requiring the full gymnasium.

The four additions to the original structure (1917, 1922, 1925, and 1931) created one of the largest high school buildings in the nation. Although intended primarily for high school students, the new gymnasiums, lunchroom, auditorium, shops, laboratories, and classrooms were used by college students as well. During these early years when most junior colleges were linked to secondary schools, JJC was indeed fortunate to share a campus and facilities with a very progressive high school.

Above the memorial fountain in the area that bridged the 1917 and 1922 additions stands the likeness of a doughboy. Conrad W. Braun donated the statue entitled *The World Soldier* in honor of the many students and faculty who served in World War I.

The 1922 addition included a modern gymnasium, generally known as the "boys' gym." It had a seating capacity of 2,000 for sporting events but could also be divided by the curtain seen here to accommodate intramural contests and gym classes. Above the gym was one of the finest indoor running tracks in the Middle West.

Left: The Eastern Avenue Baptist Church was located north of the original school and stood in the way of expansion plans. Since the School Board had been unable to acquire the property when the 1922 addition was built, architect D. H. Burnham designed a structure that virtually surrounded the church. Part of the new addition can be seen to the left (north) of the church and behind (east of) the church; the original high school building is out of the picture on the south side of the church to the right. The church was finally purchased and torn down in 1923 to make way for the second phase of the Board's expansion program.

Right: Looking north on Eastern Avenue in 1924, one sees the second phase of the expansion plan nearing completion. The Eastern Avenue Baptist Church has been razed, and a new school auditorium is being built. At the March 3, 1925, Board meeting, Superintendent Smith recommended that the following quotation from Diogenes be inscribed in the panel above the auditorium stage: "THE FOUNDATION OF EVERY STATE IS THE EDUCATIONI OF ITS YOUTH."

Left: The third phase of the building expansion program was completed in 1931 with the addition of a girls' gym. At the dedication ceremony, junior college women entertained by presenting Irish, French, Bavarian, and Polish folk dances. Participants learned their dance steps in gym class and were responsible for making their own costumes. The Polish folk dance is presented here by Winifred Kerr, Juanita Hartong, Suzanne Romanowski, Ruth Schultz, Mars Wiggim, Mary Wheeler, Irene Howell, unidentified, Rachel Bisching, Ila Bishop, Dorothy Hausser, and Emma Lou Juda.

Right: In the 1920s, most students walked or took public transportation to the junior college. A few students, however, like Edward H. Crombie, commuted by car. With the school in the background in 1928, Crombie proudly stands next to his Model T Ford coupe.

Right: In June 1911, the School Board purchased the Elwood property on the southwest corner of Jefferson Street and Eastern Avenue. The two-story brick building on the site was converted into a manual training and domestic science facility. The grounds were developed into a school campus with benches and trees. In 1938, however, the park-like property was paved for parking to accommodate the increasing number of faculty and students driving cars to school.

Left: Beginning in 1916 when Superintendent J. Stanley Brown informed students that they were no longer considered "post-graduates" but rather collegians with new privileges, officers were elected to oversee the activities and represent the interests of college students. Not until 1921, however, were photographs of junior college officers printed in school publications. The four students seen here were elected to represent the entire student body. The following year, the freshman and sophomore classes elected separate slates of officers. Pictured here are Harold Patterson (treasurer), Harriet Bush (vice president), Chalmers Miller (secretary), and Robert Fraser (president).

Right: One of JJC's most successful teams in the early years, the "basketball warriors" of 1921 lost only three of thirteen games, two of which were played on "foreign floors and in freak gyms."[18] The school yearbook boasted that Joliet Junior College was one of the most feared schools in northern Illinois. **Front:** Ray Morris A. Flint, C. Lewis, John Douglas (captain), Randall Grady, Robert Eyman. **Back:** Chalmers Miller (manager), Harold Griffin, C. J. Wagner (coach), Leland Stephen, Clarence Rogers. Freddie Heilman served as team mascot.

Left: Aubrey A. "Fizz" Wills joined the Physical Education Department in 1928 and soon enjoyed considerable success coaching the college basketball and baseball teams. Wills acquired the nickname "Fizz" as a teenager while working at the soda fountain in his father's drugstore. The teams had experienced losing conference records in the late 1920s, but Coach Wills turned around the two intercollegiate programs. Pictured here is the first JJC baseball team (1929) coached by "Fizz" Wills. **Front:** Joseph Zelko, Sherwin Leiss, Richard Calosio, Steve Smyder, Gaylord Robinson, Thomas Slattery. **Back:** Lipsey, Brutka, Edward Crombie, Aloysius Nolan, Emil Di Lorenzo, Carl Berst, Elmer Rowley, Stephen Petruska, A. A. "Fizz" Wills (coach).

Women's Athletic Association

Organized early in the 1925-26 school year, the Women's Athletic Association (W.A.A.) provided female students with opportunities to compete in sports. As the years passed, more and more athletic activities became available to women through the efforts of the W.A.A. and its faculty sponsor, Phoebe Henderson Kirby. Pictured here are members of the association in 1928. Katherine Dunham, an African-American student who later achieved world-wide acclaim as an anthropologist, writer, choreographer, and dancer, served as president. **First Row:** Virginia Powers, Cassidy, Gladys Eib, Mary Schuster, Grace Bailey, Althea Peterson, Alice Fitch, Katherine Dunham, Martha Ragnes. **Second Row:** Vera Higby, Mary Manning, Mary Lynch, Cooney, Josephine Keltie, Myrtle Patterson, Phoebe Kirby (sponsor). **Third Row:** Marie Schwab, Hazel Klint, Anna Koerner, Mary Clark, Verna Lawrence, Fraser. **Fourth Row:** Neva Robbins, Winifred Day, Mary Ashley, Elizabeth Pettigrew, Margaret O'Connell, June Hutchinson, Bourrie, Mildred Becker, Frances Barclay.

One of the W.A.A.'s most popular events was the annual basketball game with the high school all-star team. Although the 1927 players pictured here narrowly lost an exciting game, they enjoyed the enthusiastic support of other W.A.A. members cheering from the bleachers. **L-R:** Phoebe Henderson Kirby (coach), Grace Bailey, Vina Watjus, Doris Reece, Jean Grant, Neva Robbins, Ramona Powell, Lois Hartman, Ruth Mortvedt, Katherine Dunham, Hazel Conlon.

Horseback riding was added in 1931 to the growing list of activities available to members of the W.A.A. Pictured here the following year near the stables in Pilcher Park are several college women headed for a ride on the park's bridal paths. Louis Boos and Ray Daggett provided instruction for any inexperienced riders. Several club members entered three events in the annual horse show: the five-gaited, three-gaited, and musical chairs events. **L-R:** Mr. Boos, Doris Eib, Miss Turner (sponsor), Beulah Green, Elsie Rinearson, Margaret Wiswell, Mildred Kristal, Virginia Dille, Gwendolyn Davis, Betty Groth, Dorothy Westendarp (faculty sponsor), Mr. Daggett.

A popular activity sponsored by the Women's Athletic Association was swimming. Pictured here in 1932 are the junior college swimmers. **Front:** Grace Gjessing, Phyllis Tyacke, Beulah Green, Betty Groth, Gertrude Johannsen, Margaret Wiswell, Virginia Bolton. **Middle:** Elsie Rinearson, Ruth Souvenier, Gwen Davis, Guydell Schwartz, Helen Dudek, Virginia Dille, Dorothy Adams, Elizabeth Robertson, Barbara Broughton. **Back:** Margaret Skorupa, Helen Morse, Ruth Jennings, Ruth Tullock, Cecelia Branchaw, Pauline Woodrow, Louise Carlson, Janice Miller.

The Women's Rifle Club was organized in the mid-1930s to develop perseverance, patience, sportsmanship, and marksmanship. R.O.T.C. instructors coached the would-be sharpshooters in proper firing techniques for the prone, sitting, kneeling, and standing positions. Required to purchase their own ammunition, club members shot every Tuesday afternoon. Standard attire on the firing range consisted of dark blue overalls and white shirts. Pictured here are members of the 1937 Rifle Club. **Back:** Marie Berg, Ruth Smith. **Front:** Virginia Lindsley, Catherine Haller, Pearl Sutton, Genevieve Wilson, Lorraine Hedburg, Dorothy Chalstrom, Marjorie Knight, Eileen Rodgers, Marilyn Rhodes, Alice Nethery.

By the late 1930s, the Women's Athletic Association offered a wide variety of activities. In the fall, field hockey and horseback riding were popular. During the winter, basketball, rifle-shooting, volleyball, and shuffleboard were favorite activities. Golf, tennis, and baseball were enjoyed during the spring. There were also a number of all-seasonal sports and activities including swimming, tumbling, tap-dancing, and orchesis (an interpretive dance group). An Outing Club organized hiking, biking, ice skating, and tobogganing. The W.A.A. hosted Co-ed Nights in the gym and planned mixed tournaments in bowling, Ping-Pong, and badminton. It sponsored at least one "girls' choice" dance during the year, held a Christmas Tea for faculty members, and then ended its busy schedule with a Mother and Daughter Banquet in May. Pictured here in 1935 are several W.A.A. members dressed in uniforms depicting the group's various activities. **Front:** Elaine Marshall, Pauline Sweda, Marion Sieben, Mary Owens, Jennings, Sara Snure, Marie Mancuso, Gladys Gabel.

Middle: Virginia Fahrner, Willa Lou Longley, Edna Larson, Genevieve Anderson, Catherine Johnson, Viola Larson, Mary Harmon, Frances Motta, Leona Blogg. **Back:** Lucille Lentini, Rosella Canino, Helen Eaton, Dorothy Benson, Bernadine Leser, Belle Levin, Betty Johnston, Joanna Maheras, Dorothy Motta.

During the decades of the 1920s and '30s, Joliet Junior College continued to establish its own identity even though it physically remained part of a growing high school district. The superintendents who suc-ceeded J. Stanley Brown actively promoted the college as a separate entity and not merely a two-year extension of the high school experience. A variety of student clubs, social activities, publications, and

Foreign language clubs were popular on campus during the 1920s and '30s. One of the first French clubs, the Feytel Club, is seen here in 1922. Named in honor of a noted professor in France, the club enjoyed socials, formed study groups, and published a paper in French. Club members credited their group's success to faculty sponsor Minnie Babcock.

Spearheaded by Anton Olivio, Joe Duffy, and Ruth Crane, a new club known as the Growlers was organized in 1923. Meeting every third Monday evening, the organization focused on improving the social and intellectual life of the college. The meetings often featured outside speakers, debates, student talent, and musical programs followed by a social hour of dancing and games. The culminating social event of the club's first year was a traditional barn party held at the home of Florence Walz. By all accounts, the JJC wolves in attendance howled and growled and had a great time.

The Musical Club provided students an opportunity to perform in at least one musical production each year. The 1926 club members pictured here presented *Il Trovatore*. **Front:** Marjorie Livingston, Heloise Marwick, Verna Bailey, Doris Rohrbach, Jenny Westling, Carol Brewster, Mabel Hansen. **Middle:** Robert Conkling, James Lordan, C. Dana Watson, Mary Van Horn, Lease, Eleanor Metheny, Ariel Mortvedt. **Back:** Edward Harford, Dagoberto Gonzalez, Hartman, Jean Grant, Suda Norris, Paul Stewart.

The 1931 tennis team posted a perfect mark in conference play and won the championship trophy.
Front: K. Powell, Glenn Henderson, Carl Van Horn, John Howk, Francis Blogg, Lloyd Austin (captain).
Back: Coach Becker , John Baumgartner, Robert Hamlin, Edward Baskerville.

Although golf was a relatively new sport at JJC in 1931, the team won the conference championship with an unblemished record. Pictured here on the eighteenth green at Woodruff Golf Course are Hubert Zalar, Dick Stoltz, Thomas Conroy, and Tom Camp.

Joliet basketball teams were not only extremely successful in winning conference titles in the 1930s, but beginning with the first State Junior College Tournament in 1933, the Wolves also compiled an enviable record in state-wide play. Joliet won the inaugural state tournament in 1933 at La Grange and then went on to win the next two titles as well. The 1938 team again captured the first-place trophy, which gave Joliet four state championships in a six-year period. The JJC squad is pictured here in action against La Grange in the opening game of the 1933 tournament.

Opening round of the 1933 state torunament: Joliet 36, La Grange 27.

Top: John Smarker, Jack Slattery, Irving Olson.
Bottom: James Furlong, Carroll Bolton.

Coach A. A. "Fizz" Wills and the state championship trophy.

50

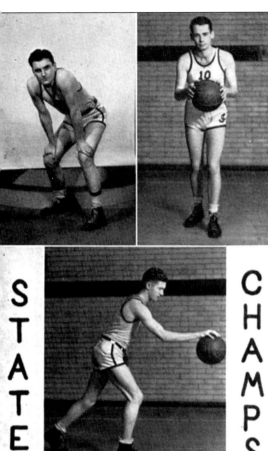

Junior college students had the most contact with members of the administrative staff pictured here. Gathered in the superintendent's office in 1937 are Grayce Stadler (secretary to the dean), Ira D. Yaggy (college dean), W. W. Haggard (superintendent), Myra Mather (dean of women), and Pauline Dillman (librarian).

This talented trio led the JJC Wolves to a state basketball title in 1938. At the end of the season, all three players were named to the All State Team. Ray McGrath (top left) was team captain; Robert Archambeault (top right) played guard; and William Knowles (bottom) was the team's leading scorer.

During his forty-eight years in Joliet, C. E. Spicer witnessed considerable change. Serving as an assistant to Superintendents Brown, Smith, and Haggard, he played an important role in the founding and early development of the nation's first public junior college. Of course, Spicer himself also changed during that time. For example, in 1891 when Spicer arrived, he had hair – everywhere. When he retired in 1939, he "barely" needed a comb.

CHAPTER 3

Years of Challenge and Change
1939-1967

Leadership in the Joliet superintendent's position changed much more frequently from 1939 to 1967 than it had during the earlier years. Whereas only three people had held the top job during the first thirty-eight years of the college's existence, a succession of six men administered the high school and junior college during the next twenty-eight. The frequent change in superintendents, especially from 1940 to 1950, came during the challenging years of World War II and its aftermath. Fortunately for JJC, remarkable stability existed in the office of college dean, an administrative position that became increasingly responsible for the operation of the college.

In 1939, the resignation of Superintendent W. W. Haggard after eleven years and the retirement of longtime Assistant Superintendent C. E. Spicer left a gaping hole in the administration. At its August meeting, the School Board hired C. L. Jordan to be the new superintendent. His most recent administrative position had been at a manual training school in Louisville, Kentucky. Jordan's status as a reserve officer in the United States Marine Corps would cut short his tenure as superintendent in Joliet. When school opened in September 1939, Germany had invaded Poland, and World War II had begun in Europe. Jordan resigned two weeks after the attack on Pearl Harbor in December 1941 when he was ordered to report for active duty.[1]

Dr. Leonard B. Wheat was released from his job at a defense plant in Dearborn, Michigan, to accept the superintendency in February 1942. The Board granted Wheat's early request to hire an assistant responsible for revising the curriculum to meet rapid social and educational changes occurring in the country. Roosevelt Basler, a doctoral candidate at Teachers College in New York, was appointed Assistant Superintendent of Curriculum and Guidance in June 1942. Six months later, Dr. Wheat resigned to take a superintendent's job in Wichita, Kansas. With Wheat gone after eleven months, the School Board promoted Basler to the district's top administrative post. The vacant office of curriculum and guidance was filled by Donald Sharpe, who had just received a doctorate

from the University of Illinois.[2]

Roosevelt Basler served as superintendent of the high school and junior college for three years but left in 1946 to take a government job as Chief of Instructional Problems in the United States Office of Education. Following recent practice, the Board offered Assistant Superintendent Sharpe the opportunity to advance to the superintendency. Less than two years later, however, Sharpe resigned due to ill health. The position was next offered in 1947 to Hugh Bonar of Oak Park, Illinois. Bonar's educational career had been spent largely at schools in Wisconsin where he had been active in state educational organizations and the North Central Association of Secondary Schools and Colleges. He brought experience and stability to the superintendent's position, qualities missing in previous years.[3] In 1960, Bonar reached mandatory retirement age and was required to resign. His successor, Dr. William French, likewise brought stability and administrative competence to the position. French led the high school and college through troubled years of crowded conditions and economic distress. By the time he left in 1967, however, the future looked bright. The district had built two new high schools, and the college had achieved Class I legal status and was in the process of severing its sixty-six year relationship with Joliet Township High School.[4]

Although certainly not insulated from the effects of frequent change in the superintendent's position, JJC enjoyed unusual stability in the office of college dean. Ira D. Yaggy served twenty-one years as dean from 1926 to 1947, and he was followed for the next twenty by Elmer W. Rowley. The various superintendents accorded the dean and his assistants considerable latitude in administering the college. From the students' perspective, the dean ran the college, and the district superintendent was a shadowy figure in the background. In truth, perception mirrored reality. Yaggy and Rowley exerted considerable influence in shaping the academic and social life of the college. Impersonal forces and world events were also important in influencing the development and direction of the college. Indeed, Pearl Harbor's bombs had an immediate impact on JJC and the college community. Not only did the school lose its superintendent to the war effort, but the vast majority of college men and several college women entered the armed forces, too. Enrollment dropped dramatically to less than half the prewar number. Social and athletic activities were curtailed or canceled, and students found ways to volunteer their services on the homefront. A Civil Pilot Training Corps was established on campus, as were rifle teams for both men and women.[5]

Ammunition plants and other war-related industries in the Joliet area begged for workers. The nation's economy shook off the stubborn effects of the Great Depression; suddenly jobs were plentiful, and wages were high. Academic schedules were rewritten to accommodate working students who needed evening and weekend classes. New courses and training programs were offered by science teachers to train powder inspectors, gauge readers, and other employees in ordnance plants. The school also tapped the talent of the Agriculture Department and participated in the nation's emergency food production program.[6]

The postwar period produced even more change that profoundly transformed the character and mission of the college. In 1944, Congress passed the Servicemen's Readjustment Act, commonly known as the GI Bill of Rights, that provided up to four years of educational benefits to veterans. The measure covered occupational training as well as traditional academic programs. Taking advantage of the GI Bill, veterans in the Joliet area began enrolling in large numbers. By the fall of 1946, almost 700 students, half of them veterans, had registered for classes. Just three years earlier, college enrollment had dipped to 179. In addition to the influx of GIs returning from war, the number of traditional students also increased due to population growth. Faculty and facilities were taxed beyond their limits. The Board of Education responded by establishing a $20 application fee, imposing enrollment restrictions, and granting admission preference to in-district students.[7]

Veterans entered college with definite goals and a wide range of educational abilities. Some had been college students before the war while others were high school dropouts who gained admission by passing the General Education Development (GED) Test. Refresher courses were offered to those who needed to improve their mathematical and verbal skills before taking advanced classes. For students uninterested in traditional academic programs, the college developed an On the Job Apprentice Training Program with courses in such areas as mechanics, painting, and plumbing, all covered by the GI Bill. "We must have both plumbers and philosophers – unless we provide quality education for both," observed John Gardner, President of the Carnegie Foundation, "neither our pipes nor our ideas will hold water." The war and its aftermath had created a need for technicians and workers with specialized training, and junior colleges adapted to meet the demand.[8]

What the Joliet community had known and experienced for many years was validated in 1947 by President Truman's Commission on Higher Education. The president appointed a group of twenty-eight leading educators to study higher education in America and to make recommendations on facilities, methods, and objectives. The Truman Commission's three-volume report touched all aspects of higher education. It particularly recognized the importance of two-year colleges, especially in democratizing education and making it readily available to the general public. Using the term "community college," the commission recommended that states establish two-year public college systems offering affordable education within easy access of all people. "Whatever form the community college takes," stated the Truman Commission, "its purpose is educational service to the entire community. It should include preparation for advanced study, vocational and technical programs, and community service. It should be dedicated to lifelong learning and be an active center for adult education." The junior college was finally recognized as an important segment of higher education and was destined to play a major role in educating the American people. Remarkably, it all began in Joliet in 1901 with six "postgraduate" students.[9]

When the Truman Commission issued its report in 1947, significant changes were occurring at Joliet Junior College. Hugh H. Bonar was hired as superintendent to replace Donald Sharpe, who had resigned for health reasons. Bonar brought stability to a district office that had seen four superintendents in the past eight years. However, Ira D. Yaggy retired in 1947, bringing to a close his twenty-one years as college dean. Yaggy was highly regarded by students and staff alike. In fact, the first college yearbook, published in 1933, was warmly dedicated to Dean

Yaggy with these words:

Realizing his sympathetic understanding, his affectionate interest, his gentle toleration toward the antics of Joliet Collegians, and his liberal attitude, we, the class of nineteen hundred and thirty-three, respectfully dedicate this first volume as a concrete manifestation of the monument we have built to him in our hearts and memories.[10]

In view of ballooning postwar enrollments and the need to broaden the college curriculum, the Board of Education decided to replace Yaggy with two full-time administrators. Elmer W. Rowley was appointed Assistant Superintendent and Dean of the College, and Harry Leinenweber was named Assistant Dean. Leinenweber resigned the position after one semester and returned to the classroom as a social science instructor. In January 1948, Susan Wood replaced Leinenweber to serve as the dean's assistant. The new dean, Elmer Rowley, was a 1929 graduate of JJC and for the previous five years had chaired the high school Agriculture Department. Moreover, he had started the Farmer's Short Course and during the war, had administered the school's food production program.[11]

Elmer Rowley served as college dean from 1947 to 1967, during which time the institution continued evolving into a true community college with a comprehensive program, including baccalaureate, vocational-technical, community service, and adult and continuing education courses. Whereas before World War II the school primarily had addressed the needs of transfer students, in the years that followed JJC made a concerted effort to serve the entire community. The curriculum became much more fluid as it adapted to the rapid social and economic changes of the postwar world. With encouragement and support from the dean, the faculty developed several new transfer and occupational programs. New transfer programs included agriculture, music, home economics, and physical education for men and women. The two-year agriculture program was the first of its kind offered at an Illinois junior college. Programs added to the vocational and technical curricula included general business, merchandising, secretarial, automotive, drafting, electricity, mechanical and machine technology, printing, wood shop, office occupations, agriculture supply, and data processing.[12]

In 1951, Rowley's role was expanded to include Director of Adult Education, and he began offering a variety of credit and non-credit courses designed for people of all ages with diverse interests. Classes ranged from knitting to cabinet making to foreign languages. Indeed, whether people in the community were interested in pursuing a hobby, sharpening a skill, or stimulating the mind, they could likely find something of interest in adult education. One of the most popular programs started in 1951 was the film lecture series "The World Today." Adult education classes and programs expanded so rapidly that in 1955 Floyd C. Tompkins was appointed to the full time position of Assistant Dean and Director of Adult Education. The program continued to grow, hampered only by limited space and budget restrictions.[13]

Campus social life and extracurricular activities also changed during the postwar era as veterans and other older students made their presence felt. Sharing a building with high school students and observing their regulations posed problems for college administrators. For example, veterans insisted on having a place to smoke and relax when not in class. A special room known as the "smoker" was finally provided, as were a new lounge and a college cafeteria. Nearby restaurants and diners also attracted students for lunch and coffee breaks. These establishments had interesting names like the Goodie Shoppe, White Shingle, Lighthouse, Cuckoo Clock, and Blast Furnace. For students with cars who were willing to risk losing their parking places, Silver Fross Drive-In with carhop service was a few blocks away, and McDonald's was a drive across town.

Students in the postwar period had ample opportunity to develop leadership skills and enjoy campus social life by playing sports, participating in clubs, running for student council or class office, and planning or attending dances, parties, and other special events. The Veteran's Club was one of the largest on campus, especially after World War II and the Korean War. Clubs brought together students with special interests in such areas as agriculture, business, medical science, engineering, teaching, photography, chess, and motor sports. The Press Club gave students the opportunity to work on college publications, while those interested in theatre could perform with the JC Players. Vocal and instrumental groups were organized for students with musical talent. Finally, intercollegiate sports, intramural sports, and various activities of the Women's Athletic Association rounded out the many extracurricular opportunities available to JJC students.

During the 1940s, JJC joined with other junior colleges to press the Illinois General Assembly for state aid. Existing state law, passed in 1937, recognized the legal existence of junior colleges but provided no source of revenue beyond local high school taxes, as noted in Chapter 2. With college enrollments dramatically increasing after the war, additional funding was necessary. At that time, all junior colleges in the state were operated by public school districts and, with the exception of Wright in Chicago, were housed on high school campuses. In the face of increasing enrollments and escalating costs in the 1940s, junior colleges struggled to stretch their modest budgets.

The Illinois Association of Junior Colleges (IAJC), organized in the 1930s, took the lead on the legislative front to secure state funding. In 1943, the first step was taken by amending the Act of 1937 to permit school districts with junior colleges to establish by referendum separate tax levies for college purposes. No record exists of the Joliet School Board ever considering such a vote. In fact, only one district in the state took advantage of the law and conducted a referendum for college funding. School boards thought it would be easier to win public support to adjust high school levies than to establish new college taxes. In Joliet during the postwar years, no additional taxes for any purpose were welcomed by the voters.

Anticipating a sudden influx of postwar students, the IAJC began preparing legislation that would provide state aid and encourage the creation of more junior colleges throughout the state. A measure introduced in the General Assembly in 1943 provided a state grant of $50 per student and encouraged the organization of new two-year colleges. The Joliet School Board sent a letter of support to Springfield, but the measure failed.[14] Later that year, the IAJC invited the University of Illinois to conduct a survey and make recommendations regarding a statewide plan for developing and supporting junior colleges. University Provost Dr. Coleman Griffith and research assistant Hortense Blackstone conducted the study and published their findings and recommendations in a 1945 book entitled *The Junior College in Illinois*. The study concluded that junior colleges should be expanded across the state within high school districts and should be funded by a combination of local taxes and state aid of $50 per full-time student. Further, a

State Board of Education should be established, said the report, with a State Superintendent of Public Instruction as the chief administrative officer. Based largely on these recommendations, the IAJC supported legislation to encourage the creation of new junior colleges as part of the common school system, with modest state funding based on student enrollment. Bills were introduced in 1945, 1947, and 1949, but each one failed to pass the General Assembly. The 1949 effort was defeated in the Senate by one vote.[15]

With no resources available from the state in the 1940s, Joliet Township High School and Junior College began to feel a financial strain. In fact, the local grade school district as well as the high school and college experienced serious budget problems. During the 1950s, studies were conducted and proposals were advanced to put Joliet schools, including the junior college, on sound financial footing. A plan to introduce greater efficiency and economy to area schools by creating a unit district was rejected by voters in a 1952 referendum. A survey conducted three years later concluded that, indeed, a unit district should be established in the Joliet area. It was unclear how the junior college would be affected if the high school district disappeared and became part of a unit system. Would the college have to be reestablished by public referendum, and would it go out of existence until such a measure was passed? There were no clear answers to these questions.[16]

Meanwhile, at the state level, the Illinois Association of Junior Colleges continued its efforts in the 1950s to secure state aid for junior colleges. Although a bill was passed in Springfield in 1951 that legally recognized junior colleges as part of the common school system, there was no provision for funding. Supporters of the measure were encouraged, however, since they believed that state resources would follow the statutory linkage of junior colleges with public schools. The 1951 law did contain a provision permitting high school districts with no junior college to levy a tax to pay tuition for residents attending any junior college in the state. Lockport was one of the few districts to approve such a tax.

During the 1950s, Joliet educators came to the forefront in the state junior college movement. In 1953, JJC's Elmer Rowley and David Heffernan of Chicago were appointed to lead the IAJC's new legislative committee. Focusing its efforts on state funding, the committee mounted a campaign to publicize the economic benefit to the state of supporting junior college education. For example, if the state granted junior colleges $100 for a full-time student, the cost would be about one-ninth as much as funding students attending state colleges and universities. Although Governor Stratton did not support the legislative efforts of the Illinois Association of Junior Colleges, he did appoint a blue-ribbon panel in 1954 to study higher education in Illinois. Joliet Superintendent Hugh Bonar was appointed to the Higher Education Commission and served on the subcommittee dealing with the expansion of junior colleges in the state.

At last, in 1955, Illinois legislators were willing to share state resources with junior colleges. Although the IAJC had asked for a funding formula of $200 for each full-time student, the law provided only $100 per student. Dean Rowley was present in the governor's office when the landmark legislation was signed. At its next biennial session, in 1957, the General Assembly increased the reimbursement formula to $200 as recommended by the report of the Governor's Commission on Higher Education. The commission's report also renewed public interest in creating a state-wide system of junior colleges; it recommended that junior colleges should be established within commuting distance of every high school graduate in Illinois. After consulting Dr. Robert Johns, chairman of the commission, Dean Elmer Rowley and Assistant Superintendent James H. Cherry, both of Joliet, drafted a bill that would encourage the creation of junior college districts throughout the state. Joliet-area Representative Louis Bottino introduced the measure, which passed in July 1959. For the first time, separate junior college districts were authorized in Illinois. The state apportionment formula also changed in 1959 from a flat $200 per full-time student to a grant of $7.60 for each semester credit hour taken by students.[17]

Although JJC began receiving state funds in the mid-1950s, the school district continued to struggle with tight budgets and space shortages. Especially pressing was the need for additional room and resources to develop vocational and technical programs. Buildings across Jefferson Street that housed the Vocational Department were crowded and dilapidated. In 1955, voters decisively defeated a referendum for a new vocational-technical building. Another attempt the following year produced success but with

a scaled-down version of the original plan. The White Shingle, a popular student hangout for many years, was razed to make way for the new building at the corner of Van Buren and Collins Streets.[18]

The new vocational-technical facility brought some relief in 1958 to crowded conditions, but the problem persisted as high school and college enrollments continued to climb. One School Board member suggested that perhaps it was time to separate the college from the high school as provided in the law written by Rowley and Cherry, but the rest of the Board rejected the notion. Superintendent Bonar floated a plan at a study session that envisioned a county-wide school system with one board administering all levels of education from kindergarten through junior college. The proposal quietly died for lack of interest. Another attempt by a community group to establish a unit district was also voted down in a 1960 referendum.[19]

The new superintendent, Dr. William C. French, recommended that the Board hold a referendum to build two freshman-sophomore feeder schools that would each accommodate 1,500 students. District voters defeated the proposition in May 1961. With 5,000 students crowded into a building designed for 3,500, the Board turned to a team of consultants from Northwestern University to study the district and propose a course of action. Lead consultant Dr. Jack Childress recommended that two four-year schools be built immediately and that eventually a separate junior college for 2,000 students be constructed on the far west side of town near the stadium. In December 1961, a referendum was passed to build Joliet West and Joliet East High Schools. Two Board members suggested that the building on the east side of town should house the junior college instead of a high school. Other members did not agree; after all, voters had approved two new high schools.[20]

The new schools opened in the fall of 1964 and immediately solved the problem of space, but, at the same time, exacerbated the district's financial woes. Not enough money existed to staff and operate three high schools and a rapidly growing junior college. State funding was not nearly enough to operate the college, nor were the incidental fees paid by students. Superintendent French advised the School Board that a 1963 law permitted districts like Joliet to levy college taxes simply by passing a resolution. However, if 10 percent of the district's eligible voters filed a petition within thirty days challenging the resolution, the Board would then have to conduct a public referendum. The School Board passed a tax resolution to levy 17.5 cents for a college education fund and 7.5 cents for a building fund. A petition drive was soon underway organized by local politicians Sammy Berk and Arthur O'Neil. The petitions submitted to the Board were not notarized and therefore were of questionable legality. "Petitions being submitted that are not verified," said one Board member, "it sickens me." Nevertheless, the Board decided to hold a referendum.[21]

On November 21, 1964, voters rejected college tax levies by a 2-1 margin. The Board decided it was time to begin charging in-district students tuition. Although township residents had been charged a fee of $35 during the Great Depression and war years, this fee had been discontinued in 1949. This time the tuition fee had the feel of permanence. Beginning with the 1965 spring semester, a tuition payment of $7 per semester hour was required. Non-resident students paid a higher rate of $21.93 an hour. Before the fall semester began, rates were raised to $10 per hour for in-district students and $30 for non-residents. The only students who attended free were those who lived in Lockport and had their tuition paid through a special tax.[22]

Despite the new tuition revenue, the future of the college still looked bleak. At the June 1965 Board meeting, Superintendent French reported that the district was in "alarming financial condition," caused primarily by the cost of operating the college. Additional funds were immediately needed if the district wished to continue operating JJC. "It would be very unfortunate," observed one Board member, "if this, the first junior college in the nation, should also become the first in the nation to disband because of public apathy." The Board again decided to try levying college taxes by resolution. Once again, Berk and O'Neil launched a petition drive to challenge the tax resolution and require a referendum. This time, the petitions were even more questionable than before. As many as 3,000 of the 8,200 signatures were obviously invalid or fraudulent. For example, all the names on several sheets appeared to be in the same handwriting, and most of the petitions had not been signed and verified by the person circulating them. Disappointed and disgusted, the Board submitted the petitions to the state's attorney for appropriate legal action and proceeded to conduct another referendum,

despite the irregularities. On September 7, 1965, voters again soundly defeated the proposed junior college levy. The state's attorney reported that although wrongdoing was clearly evident, there was no reasonable recourse for legal remedy.[23]

The Board of Education persisted in its efforts to raise taxes and went back to the voters in September 1966, this time asking for an increase in the high school levy from 84 to 98 cents. The public was just as persistent in rejecting these taxes, too. The Board president remarked that "the general lack of concern on the part of the community has placed the district in a needlessly crippled situation." Steps were immediately taken to cut costs by curtailing the school program. All buildings were closed on weekends and at 5:00 p.m. on weekdays; the evening school and adult education programs were reduced to two nights a week, with all evening classes canceled on the east and west campuses. Extracurricular activities were seriously curtailed for both high school and college students. For example, all school-sponsored dances on and off campus were prohibited. Furthermore, the Board announced that additional cuts would soon be announced.[24]

The district's financial problems were especially onerous to faculty members and other school employees who year after year received little or no salary increase. Since Joliet was a blue-collar community with a strong union tradition, it is not surprising that school employees organized to improve working conditions. Teachers were much slower to unionize than maintenance workers, who reported to the Board in January 1939 that a majority of them had joined a local union affiliated with the International Brotherhood of Firemen and Oilers, A. F. of L. Beginning in 1947, union teachers became active in making their requests known to the School Board. During the 1950s and early '60s, union membership increased as high school and college teachers left the Teacher's Association, an Illinois Education Association (IEA) affiliate, and joined Local 604 of the American Federation of Teachers (AFT). For several years, the two groups worked together to jointly present salary and benefit proposals to the School Board.[25]

As its membership grew in the 1960s, the teachers' union became more active in unilaterally pressing for improvements in salary and benefits. Differences and divisions between the association and union were becoming more apparent and more public. At an April 1966 Board meeting, Robert

Burke, President of AFT Local 604, read a statement pointing out that teachers had worked for two years without a raise and that there would be "serious consequences" if there was no increase the next year. During the following month, the union presented a bargaining rights petition requesting an election to name a teachers' organization as the sole bargaining agent for all faculty members. The IEA-affiliated Teacher's Association objected, claiming that such action was ill-advised and illegal. The School Board twice rejected the request before finally consenting in October 1966 to a collective bargaining election. In a secret ballot, high school and college faculty chose AFT Local 604 to be their sole bargaining agent. The Board approved a temporary agreement to negotiate with representatives of the teachers and to enter into a formal contract with the faculty on January 20, 1967. When no agreement was reached by that date, union members voted to strike on January 25. School lawyers went to court and obtained an injunction to end the strike; however, teachers ignored the injunction and continued the work stoppage. With the Joliet Ecumenical Clergy Association acting as an intermediary, the two sides reached an agreement and ended the strike. On April 11, 1967, the Board of Trustees ratified a formal contract with high school and college faculty represented by AFT Local 604.[26]

While the Joliet high school and junior college district was struggling with finances and employee unrest, the General Assembly passed the Junior College Act of 1965. The master plan for junior colleges under the new law offered a partial solution to the district's problems. If JJC became a separate Class I college as defined by the statute, the state would pay three-fourths of the cost to acquire a site and build a campus. It would also reimburse the college at a rate of $11.50 for each semester credit hour earned by students. Furthermore, the creation of an expanded junior college district would broaden the tax base and lower the tax rate. If under the 1965 law the college retained a Class II standing, it was entitled to only $9.50 per credit hour. In order to achieve Class I status, a feasibility study would have to be conducted, district boundaries established, and a tax rate set. An application would have to be approved by the Illinois Junior College Board and the Board of Higher Education, followed by a successful referendum in the proposed district.[27]

A Coordinating Council on Education, composed of some twenty civic and social organizations and headed by George Travers, developed a three-part plan for dealing with the financial crisis in Joliet's public schools, from elementary through junior college. Concerned citizens and school leaders would make a concerted effort, first, to pass tax referendums for both the grade school and high school districts; second, to establish a Class I junior college and finally, to pass a bond issue for new elementary classrooms. The committee stressed the importance of everyone working equally hard on all three propositions. Local attorney and JJC graduate Kenneth Timm chaired the subcommittee responsible for creating a Class I junior college district. A broad-based committee representing several communities in the Joliet region studied the matter and proposed that a Class I college be created from twelve high school districts encompassing all or part of Will, Grundy, Kendall, Kankakee, and LaSalle Counties. The committee proposed a tax rate of 9.5 cents, among the lowest of any junior college district in the state. Certainly, this would be a selling point to Joliet voters who had turned down two junior college tax levies in the past three years. The state quickly approved the committee's plan; now it was up to the voters.[28]

John Racich, a Joliet banker and college alumnus, led the drive to publicize the plan and encourage voters throughout the proposed district to support the proposition. Max Kuster, a junior college instructor and Chairman of the Research and Information Committee, helped recruit speakers and mobilize volunteers. On December 10, 1966, an unprecedented 20,000 Joliet voters turned out and passed the grade school and high school referendums by the slim margin of 200 votes. Buoyed by its initial success, the Coordinating Council on Education next focused its efforts on the junior college referendum two months later. On February 18, 1967, America's oldest public junior college attained Class I legal status by an overwhelming total of 20,043 to 5,032 votes. JJC's future looked much brighter.[29]

Joliet Junior College experienced a period of challenge and change between 1939 and 1967. During this critical time in the school's development, six different people served as superintendent of Joliet Township High School and Junior College. The superintendents devoted most of their time to administering the high school and delegated to the college dean and his assistants the responsibility for operating the college. Leadership of the college during these years remained stable. Ira D. Yaggy served as dean from 1926 to 1947, followed by Elmer Rowley from 1947 to 1967. During Rowley's tenure as dean, he was assisted by Susan Wood, Walter Zaida, and Floyd Tompkins.

C. L. Jordan,
Superintendent,
1939-41

Dr. Leonard B.
Wheat,
Superintendent,
1942-43

Dr. Roosevelt
Basler,
Superintendent,
1943-46

Donald M. Sharpe,
Superintendent,
1946-47

Hugh H. Bonar,
Superintendent,
1947-60

Dr. William C.
French,
Superintendent,
1960-67

Elmer W. Rowley,
Dean, 1947-67

Susan Wood, Assistant Dean, 1948-67

Ira D. Yaggy, Dean, 1926-47

Walter F. Zaida, Assistant to the Dean,
1961-67

Floyd Tompkins, Assistant Dean and
Director of Adult Education, 1955-67

Secretaries

The 1943 yearbook was dedicated to Grayce Stadler, the attractive, personable secretary to Dean I. D. Yaggy. Because of her position in the dean's office, Miss Stadler frequently dealt with students who needed questions answered and problems solved. Next to her photograph on the dedication page, the class of '43 expressed its "sincerest appreciation" to Grayce, who "aids us in every way" and always with a "gracious smile." Seven years later, the Class of 1949 also dedicated its yearbook to Miss Stadler, citing her "kindness, understanding, and friendship" as the reason for the honor.[30]

In 1967, Grayce Stadler (seated) was still assisting students as an administrative secretary, as was Claire Poole (standing).

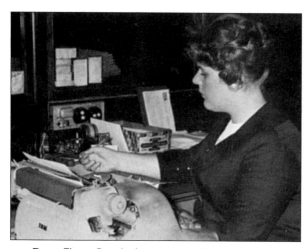

Dean Elmer Rowley's secretary, Sondra Flint, is pictured here in 1961.

In 1967, secretaries Edith Stewart and Helen Ford offered friendly and professional assistance to students and staff alike. They and others like them in administrative and department offices were important in the day-to-day operation of the college.

Custodians and maintenance men kept the building in tip-top shape. Seated around the table are John Anderson, Andy Zahm, Vince Smith, William Jackson, Raymond Becker, Otto Pearson, Herbert Forsell, and building policeman Lawrence Anderson. Standing are Harry Johnson and John Krakar. Although their work was often routine and performed when few people were around, occasionally they were required to deal with monumental messes created by large crowds or Mother Nature.

Pictured here is the woodshop floor buckled by floodwaters in July 1957. Surveying the damage and the magnitude of the cleanup is Superintendent of Buildings and Grounds Bror Anderson (white shirt).

World War II Impacts JJC

World War II had a tremendous impact on the history and development of the college, even greater than World War I some twenty-five years earlier. The shock waves of Pearl Harbor's bombs were virtually felt in the hallways and classrooms of Joliet Junior College. In less than two years, enrollment dropped from 387 students to 179, most of whom were women.

Approximately 300 JJC students served in the armed forces during the war. So few men were left on campus that even the school's highly successful basketball program was dropped in 1943. Red Cross meetings became commonplace as students at home looked for ways to support the war effort. History classes sold War Savings Stamps, and special parties were held to honor servicemen and women home on furlough.

The war ended the lingering effects of the Great Depression in the Joliet area by creating numerous jobs in war-related industries. Workers were especially needed in the nearby ordnance plants and shipyard. Twilight, evening, and weekend classes were added to the schedule to accommodate students who decided to work. The school's Science and Agriculture Departments provided training and technical assistance during the war. Science instructors R. L Frisbie, C.M. Eggman, and Everett Nelsen taught intensive classes to train gauge readers and powder inspectors. With much of the male labor force depleted by the war, an increasing number of women found employment outside the home. In fact, one training class in the manufacture of explosives was attended entirely by females employed in ammunition plants.

In 1942, the head of vocational education, Drew Castle, was named Supervisor of Defense and placed in charge of developing special classes to produce items and commodities needed for the war. During the following year, the high school and junior college became a center for the production and canning of food. Elmer Rowley, Chair of the high school Agriculture Department, administered the school's overall food program that included instruction in planting "victory gardens," instruction in food production, and the operation of three centers for canning

Science instructors Eggman, Frisbie, Nelsen, and Larson.

Student Federalists in 1947.
Standing: Marjorie Parkhurst, Robert Smolich, Madeline Niznik, Edward Bergquist, Lloyd Raridon, Richard Briick, Florine Klatt, Reichman, Lloyd Howerton. **Seated:** Elizabeth Barns (faculty sponsor).

Employees of the Elwood Ordnance Plant near Joliet are seen assembling boosters for shells during World War II.

uits, vegetables, and meats.[31]

On campus, students became actively involved in he National Defense Program. The 1942 college earbook proudly announced that JJC men were reparing to defend the country "with wings and ifles" and that JJC women were also doing their art with a rifle team. A Civil Pilot Training Corps as established on campus with ten men and two lternates receiving instruction to eventually earn heir wings and enter the Army Air Corps. A men's ifle team was organized under the supervision of OTC instructors for the purpose of "hit[ting] the foe ith a blitzkreig which our enemy has invented to dd our country to their long list of prey."[32] The proximity of Joliet to nearby ammunition plants kept the ity on alert during the early phase of the war. In anuary 1942, the School Board cooperated with civil efense efforts by designating the cafeteria as an mergency hospital. On April 24, 1942, an air raid rill was conducted on campus. When the sirens egan to wail, students quickly left their classes and marched downstairs to lower corridors, where they stood in hallways away from glass until the "all clear" was sounded.[33]

In social science classes, students sold war stamps and discussed the causes of the war and what could be done to prevent such a crisis in the future. Some students were drawn to the idea that extreme nationalism had contributed to the war and that lasting peace could be achieved only through the creation of a federal world government. Under the direction of faculty sponsor Elizabeth Barns, an organization called Student Federalists was established in 1947. The group explained in a letter to *The Blazer* that "Student Federalists believe that the world has become a single great community, and it will either be united under law or destroyed by an atomic or bacteriological war." Indeed, individual students and the college as a whole adapted and responded to the economic, social, ideological, and military challenges of World War II.[34]

Men's Rifle Team

Students quickly moved from classrooms to basement corridors during a 1942 air raid drill.

Civil Pilot Training Corps members James Scofield, Raymond Herkert, James MacDonald, August Perino, John Airoldi, Robert Cirasole, Warren Armstrong, Lambert, and Leo Fay.

"In-Line" Registration

Students who stood in long, slow-moving lines to register for classes would be envious, indeed, of today's students who use home computers to register online. The first step in the registration process was to choose a major and select courses that fit the desired program. Prior to the mid-1950s, all students met with the college dean to make out a schedule of classes. Six faculty advisors were appointed in 195? to assist students in developing class schedule? designed to achieve their educational goals. Over th? years, the number of advisors increased in proportio? to college enrollment and the popularity of programs. With schedule in hand, students stood in line outsid? the college library on registration day and waite?

Georgina Smith (left) was one of the original advisors appointed in 1955. She is pictured here in 1963 with Vera Smith (right), who also advised students in the pre-education curriculum.

In 1963, the business and pre-commerce programs were popular with students who were assigned to one of the advisors seen here: Elmer Jamnik, John Birkholz, John Corradetti, and Lola A. Emery.

Every freshman student was required to take placement tests that advisors used when helping students choose programs and courses.

Assistant deans Walter Zaida and Susan Wood are seen helping Dean Elmer Rowley (seated) prepare materials for Station 1 on registration day.

their turn to enter the door, only to wait some more. Snaking their way from station to station, they learned lessons in patience and disappointment. Sometimes, classes were closed or canceled, and it was necessary to revisit the advisor and start all over again. What a relief to finally reach the last station, even if it was the cashier ready to take that hard-earned money. Whenever students wrote retrospectives in yearbooks and other publications, they vividly recalled the registration ordeal and the long, interminable lines. These reminiscences usually concluded with the sentiment, "There must be a better way!"

Students stood in line outside the college library and filled out last-minute forms while waiting their turn to register for classes.

Year after year, little changed — except larger enrollments and longer lines.

Once inside the registration area, students slowly moved from table to table, sometimes discovering that a class was closed or a prerequisite had not been met.

"Who's next? Sorry, you're in the wrong line. You should be over there!"

The final step in the registration ordeal was fittingly the most painful — paying the bill.

66

Parking

Parking problems grew steadily worse as enrollment increased and students became more affluent and mobile. A student-faculty committee in 1959, for example, determined that there were eighty-five parking spaces available for students. The criteria established for issuing permits gave priority to students who commuted to classes from outside the district. Other factors considered were health conditions, married students with jobs, and service to the college. A 1964 survey found that half of the students owned cars and drove to school. From the students' perspective, it seemed that "No Parking" signs were much more plentiful than places to park. Taking a chance on parking illegally meant risking a dreaded $3 ticket or, worse yet, a towed car and a steeper fine. *The Blazer* empathized with frustrated students, complaining that there were "cars, cars everywhere, but not a place to park."[35]

Books

During the years that JJC shared facilities with the high school, there was no college bookstore. The Student Council often operated a book exchange that facilitated the buying and selling of used books. Students would drop off their books, appropriately marked with a selling price. If the books were sold, 10 percent was deducted from the seller's proceeds and placed in a scholarship fund for a needy sophomore student. Jim Arnold is seen here assisting Karen Brode in 1963.

School Picnic

The first social activity of the school year was the annual picnic at Inwood Park. After a variety of get-acquainted activities and team games, such as tug-of-war, a traditional picnic dinner of barbecues, sandwiches, beans, potato salad, and cake was served. Table conversation often turned to class schedules and the frustration of registration. The evening usually ended with a college "mixer" or dance.

The fall picnic during registration week was a time for students to enjoy themselves and establish new friendships. The young men seen here amuse a female companion by demonstrating various methods of opening a soft drink without a bottle opener.

Seated near to far on right, students Donna Swinford, Verna Fretty, and Joyce Speckman shared a table with faculty member Steve Lenich and his wife in 1961.

Playing tug-of-war at the 1970 picnic got a little muddy . . .

. . . really muddy!

Diane Isberg, Bev Bettenhausen, Sandy Starr, Wilma Schuldt, and Barb Butterfield added a secret ingredient to the beans at the 1959 picnic.

Focus on Faculty

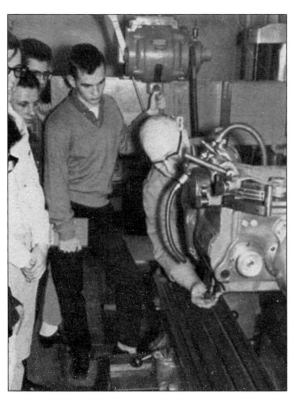

Max Kuster explains to his students in 1963 why this Deere has not been "running like a deer."

In 1965, Lloyd Zimmer shows students how to make an adjustment in machine shop.

Department Chair and advisor Al Racchini uses a hands-on method to teach auto shop in 1968.

In 1961, under the watchful eye of instructor Renee Slatton (hidden from view), Sandy Balog, Joyce Speckman, and Sally Booth work on a recipe in a home economics class.

Mrs. Barbee demonstrates the art of sewing with a Singer in a clothing construction class in 1966.

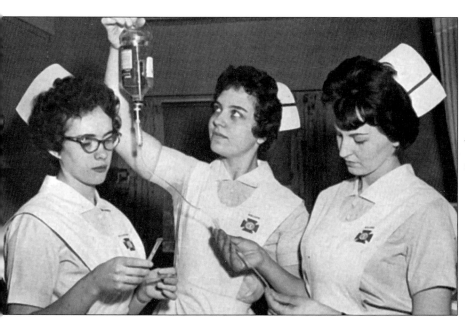

JJC partnered with Silver Cross Hospital to offer general education and science classes to student nurses. Pictured here in 1963 are Patricia Christensen, Sharon DePratt, and Lareene Haas.

Data processing instructor Eugene Small offers instruction in operating a key punch machine in 1966.

Richard Manthei, data processing student in 1967, operates an IBM card reader providing input into the computer.

Members of the Social Science Department hold a meeting in 1942: Harry D. Leinenweber, Glenn Evans, Elizabeth Barns, C. O. Burden, and Olin McReynolds.

Erma Smith, Paul Lester, Bruce Houseknecht, and Catherine Wood of the Fine Arts Department pose for a yearbook picture in 1948.

In 1950, child education students Roberta Morrissey and Estelle Voira work with youngsters in the new nursery school operated by JJC as a training center for curriculum enhancement.

Catherine Adler announces the term paper due date to her freshman rhetoric class in 1966.

Ted Thompson makes a point in his rhetoric class in 1968.

In 1968, English Department Chair Robert Burke conducts a lecture in American literature.

Art Department Chair Earl Kurtz demonstrates his own artistic ability in 1967.

Although nude models were not yet used in 1967, the subject's attire reveals the lines and curves of the human body for student artists learning to draw.

Instructor Ed Puddicombe introduces students in his 1960 physiology class to "George" and "Henrietta," two models who are nothing but bones.

Chemistry instructor Duane Converse conducts an experiment in 1967.

Everett Nelsen points out the internal features of a frog's anatomy to zoology students Ken Bromberek and Mary Ann Lambakis.

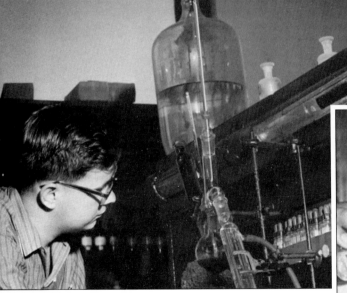

The distinct smell of rotten eggs often emanated from the "department of odors and vapors." Peering in for a closer look, these students are fortunately wearing their safety glasses.

Sitting at his desk in 1967, math instructor Si Ellingson answers a student's question.

Art Wagner, Chair of the Biological Sciences Department, responds to a student question in 1968.

In 1968, James Egly consults his notes in Economics 101.

Economics instructor and assistant football coach William Brinkman explains the principle of supply and demand to his class in 1967.

Keeping busy at their desks between classes in 1968 are Ken Parker, Chair of Physical Education, and Neil Lance, Director of Intramural Sports.

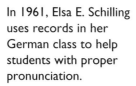

In 1961, Elsa E. Schilling uses records in her German class to help students with proper pronunciation.

Library

Under the supervision of librarian Lottie Skidmore, students use "listening posts" in the college library to review material for language and music classes.

Some students preferred studying outside the library away from the watchful gaze and occasional "ssshhh" of librarian George Fox.

The college library was remodeled from time to time to improve lighting and expand shelf space for the growing collection. Doing research for a class report or term paper kept some students working right up to closing time at 9:00 p.m. Bill Cernugel consults a book in the reference section, while Kaye Krohn checks the card catalogue. There were no interlibrary loan services or online sources available to students at this time.

The Smoker

In 1947, *The Blazer* announced under the heading "Believe It or Not" that a smoking room had been established for college students in the custodian's office. Noting that smoking had always been a very serious offense, the article explained that the "great change in attitude" was due largely to the number of returned servicemen on campus to whom "smoking has become a near necessity." Although initially restricted to male students, within a few years the "smoker" was relocated, refurnished, and opened to women. A TV was installed in 1955, a welcome addition to the room's "creature comforts." *The Blazer* periodically scolded the few creatures who littered the room and misused the furniture and pointedly suggested that they "treat it as civilized people would."[36]

The college smoker was one of the most popular and controversial places on campus. It served as a place to relax and socialize and to have a quick smoke and a Coke before class. For others, it became a hangout and a place to play cards when "ditching" class. School administrators kept an eye on the room, sometimes breaking up card games and admonishing players that it was time to shuffle off to class. When the music and noise got too loud or the

Seats in the smoker were often at a premium, causing some to peer in and pass by.

A smoke and a Coke, then off to class.

Desperate times called for desperate measures — the smoker had been administratively closed until further notice.

Final exam week created anxiety and extreme nervousness in the smoker.

litter on the floor got too deep, the smoker would be suddenly closed until further notice. Inevitably, students would complain, *The Blazer* would lecture readers on keeping butts and Coke cups off the floor, and the Student Council would hold meetings with administrators to negotiate the reopening of the room.[37]

A reporter for *The Blazer* captured the ambiance of the smoker prior to a temporary closing in 1961: "Through the thick white film of smoke, dim figures could be seen clapping hands and beating their feet in rhythm with the record 'Runaround Sue.' In short, it was paradise complete." The same writer noted that when the "cough chamber" was reopened two days later, someone had put a sign on the window: "Please Do Not Feed The Animals." In 1962, the smoker was closed for a month, during which time a survey was conducted to determine whether students really wanted such a place. The result was a resounding 94 percent in favor of its reopening. Clearly, students in the '60s were not interested in a smoke free-campus.[38]

Topics of Conversation in the Smoker and Lounge

Year	Top Tunes	Major Movies
1955	Rock Around the Clock Ain't That A Shame Love is a Many Splendored Thing	Marty Mister Roberts The Rose Tattoo
1956	Hound Dog Blue Suede Shoes Tutti Frutti	Around the World in 80 Days The Ten Commandments The King and I
1957	All Shook Up Bye Bye Love Wake Up Little Susie	The Bridge on the River Kwai Peyton Place Twelve Angry Men
1958	At the Hop Great Balls of Fire All I Have to Do is Dream	Gigi Cat on a Hot Tin Roof The Defiant Ones
1959	Mack the Knife There Goes My Baby Smoke Gets in Your Eyes	Ben Hur The Diary of Anne Frank Anatomy of a Murder
1960	Its Now or Never Only The Lonely Kathy's Clown	The Apartment Elmer Gantry Psycho
1961	Moon River Are You Lonesome Tonight Will You Still Love Me Tomorrow	West Side Story The Hustler Judgment at Nuremburg
1962	I Can't Stop Loving You The Loco-Motion Let's Twist Again	Lawrence of Arabia The Music Man To Kill a Mockingbird
1963	She Loves You If I Had a Hammer It's My Party	Tom Jones Cleopatra How the West Was Won
1964	I Want to Hold Your Hand Walk on By Can't Buy Me Love	My Fair Lady Becket Mary Poppins
1965	The Times They Are A – Changin' California Girls A Hard Day's Night	The Sound of Music Doctor Zhivago Ship of Fools

College Lounge and Cafeteria

Originally known as the rec (recreation) room, the college lounge had a different look and smell than the smoker. It was one of the favorite places on campus for students to gather. Some socialized with friends, others did their homework at one of the tables, and still others sat quietly as spectators of student life. Occasionally, someone who had studied or partied long into the night could be seen taking a nap.

In 1952, some students campaigned to have a TV installed in the lounge, especially since school authorities were cracking down on playing cards. *The Blazer* joined the debate and wondered "whether television would be damaging to the morals of the college students." The liquor advertisements and portrayal of crime on the screen might contribute to a "distorted code of morals," observed the writer. Despite these dangers, a TV was purchased for the lounge in 1953, and then the subject turned to daytime programming. What would the students watch? The choices ranged from the *Arthur Godfrey Show* to *Ding Dong Nursery School*. Students learned the art of compromise whenever there were disagreements in program selection. When the TV was new and still a novelty, there was often more "sshhing" in the lounge than in the library.[39]

Student behavior in the college lounge sometimes became an issue. Feet on the furniture and filth on the floor brought reprimands from school administrators. Occasionally, the room was temporarily closed until student leaders addressed the problem. Following a $4,000 renovation in 1955, students were informed that now they were expected to be on their very best behavior. For several weeks, the student council arranged "hosts" for the lounge to monitor its use and to remind users that this room was a privilege and not an entitlement. The lounge was described as the heart of the college socially, one of the first places that students looked when trying to locate their friends. Pictured in the **top photo on the opposite page** is the reception held to celebrate the opening of the remodeled lounge in 1955.[40]

Graduation

During the early 1960s, several changes were made in the annual graduation ceremony. The college discontinued the practice of holding a combined ceremony with high school seniors in an outdoor setting at the stadium and began conducting separate graduation exercises in the school auditorium. The new format featured student speakers as well as prominent guests. Pictured here in 1964 is student speaker Janice Johnson. After all the awards were given and the speeches were made, Dr. Suren Seron, President of the Board of Education, presented diplomas to the proud graduates. Among the first to cross the stage and accept the congratulations of Assistant Dean Susan Wood, Dean Elmer Rowley, and Dr. Seron are Carol Sue Burnham and William Ciluffo.

"Leaders are made, not born," declared Dr. Del Kinney at the annual Leadership Conference in 1963. Attended by class officers, student council members, and officers of various clubs, JJC students spent an October weekend at George Williams College Camp in Lake Geneva, Wisconsin. Kinney led the students in analyzing the college and understanding their role as student leaders. They learned how to plan and conduct meetings and practiced various problem-solving techniques. Assistant Dean Walter Zaida is seen here distributing materials at the opening session.

Leaders of the 1963 freshman class were president Russ Wunderlich, secretary-treasurer Mary Ann Ross, and vice president Jack Mork.

Organized in 1948 by the students pictured here, Students of Medical Science was one of the most active clubs on campus. Under the direction of faculty sponsor Ed Puddicombe, SMS watched films, heard guest speakers, and took numerous field trips to regional hospitals and professional schools. Students were occasionally permitted to observe surgeries, sometimes performed by JJC graduates in the medical profession. One of the longest trips taken by the club was to Mayo Clinic in Rochester, Minnesota, in 1966. Also, in a joint effort with the college Adult Education Office, SMS co-sponsored the popular program *Your Doctor Speaks.* Original club members are pictured. **Front:** John Coady, John Bedesky, Mark Meers, Bob Riffel, and Ralph Deuschman. **Back:** Gus Samios, Jim Blackburn, Jack Briick, John Klocke, and Art Wilhelmi.

During the 1950s, the Veteran's Club became one of the largest on campus as Korean War vets returned to college. The club sponsored an annual Christmas project collecting food and toys for needy families in the area. Members are pictured here in 1957. **Front:** Ronald Goldenstern, Harold Swinford, Richard Kittrell, Ted Zuck, Willard Curtis, John Mahan, Ronald Ludeman, Willard Prynn. **Middle:** Joe Remko, Merle Drew, Richard Maske, George Economides, Robert McIntyre, Jack Albert, Matthew Picciolo, Edward Stefancic. **Back:** James Slobodnik, Paul Belin, Carl Batson, Harry Woodhouse, LaVerne Kastman, Gil Nicoll, Dallas Munter, Lou Vargas, Matt Racich.

The Motor Sports Club encouraged the ownership and appreciation of motor-sports vehicles. The club held rallies, planned speed and distance contests, and attended auto shows and races. Pictured here are members in 1964. **Front:** Bill Piner, Mike Lenich, Ken King, and Ray Friday. **Back:** Jim Wellman, Roger Tracy, Jack Wicke, Chuck Marshall, Jerry Frattini, Phil Bjekich, Lee Bettenhausen, Ron Smego, Milton Sheffield, Al Zanzola, and Al Chesko.

The Spanish Club, pictured here in 1966, was organized to promote the study and appreciation of the Spanish language and culture. **Front:** Sylvia Ponce, Pam Scriber, Marge Sauer, Flip Jerzycke, and faculty sponsor Dulce Hornvale. **Back:** Charles Meyer, Dave Kramer, and Tom Newberry.

Stop the presses! Scores of junior college students gained valuable experience over the years as members of the Press Club. Writing, editing, and publishing skills were developed and sharpened as students met deadlines and produced a variety of publications including *The Blazer, Shield, College Casuals,* and "The Wolf Call," a weekly column in local newspapers. Officers of the 1965 Press Club were vice president Maribeth Sullivan, president Joe Baltz, and secretary-treasurer Norma Barone

The Camera Club was a fairly new organization in 1943 when members were photographed here examining a camera used to take pictures for the yearbook. Students learned darkroom techniques necessary for developing film and printing photographs. The only requirements for membership were an interest in taking pictures and the ability to work in the dark. **Seated:** Leona Braman, Florence Hojnacki, and Milton Lewis. **Standing:** Robert Markelz, Franklin Sidell, and Connors.

Organized in the mid-1940s, the Engineer's Club was composed of students interested in learning about the engineering profession. Under the guidance of faculty sponsor Drew Castle, the club watched educational movies, heard guest speakers, and went on field trips to regional companies. The 1956 club pictured here was the first to have female members. **Front:** Edward Sparks, Henry Frieh, Joyce Potter, Judy Sanders, Val Spreitzer, Palmer Kloster, Phil Egizio. **Middle:** Andrew Prophet, Gordon Fabian, James Krizmanic, Joseph Dezelan, Henry Atkinson, Drew Castle (faculty sponsor), James St. Germain. **Back:** Jesse Roa, Roger Geske, Robert Davis, Krakar, Richard Barklow, Jim Yakich, William Verd.

Members of the 1965 Chess Club study their next moves as they try to out-strategize their opponents. The club was organized to promote the game and to make matches available to chess enthusiasts.

Composed of both high school and junior college students, the FDA (Future Distributors of America) Club was limited to those enrolled in distributive education classes. Students attended classes in the morning and worked in local businesses in the afternoon. They were paid regular wages for the hours they worked and received credit for their time both in class and on the job. Distributive Education Coordinator Duane Kirchoff served as FDA Club sponsor. **Seated:** Chris Dragatsis, Joyce Bauch, Elsie Shaubel, Darlene Reece, Marilyn Chesko, Betty Peart, and Lorraine Tezak. **Standing:** Wayne Massey, Andy Orsini, Don Beno, Wally Sharp, Richard Rachick, Jim Gillette, and sponsor Duane Kirchoff.

The Associated Business Students, or the Business Club as it was generally known, met once a month and welcomed all students interested in pursuing business careers. Men and women from the business world often attended club meetings and shared information on the requirements and opportunities in their chosen fields. The social highlight of the year was a spring banquet climaxed by the presentation of awards and scholarships and the announcement of newly elected officers. Pictured here are club members in 1961. **Front:** Faculty sponsor John Corradetti, Leslie Yunker, Fred Baldazzi, Mary Ann Lambakis, Doris Hareld, Janice Whitler, Janet Judnick, Lynn Herbst, Jim Benson, and Jim Norris. **Back:** Chuck Allen, Dennis Taylor, Jim McGuire, Steve Kochevar, Lou Marello, Rich Eyrich, Dave Kettwig, Bob Becker, Bill Laken, Jim Troutman, and Richard Butterbach.

In February 1966, the Social Science Club sponsored a program in observance of Brotherhood Week featuring Rabbi Morris M. Hershman of the Joliet Jewish Congregation (pictured here) and Father Epple, Chaplain of Lewis College. In speaking on "The Implementation of Brotherhood," Rabbi Hershman stated that "we must come to a realization that our world and nations are made up of minorities, and all have something to contribute. Everyone has something to contribute to society." At its monthly meetings, club members discussed such topics as the conflict in Vietnam, the Civil Rights Acts of 1964 and 1965, and social change in America.[42]

In 1961, the teacher education program began the practice of placing sophomore students in nearby elementary and high schools to gain a practical understanding of the teaching-learning process. Students observed cooperating teachers at work and then met once a week with their college instructor to share and discuss their experiences. These discussions of best teaching practices often carried over into meetings of the Student Education Association, the student club for future teachers. Several sophomores are seen here leaving campus to observe classes in 1963: Rosemarie Varju, John Bertino, Sandy Brown, Sue Manner, Marilyn Simonetti, Lucile Allen, Rita Roy, Carolyn Schaeffer, Rose Bennett, and Clyde Andrews.

In 1951, Joliet Junior College celebrated its Golden Anniversary with a banquet. Addressing the attendees, who came from all over the country, is former Superintendent Roosevelt Basler. Seated on his right is Dean Elmer Rowley, and on his left is Assistant Dean Susan Wood. Next to Miss Wood is Dr. Jesse Bogue, Executive Secretary of the American Association of Junior Colleges. To his left is Mrs. Bonar and Superintendent Hugh Bonar. Included in the program were reminiscences of retired faculty members and a roll call by classes. Many former teachers and students who could not attend sent letters of greeting.

In January 1953, the XI chapter of Sigma Mu Sigma Fraternity was chartered at JJC, the first four-year fraternity organized on a community college campus. Sigma Mu Sigma was a general social fraternity established to promote fellowship among members, service to community, and reverence for God. Faculty sponsors were Almond Fairfield and John Schneider, both of whom were national officers of the fraternity. Charter members initially constructed a chapter room in Mr. Fairfield's basement, but eventually acquired a house at 108 Richards Street. The fraternity "rushed" pledges, initiated new members, and planned a variety of social activities. In November 1955, Orrie Seron was chosen as the group's first "Sweetheart of Sigma Mu." Superintendent Bonar informed the School Board in June 1958 that a legal opinion held that fraternities and sororities could not legally exist on junior college campuses. The Board immediately passed a resolution declaring that students connected in any way with such organizations would be immediately expelled from school. Pictured here in 1954 are officers of Sigma Mu Sigma. **Seated:** Dave Mraz, treasurer; Bob Fraser, president; Jack Shaw, junior vice president. **Standing:** Jerry Algeo, guard; Don Thornburg, senior vice president; Joe Kuhar, secretary.

In 1966, Dean Elmer Rowley prepares to open the Bulletin Board to install a new sign stating that JJC is America's oldest public junior college. Assisting and observing with approval are Petra Ziegner (holding sign), Ken Bazaar, Judy Lutz, and Assistant Dean Robert Mitchell.

AMERICA'S OLDEST PUBLIC JUNIOR COLLEGE

Activities

Recognizing the importance of school activities in the overall learning experience, Joliet Junior College has historically offered its students opportunities for involvement in clubs, special programs, and social events. Students are encouraged to participate fully in campus life but are free to choose their level of involvement. Although jobs and family commitments leave little free time for some students, those who are able to participate in campus activities maximize their college experience and often learn lessons not taught in class.

In October 1952, Senator William Fulbright, an Arkansas Democrat, and Governor Val Peterson, a Nebraska Republican, squared off in the school auditorium to discuss the 1952 presidential candidates. The two politicians were in Joliet as participants in "America's Town Meeting of the Air," a program sponsored locally by JJC's "World Today" series. Fulbright and Peterson discussed the differences between General Dwight D. Eisenhower and Governor Adlai E. Stevenson and expressed sharp disagreement over which candidate would make the better president. The program filled the auditorium and was also broadcast by ABC. Pictured here on stage are Assistant Dean Susan Wood, Governor Val Peterson, Dr. Orville Hitchcock (moderator), and Senator William Fulbright.

In the fall of 1947, the college began broadcasting biweekly programs on WJOL radio. The format was broad enough to include musical performances, discussions, dramatizations, and interpretive readings by students and staff. Miss Erma Smith, a new speech and English instructor, served as faculty sponsor and helped students polish their scripts and showcase their talent. Pictured here are Jimmy Scheppach, Mary Ellen Scheppach, Henry Simpson, Noblitt, Ted Berst and Ronald Cook.

he annual ski trip etween semesters gave oth experienced skiers id those new to the sport i opportunity to hit the opes. Pictured here in 958 are JJC "schussoomers" at Ishpeming, ichigan, with faculty sponor Eugene Bondar (kneelig with glasses).

i 1946, a Men's Glee Club was organized with twentyve members. Director Paul Lester met with the oup twice a week for practice. Whenever special iusic was needed at school assemblies or civic gatherigs, the Glee Club was ready to perform.

Planning the annual ski trip and sharing survival stories later were almost as much fun as the downhill runs. Pictured here at a 1963 planning session with a sign reading "Mt. Telemark or Bust!!!" are Karen Behling, Alex Francois, and Barbara Johnson in front and Aija Jekabsons, Lynn Mauer, and Jim Lois in back.

In 1965, Ron Jugenitz recounts the ordeal of how he "busted" his ski — but fortunately not his leg. Looking on are Melanie Berta, Jan Hanley, Paul Spittal, and Joy Nembic.

95

Over the years, numerous entertainers and nationally known speakers have appeared on campus. One of the most memorable humorous programs was presented by the Smothers Brothers in 1963. Lacing songs with satire, Tom and Dick Smothers delighted the huge crowd with their sibling rivalry and Tom's wacky jibes and comments.

Roller skating parties were especially popular in the 1940s and '50s. Here, in 1957, John Racich manages to remain upright with a little assistance from Eugene "Jug" Matesi while Fred Norton appears to be an experienced skater as he overtakes the unsteady pair. Meanwhile, Everett "Sparky" Hauck has made an unscheduled landing on the hardwood. Their facial expressions and body language reveal the challenge and enjoyment of partying on wheels.

Choir performances in 1949 featured the duet of Bill Rutter and Elaine Ott with Phyllis Hedstrom at the piano. The three musicians provided entertainment at the annual Junior College Conference with such popular love songs as "Wanting You" and "Love Me Tonight." According to *The Blazer*, Rutter's linen-like notes were a real hit with college women in the audience.[43]

The JC Players entertained appreciative audiences over the years while learning the art and craft of acting. Under the direction of Robert Mallary, the Players presented the three-act play *The Angry Twelve.* Seen here rehearsing in 1958 are Dolores Pagliei, Marie Chalstrom, James Padley, Lester Nelson, David Imig, Richard Wilhelmi, Genevieve Coulson, Allen McCowan, Wayne Barnett, Guy Sell, and Mary Ann Milner.

First organized in 1946 by Jack Hinton and then reorganized in 1949 by Dr. Hal Dellinger, the swing band drew musicians from the rich pool of talent in the Joliet area. The band played at a variety of school assemblies, dances, sporting events, and community functions. Together with the college choir, the swing band annually toured area high schools. Members are pictured here in 1950. **First Row:** Jack Meyer, Glenn Young, Mary Armstrong, Zoe Ann Schneiter, Joseph Lazzaro, Joan Briick. **Second Row:** Richard Comer, Donald Kramer, Charles Ursitti, Doris Kahn, Fred McGuire, Herman Kuntz. **Third Row:** Robert Riffel, John Howard. **Fourth Row:** Dr. Hal Dellinger, Sandro Brandolino, Angelo Principali, Tom Winterstein.

The JJC Choir in 1963 boasted fifty-five voices under the direction of Dr. Hal Dellinger. During the fall, the choir joined the swing band on a tour of area high schools to entertain and recruit students. The Christmas season found the choir presenting holiday programs to civic and social groups. The major event of the year was the annual spring musical, which featured various soloists and ensembles.
First Row: Michele Tinder, Sue Manner, Lila Kenyon, Judy Schempf, Addie Withers, Diane Ball, Barbara Johnson, Karyn Chizmark, Vicky Smith, Charlene Potter, Lynn Spencer, Sharon Maitland, Dr. Hal Dellinger. **Second Row:** Joan Dawson, Judy Crackel, Martha Huxtable, Judy Neutzman, Barbara Dorn, Beverly Startz, Linda Sandbloom, Grace Bachman, Joan Gustafson, Barbara Almberg, Penny Gregory. **Third Row:** Phillip Kaveny, Noble Allen, Joseph Kociuba, Phillip Pellouchoud, David Chelini, Dwight Ferryance, Thom Barber, John Rice, Vincent Gelsomino, Frank Gutierrez, Clyde Andrews. **Fourth Row:** Donald Young, Jerry Jackson, Randy Sala, Bob Cary, Kenneth Palmer, Larry Peet, Russell Wunderlich, Ronald Silc, William Holt, Arthur Kureghian, Joseph Maielli.

We Could Have Danced All Night

Although several generations of students have attended Joliet Junior College, one constant over the years has been the planning and enjoyment of dances. Music and dance steps have evolved and changed, but the fun and excitement of going to a dance with someone special have remained the same. Planning committees have worked long and hard to select a theme, choose a band, decorate the room, prepare refreshments, and attend to all the details that ensure a successful event. Some dances have been casual and others formal. They have been called mixers, hops, swings, and stomps. Dances were sometimes held to observe special events like homecoming or New Year's Eve, and often queens were elected and crowned. Indeed, throughout the years, dances have been the mainstay of the college social calendar.

During the 1940s, brooms with horses' heads were commonplace at mixers and casual dances. If a man on the side wanted to cut in, he would dance out on the floor with a horse-head broom and hand it to a woman's partner. The recipient of the broom was obliged to waltz off with his new horse-head partner and permit the cut to occur.

Decorating for dances often included interesting props for taking pictures. In keeping with the theme "The Gay Nineties," the 1943 Fall Formal featured a surrey with fringe on top. Posing for a group photograph are Ruth Markel, Richard Sokatch, Lois Damen, and Donald Wilhelmi.

There were always the mystery and excitement of the unknown when attending a box lunch social. Female students fixed the food, packed the unmarked boxes, and waited in suspense for theirs to be auctioned. The young men seen here in 1943 were just as anxious to discover whether good food and a fun dinner partner awaited their winning bid.

Opposite page: The committee pictured here planned the Fall Formal in 1966 with the theme "Noche de Fantasia." Roy Gordon's Orchestra furnished the music for the dance, which was held at D'Amico's 214 (now the City Center Campus). A highlight of the evening was the crowning of the yearbook queen, "Miss Shield." Serving on the planning committee were Susan Pierson, Rose Jovanovich, Petra Ziegner, Audrey Hornvale, Gary Nelson, Rena Wheeler, Barbara Kochevar, and Cindy Ringo.

Announcing the yearbook queen and crowning the new "Miss Shield" was the highlight of the annual Fall Formal. "Mediterranean Moonlight," the theme of the 1967 dance, set a romantic mood for the crowning of Nancy Myers. Placing the crown on her head is Marlene Samios, a former beauty queen herself. The new queen had the honor of leading the next dance to the applause of her friends and the music of Roy Gordon's Orchestra.

Faculty members and school administrators attended dances as sponsors and chaperones. Perhaps a line of chaperones like the one pictured here at the 1958 Spring Formal inspired "Varsity" to pen the poem that appeared in *The Blazer:*

> Gather your kisses while you may,
> For time brings only sorrow.
> The girls who are so free today,
> Are the chaperones of tomorrow.[44]

Decorating the gym for a dance required hours of work in constructing a false ceiling of crepe paper. Pictured here in 1955 is the grand march at the Winter Formal.

New Year's Eve was often celebrated at a college dance. JJC students in 1961 are in a festive mood as they usher in the New Year.

"Gettin' on down" at a college dance took on new meaning in 1962 when this couple won the twist contest. A *Blazer* reporter interviewed several people on campus to see what they thought of the new dance. Responses ranged from enthusiastic support expressed by some students to instructor Harry Leinenweber's comment: "I don't think much of it as a dance." One person wondered how the twist would affect one's back.[45]

FALL FORMAL

Several well-known musicians and bands performed at junior college dances, including Roy Gordon, Stan Kenton, Sammy Kaye, Si Zentner, and Louis "Satchmo" Armstrong. America's ambassador of jazz, Louie Armstrong, performed in 1958 at the Fall Formal. The gym was decorated with a false ceiling and silhouettes of jazz musicians covering the walls. Several couples are seen here enjoying refreshments during intermission.

Sadie Hawkins Week

Beginning in 1960 and lasting into the 1970s, JJC annually observed TWIRP Week with a full schedule of Sadie Hawkins activities. For those new to the concept, *The Blazer* explained to students that TWIRP meant "The Woman Is Requested To Pay." Female students were expected to reverse roles and take the lead in dating and showing deference to men by driving on dates, opening doors, helping with coats, carrying books, and paying for food and entertainment. Coupled with Sadie Hawkins activities, TWIRP Week had a definite hill-country flavor.

Based on the comic strip "Lil' Abner," Sadie Hawkins Day was a time in Dogpatch when wily and aggressive women had a chance to catch a husband.

Dressed for Sadie Hawkins Week in 1962 are Penny Wills, Sandy Celeznik, Leona Wicburg, Sue Grimpe, Diane Lockwood, and Sally Wohlgemuth.

Sporting beards, guns, jugs, and Dogpatch hats, these Lil' Abner look-alikes are ready for the hoedown: Robert Querio, Robert Sandberg, Andy Kotowicz, Neal MacDonald, David Warthen, and Tom Kienlen.

Carrying out the tradition of TWIRP Week, Barb Merrell, Melanie Schroeder, and Bertha Schultz carry books for Larry Kienlen, Ralph Alderman, and Neal MacDonald.

Daisy Mae and Lil' Abner outfits were proper attire at the week's activities. Pigtails on women, beards on men, clothes with patches, and tattered overalls were commonplace. The culminating event on Friday night was the Sadie Hawkins Dance to which women invited their dates. Prizes were awarded to the worst-dressed couple and to the men with the longest, shortest, and scrawniest beards. At some point in the evening, the room was usually darkened, and women armed with flashlights searched for their man to haul off to Marryin' Sam. For a few years during the 1970s, a Daisy Mae bikini contest was added to the festivities. Changing times and social sensibilities brought an end to TWIRP Week and Sadie Hawkins activities.[46]

Contestants in the Dogpatch bikini contest in 1971 were Sandy Adams, Cheryl Foster, Debbie Gilbert, Jane Hritz, Maureen Kennedy, Cherie Long, Joanne Masek, and Kathy Remus.

Debbie Gilbert was the winner.

Homecoming Weekend

Joliet Junior College held its first Homecoming Weekend in 1955, more than fifty years after its founding. For several years, the festivities followed a similar format. College clubs and organizations selected candidates for homecoming king and queen and began campaigning with signs and banners drap- ing halls and covering walls. At the bonfire on Friday night, coaches introduced members of the football team, and the Student Council president announced the king and queen. Often spontaneous, but some- times planned, a snake dance moved the fun-filled gathering from the embers of the fire to the grand-

Huge eye-catching banners spanning hallways were a sure sign that campaigning for homecoming royalty was underway. Supporters of each candidate tried to outdo the others in capturing the attention of passing students.

Campaigning ended, and it was time to vote. Barring a lengthy recount, the king and queen were announced at the bonfire pep rally on Friday night.

Standing next to a roaring fire in 1956, the coach introduced his players and thanked the students for their support. Somehow, victory seemed certain at a homecoming bonfire.

104

stand where cheerleaders held a pep rally. The evening usually ended with a casual party or mixer.

On Saturday morning, club members frantically put the finishing touches on their floats in preparation for the parade and motorcade to the stadium. At half time of the football game, the king and queen were introduced, and the floats circled the stadium. Judges then announced the winning entries, usually in several categories. Following the game, Homecoming Weekend ended with a dance and, if all went well, a victory celebration.

Students hammered, sawed, painted, and stuffed chicken wire with thousands of napkins as they worked feverishly to finish homecoming floats in time for the big parade. The task of creating a prize-winning float required both consultants and builders. Pictured here at work on their entry in 1957 are Kaye Powell, Thurm Bolerjack, Sharon Hutchins, Nancy Ahrens, Carole Sue Johnson, Judy Speckman, Carole Fris, and Bobbie Smith.

Led by mascot Wily Wolf and cheerleaders in 1968, a snake dance begins to wind its way from the dying bonfire to a rousing pep rally.

Frozen in time by the click of a camera, students at a pep rally in 1957 appear to be enjoying themselves.

The first homecoming queen and her court are leading the parade to the stadium in 1955: Connie Robinson, Dolores Davis, Madeline Martin, Queen Phyllis Olivo, Gerry Scaccia, Jo Sigwalt, Judy Lukanich.

The Booster Club float in 1955 proclaims "Wolves on the Warpath" and "Pierce Thornton." Riding atop the float are cheerleaders Bonnie Reid, Georgiana Dodge, Sue Montgomery, and Robert Johnson.

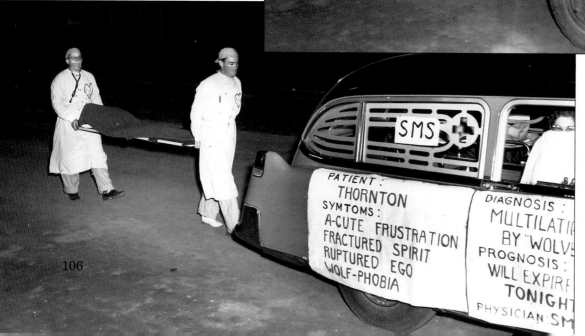

In keeping with the image of their club, Students of Medical Science (SMS) portray Thornton, JJC's homecoming opponent in 1955, as a hopeless patient with a variety of problems.

The Cultural Cinema Club entered the 1967 homecoming motorcade sporting Hollywood shades and a movie camera prop.

JJC mascot Wily Wolf sometimes showed a softer side when tenderly consoling a cheerleader after a heartbreaking loss. However, on other occasions, it was abundantly clear that underneath it all Wily was really a wolf in wolf's clothing.

Spotlight on Sports

Throughout the years, many outstanding athletes and championship teams have donned purple and white and performed exceptionally well for JJC. Given the constraints of limited space and available photographs, the athletes pictured here represent just a few of the many students who deserve recognition for their excellent play and the acclaim they achieved for the college. Many of these athletes transferred into senior institutions and continued to perform at a very high level.

Football

Responding to growing community interest reflected in a petition containing 22,000 signatures, the Joliet Park Board began to seriously consider the construction of a stadium in the late 1940s. JJC students joined the drive to have a stadium built. A *Blazer* reporter in 1947 polled students and staff for their ideas on where the stadium should be built. Several suggested that it should be within walking distance of the school. Others thought that the proposed location on the far west side of Joliet near Inwood Golf Course would provide plenty of space far away from traffic jams.[47]

The Joliet Park Board settled on the Inwood site and began construction in 1950. The new 10,000-seat stadium was completed in 1951 in time for JJC to move its football schedule from Richards Street Field to the new facility. Playing in a large stadium with towering lights added to the players' excitement. The press booth, camera deck, public address system, lighted scoreboard, and concession stands were amenities that added to the comfort and enjoyment of reporters and fans. With Inwood Golf Course and the airport runway in the background, this aerial view of Joliet Memorial Stadium shows that its location on West Jefferson Street was removed from city congestion in the 1950s.

JJC fielded its first football team in the fall of 1951. Spearheaded by the Student Council in 1950, students voted to discontinue publishing a traditional yearbook and to use the allotted funds to start a football program. The School Board approved the plan and appointed Herm Walser and Roy Carlson to recruit and coach the team. Playing with secondhand equipment, the team turned in a first class performance. Surprisingly, the squad compiled a season record of 7 wins and 1 loss. Even more remarkably, five players were named to the Junior College All-Star Team: quarterback John Bourg (No. 36), end Bob Brophy (No. 35), guard Matt Connors (No. 40), tackle Jack Ostrem (No. 37), and guard Tom Winterstein (No. 33). At the end of the season, the team was invited to California to play in the "Little Rose Bowl," where it was defeated by a more experienced squad from Compton, California.

oe Mussario won All-American honors in 1957 and was the eam's leading rusher two years n a row with an average of 6.6 ards per carry.

Playing guard and serving as team captain, Joe Gariboldi was named to two All-American teams in 1958.

Flanked by teammates on the sidelines, offensive end Ed Matesevac (No. 47) won All-American honors in 1960.

Grinding out tough yards, Jack Dinoffri led conference fullbacks in rushing and was named to the All-American team in 1960.

Coach Gil Bell congratulates Vern Voss on being named to the 1963 All-American football team. Voss was a standout at defensive end and offensive guard. When Bell needed a fullback late in the season, Voss took over the position for his injured teammate and averaged 6.2 yards per carry. Vern was also an outstanding wrestler for two years.

Vern Voss blocks an opponent to clear the way for a long gain

Coaches cautioned players that a sloppy field was no excuse for sloppy play. Pictured here in 1962 are Dan LeGrand (No. 45) and Ken Pellegrini (No. 40) taking a break from playing in the mud.

Helping an injured player from the field was almost as painful for a coach as the player. Here Gil Bell (right) assists Joe Smyder (center) to the sidelines.

Winning All-American honors in 1965, linebacker Mike LeGrand (No. 53) is seen here waiting for the ball to be snapped.

Basketball

The 1940-41 basketball team posted an impressive 27-5 record and won the junior college state title. Wolves' pivot man Joe Blum was named to the All-State Team. **Sitting:** Gordon Graham, David Webb, William Smith, Harvey Vollmer, Coach A. A. Wills. **Kneeling:** Joseph Blum, Al Waznis. **Standing:** George Shepley, Arthur Rimmke, Russell Stevens, Robert Spangler, Richard Pearson.

Under Coach James Rickhoff, Tony Gutierrez helped lead the Wolves to a state championship in 1946 with his accurate shooting and all-around excellent floor play.

In 1950, Joliet was selected to host the state basketball tournament. The JJC squad easily defeated its first two opponents to move into the championship game. With the score knotted at 49 with 10 seconds remaining, team captain Tom Williams hit a jump shot to win the game and thrill the huge crowd of hometown fans. The team ended the season with 28 wins and 5 losses. **Kneeling:** Rich Juricic, Bob McEvilly, Jack Major, Carl Adams, Al Denovellis. **Standing:** Charles Book (team manager), Tom Williams, Moose Broadrick, Jim Fagan, Bob Whyte, Bill Mooney, Rudy Skul, Coach A. A. Wills.

Although the 1956-57 team did not possess much height, it ran the ball well and generated a lot of offense. In eleven of its thirty-two games, the JJC squad scored over 100 points. Bill Tuffli, a 6'2" forward, was the fifth highest scorer in the nation with a 26-point average per game. **Kneeling:** Spiro Bruskas (team manager), Ray Chaloka, Don Flatt, Bill Tuffli, Jim Sparlin. **Standing:** Ted James, Jim Miller, Tom Broderick, Gil Nicoll, Matt Vigliocco, Rick Anderson, and Coach A. A. Wills.

During the late 1950s and early '60s, JJC traveled by bus to Binghamton, New York, to compete in the Broome Tech Holiday Tournament. Team members are all smiles as they prepare to leave Joliet in 1958. After winning first place, the ride home was even more enjoyable. **L-R:** Tom Phelps, Jack McCarthy, Harry Ayers, Joe Pasavento, Coach A. A. Wills, Ken Norton, Larry Voss, and Ken Barone.

For many years John Corradetti was a familiar sight selling tickets at basketball games.

Joliet took second place in the Broome Tech Tournament in 1959. Coach Wills is seen here posing with the team trophy and two JJC players who were named to the tournament All-Star Team, Joe Pesavento (left) and Bill Sparlin (right). Sparlin was the squad's overall leading scorer both years that he played and was awarded third team All-American honors for the 1960-61 season.

For two years, the pivot position was played by 6'1" Ted James. Although much shorter than opposing centers, James' quick moves under the basket made him one of the most effective players in the conference. During the 1957-58 season, Ted scored 596 points, including an amazing 50 free throws in a row. With no apparent place to go, Ted James (No. 27) is about to split the defenders and head for the basket.

112

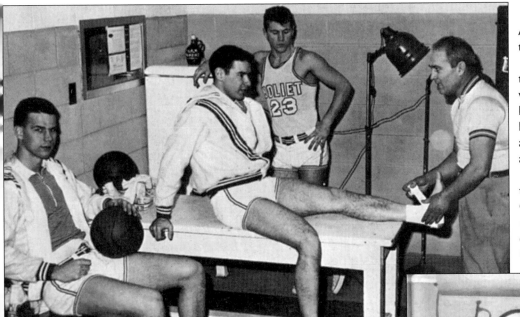

Athletic trainer Jim Catarello is seen taping the ankle of Jerry Widlowski in 1961 while other players wait their turns. "Cat's" humor and wry wit, as well as his expert care, made him popular with athletes over the years. He was honored in 1964 by being selected to attend the Olympic Games in Tokyo as a trainer.

Other ailments might require a visit to the school nurse. Unlike Trainer Catarello, Nurse Ruthenbeck's powers reached beyond the art of healing to excusing students from class. Some athletes got to know her very well.

Converse All Stars were the shoes of choice in the 1950s and '60s

One of the most popular and exciting players to watch in the early 1960s was the diminutive Charlie Brown. An exceptional ball handler and an accurate shooter, Brown led the team in 1962 in every statistic except rebounding. During his two years at JJC, he won several all-conference, all-tournament, and most valuable player honors. Hampered by a lack of size for many years, Coach Wills was pleased to welcome 6'10" Dwight Toland to the team in 1962. Pictured here in the college yearbook, Toland towers over teammate Brown.

Marv Evans is about to sink another free throw. During the 1966-67 season, the sharp-shooting guard scored a team record 50 points in a single game.

In 1965, the Wolves captured sixth place in the national tournament and were led by Willie Boyce and Tom Moran with 22.3 and 20.1 scoring averages respectively. The previous year, Boyce broke the team's single season scoring record with 759 points even though he was usually double-teamed or guarded by the opponent's best defensive player. Boyce and Moran accumulated a number of all-tournament, all conference, and most valuable player awards. Willie's outstanding career at JJC was capped off with an All-American Team honorable mention in 1965. He is pictured here in a familiar pose, shooting his deadly jump shot.

The end of the 1966-67 basketball season brought the long coaching career of Aubrey A. "Fizz" Wills to a close. The week of February 13-18 was celebrated on campus as Wills Week. Looking back over his thirty-nine years at the high school and college, Wills said, "I hate to see it end." During that time, he compiled an impressive record of 668 victories and 198 losses. His most successful team was the 1951-52 squad with a 27-2 record; his last team in 1966-67 was the least successful with 15 wins and 11 losses. Wills is pictured here reflecting on his many years of prowling the sidelines and celebrating victories. Fittingly, the gymnasium built a few years

later on the new college campus was named in Coach Wills' honor.[48]

Following his retirement from teaching and coaching, Wills ran for several public offices. He was elected to serve on both the JJC Board of Trustees and the Joliet Park District Board. In 1965, he was narrowly defeated in the mayoral election for the City of Joliet. Wills was honored on May 1, 1976, when he was recognized as the nation's winningest community college basketball coach and inducted into the Illinois Basketball Hall of Fame. His name also appears with that of Floyd "Pop" Wagstaff of Tyler, Texas, on the trophy – the Wills-Wagstaff Trophy — presented annually to the most valuable player in national junior college basketball.[49]

114

Baseball

After a thirteen-year dry spell, the 1948 baseball team won the conference title. First baseman Frank Gabrys led the team with a .458 batting average. Gabrys went on to play in the Chicago White Sox farm system but had his career cut short by an injury. **Front:** Glenn Schultz, Richard Williams, Jack Kostelz, Clair Moore, Patrick Cleary, Daniel Thom. **Back:** Gene Stevens, Edward Smith, Coach A. A. Wills, Frank Gabrys, Keith Staats.

The baseball team had an excellent season in 1965, winning conference and state titles and finishing second in the North Central States Tournament in Iowa. **Front:** Robert Hill, John Paul, Earl Maxwell, Harold Reiss, John Killian. **Middle:** Robert Fitzer, Michael O'Brien, John Weilgosz, Robert Keefer, Robert Rocks. **Back:** Thomas Kosmerl, John Mackender, Coach Gil Bell, Peter Fulton, Bernie Valek, Jerry Klover.

Wrestling

In 1961, several athletes approached Athletic Director Herman Walser with the request to reinstate a wrestling program at JJC. The following year, John Swalec was hired from Oak Lawn High School, where he had been a very successful wrestling coach. A schedule was established for the 1962-63 season, and a team was assembled. Here Coach Swalec works with John Young in improving his sit-out technique. The new team closed the season with an impressive 12-1 record and established the groundwork for Joliet to become a wrestling powerhouse during the 1960s.

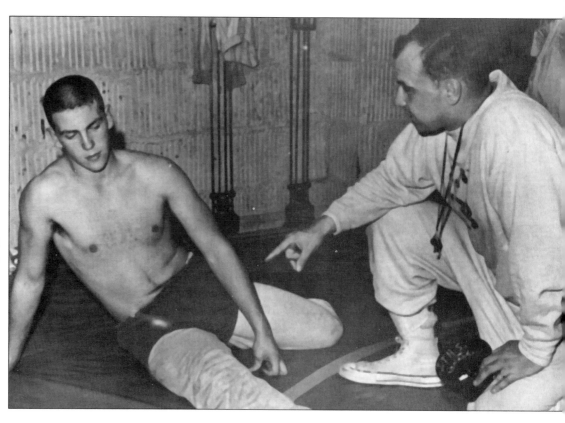

In its second year, 1963-64, the wrestling team was undefeated in dual meets and tied for first place at the National Junior College Wrestling Tournament in Worthington, Minnesota. Bob Furlan and Milt Thomas capped perfect seasons by winning national championships. Wrestling at 137 pounds, Furlan was 19-0 and pinned his opponents in 13 matches. Thomas had 18 pins in compiling a 20-0 record. **Kneeling:** Jesse Edwards, Marty Clegg, Sam Epps, Bob Furlan, Milt Thomas. **Standing:** Rod Landorf, Ray Matesevac, Ted Lincoln, Vern Voss, John Manner.

In 1964 Coach Swalec left JJC, but the team continued its winning ways under Henry Pillard. By the time Pillard (pictured here) temporarily handed the reins to his successor in 1968, the team enjoyed a winning streak of sixty consecutive victories, dating back to March 1964, and had won five consecutive conference titles. Pillard returned in 1970 and coached the squad for the next fifteen years.

Bob Furlan,
National Champ

Milt Thomas
National Champ

The facial expressions and body language of Coach Pillard and the team suggest that a Joliet wrestler is about to pin his opponent and add to the score.

From 1964-66, Wayne Watson led the team to back-to-back fourth place finishes in the National Junior College Tournament. Watson won the championship crown in 1965 at 115 pounds.

The wrestling team ended the 1967-68 season with a perfect 19-0 record and went on to take fourth place at the national championships. The team leader and outstanding performer was Canadian-born Harry Geris, who had an undefeated season. Wrestling in the heavyweight division, Geris won the National Junior College Championship and was named first-team All-American. At the end of the season, he began training for the Olympic Games in Mexico. Geris had won the Canadian National Heavyweight Wrestling Title in 1966 and 1968 and decided to represent Canada in the Olympics. Geris returned to JJC to wrestle in 1968-69 under Coach Jerry Yost. Although he had another outstanding season, he lost his final match at the national tournament to a 380-pound heavyweight by a score of 3-2.

Midway through the 1968-69 schedule, the team's string of 60-plus consecutive victories was broken. However, the season ended on a strong note. Mike Bay captured first place in the 191-pound class at the National Junior College Tournament and led JJC to a second place finish. This was the team's best showing in the Nationals since 1964 when it tied for first place.

117

Golf

The 1940 JJC golf team pictured here won the state tournament with individual highest honors going to Carlstrom. The team won all its matches and claimed the conference title. Russell Stevens distinguished himself by shooting a 63 to break the record at Joliet's Woodruff Golf Course. **L-R:** Carlstrom, Ernest DeSignor, Russell Stevens, Frank Prange.

In 1946, Paul Hudak captained the college golf team and won top honors with the lowest score at the state tournament.

Tennis

The 1963 tennis team posted a perfect 10-0 record in winning the conference championship. Dean Elmer Rowley is pictured here with the team and their trophy. **L-R:** David Hicks, Dean Rowley, Robert Saieg, Dwight Toland (conference singles champion), William Smilie, Coach Howard Scheidt, Al Levering.

Swimming

Organized by the students themselves in 1947, JJC's first swimming team had a very successful season by placing second in the conference and fourth in the state. **Front:** John Skoog, Donald Muhlig, Charles Repenn, Robert Mitchell, William Hogan. **Back:** Richard Donahue, John Pearson, Earl Osborne, Andre Bayle, Ralph Repenn, Donald Schofield, Coach Beryl Longman. The team's leading diver was Robert Mitchell, seen here leaving the springboard.

Lettermen

The Lettermen's Club was composed of athletes who earned letters in JJC sports. Jackets were awarded to club members who had participated in their sports for a certain number of minutes. Besides rehashing games and discussing sports, club members sponsored parties and dances and planned an annual banquet at which awards were presented to most valuable players. Pictured here are members in 1960. **Front:** Herman Walser (sponsor), Don Brown, Herb Boginis, Gil Bell (sponsor). **Middle:** Paul Seaborg, Bob Kujawa, Terry Small, Dan Racich, Jerry Widlowski, Bill Sparlin. **Back:** Jim Garrison, John Gabel, Gordon Kay, Gary Lichtenwalter, Bob Madjak, Joe Pesavento, Don Weber.

Bowling

Intramural bowling was introduced in 1941 and proved to be a popular sport. The first place team is pictured here together with the bowler rolling the highest game. **Seated:** Richard Zalar, John Williamson, James Elens. **Standing:** Ned Grabavoy, George Volling (high score), and Richard Oldani (team captain).

P.E. Class

The wry wit of instructor Ken Parker took some of the pain out of doing calisthenics in physical education class. However, running laps on the indoor track above the gym was dreaded by most students, despite the coach's good humor. A *Blazer* article in 1960 described the "heroic efforts" of PE teachers to insure that the young men of JJC got as much exertion as possible in gym class. Typically, sixteen brisk laps around the track followed "smartly executed calisthenics." Another article put a different spin on the experience: "Our calisthenics include sit-ups, push-ups, back-breakers, rib-crackers, arm-busters, and any number of other contortionist exercises. You name it, we do it."[50]

A new weight-lifting machine in 1967 added to the pleasure of PE.

Cheerleaders

The earliest cheerleaders, or yell leaders, as they were called, were male students who were chosen for their ability to yell encouragement to the players and keep up the fans' spirits. One of the first organized cheers was "Yeah purple, yeah white, yeah Joliet, let's fight." Among the first cheerleaders were Frank Gates and Art Liebermann.

Since there were not enough players to field teams during World War II, there was no longer a need for cheerleaders. After the war however, sports became popular again, and cheerleading squads, predominantly female, were chosen. Pictured here in purple and white is the 1955-56 squad. **L-R:** Orie Seron, Bonnie Reid, Robert Johnson, Mary Brett, Judy Zusag.
> Boom Chicka Boom, Boom Chicka Boom,
> Boom-Chicka-Ricka-Chicka Ricka-Chicka-Boom,
> Siss Boom Bah, Siss Boom Bah,
> Joliet, Joliet, Rah! Rah! Rah!

The newly organized pompon squad made its first appearance at the 1956 homecoming game. Dressed in white skirts and sweaters and carrying purple and white pompons, the squad added considerably to the enthusiasm of fans with such cheers as "One for the money; two for the show; three to get ready;

now go, Wolves go!" **Front:** Judy Yahn, Kay Weiss, Rosemary Robbins, Jonna Frosch, Carol Colstock. **Back:** Judy Speckman, Barbara Seffens, Rosemary Anderson, Sue Carnaghi, Dolores Pagliei.

Sometimes the auxiliary cheerleaders appeared at pep rallies to whip the crowd into a frenzy. As a rule, however, they made infrequent appearances – thankfully.
> Put them in the bathtub, pull out the plug.
> Down goes (the opponent), Glug! Glug! Glug!

A familiar sight during a timeout was the cheerleaders hurriedly leading a cheer before the game resumed. The 1961-62 squad is pictured here.

Women's Athletics

Declining enrollments during the war years made it impossible for the Women's Athletic Association to continue its full range of activities. Although the W.A.A. scaled back its program during the 1940s, it remained a viable organization on campus until the '50s when interest continued to wane. In 1958, th[e] Women's Athletic League (W.A.L.) was organized t[o] take over certain activities and programs of th[e] defunct W.A.A. However, during the 1960s an[d] beyond, the school played a diminished role in provid[ing]

Father-Daughter Sport Night, 1940.

Baseball, 1941 - Wilma Grell, Dorothy Burr, Kathryn Kirinich.

Hiking, 1941 – Dara Prew, Oleta Lankenau, Lowe.

Swimming, 1942 – Marion Meyer.

Tap Dancing, 1941 – Fisher, Patricia Burress, June Schiek, Marge Dillman.

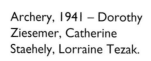

Archery, 1941 – Dorothy Ziesemer, Catherine Staehely, Lorraine Tezak.

Clayton Wintersteen displayed his sign during the teachers' strike that closed the high school and junior college four days.

r. Hal Dellinger and Ben Day worked the picket line dur-
g the strike.

Ignoring a court injunction, faculty members continued to picket until a settlement was reached.

Class I Referendum

Max Kuster served as Chairman of the Research and Information Committee and traveled widely throughout the area, explaining the benefits of Class I status for the junior college. As head of the Agriculture Department, Kuster was especially well known in rural areas of the proposed district. He had been the guest speaker at many Future Farmers of America (FFA) banquets and had also conducted Young Farmers classes as well as the college's annual Farmer's Short Course. Kuster was an engaging speaker and the ideal person to encourage outlying communities to join with Joliet in establishing a new Class I junior college. Many other faculty and staff members joined Kuster in actively supporting the referendum throughout the entire proposed district.

For Superintendent French, the first two months of 1967 produced bitter-sweet feelings toward the high school and junior college faculty. In January, he was very critical of most of his teachers who, as union members, went on strike to secure bargaining rights and a salary increase. The next month, he praised many of the same faculty members for working hard to pass the Class I junior college referendum. Within the boundaries of Joliet Township High School and Junior College District No. 204, the vote totals were 10,758 for and 3,602 against Class I status. In the outlying areas that were being incorporated into the expanded junior college district, the results were 9,285 in favor of the proposition and 1,430 opposed.

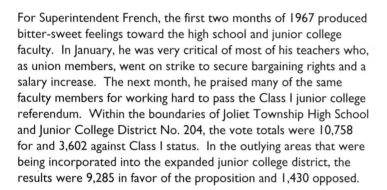

JOLIET TOWNSHIP HIGH SCHOOLS & JUNIOR COLLEGE
Dr. William C. French, Superintendent

February 20, 1967

To: ALL STAFF MEMBERS OF DISTRICT #204

From: William C. French

On behalf of District #204, I would like to express appreciation to all of those staff members who worked to make the establishment of a Class I Junior College in this area a success. The election was a solid victory for education and insures the future of the junior college opportunity in the years to come.

The success of the February 18th election completes the basic plan developed for District #204 some years ago. This plan included the development of expanded high school facilities, the improvement of the district educational tax rate, and the establishment of a separate tax base for the junior college. The fact that these three goals took a long time to achieve does not make their accomplishment any less satisfying.

Congratulations to all who worked so hard to make this issue a successful one.

CHAPTER 4

A New Home on Houbolt Road: 1967 to 2000

When Joliet Junior College became a Class I district on February 18, 1967, a sixty-six year relationship with Joliet Township High School District 204 was legally severed, and JJC embarked on a new course as Illinois Junior College District 525. An election was held on April 15, 1967, to select a seven-member board of trustees. Until a junior college board was elected and prepared to take over college operations, the high school would continue to administer the business and academic affairs of the college. From a field of thirty-five candidates, the seven men endorsed by the Central Steering Committee headed by Kenneth Timm were elected. They were William Glasscock, a Joliet Township farmer and JJC alumnus; Dr. Cecil W. Ingmire, a Joliet veterinarian; Ronald M. Whitaker, a New Lenox insurance broker and JJC alumnus; H. Allen Holler, a Mazon farmer; Victor Scott, a Joliet realtor with residence in Plainfield Township; Samuel Saxon, a Plainfield attorney; and Daniel L. Kennedy, a Joliet attorney. Glasscock was elected president of the Board, and Dr. Ingmire was named vice president. Whitaker was selected to serve as Board secretary while Kenneth Timm was retained as Board attorney.[1]

JJC's long relationship with the high school district created problems for determining ownership of assets. Although college students had paid tuition between 1933 and 1949 and from 1965 to 1967, no separate educational fund existed for the junior college; and even college money received in state aid since 1955 had been placed in the general fund of the high school. Other problems seemed just as perplexing. Would the college now rent facilities from the high school? If so, at what price? The 9.5 cent tax rate approved by the voters would not be collected until the following year, and the $11.50 per student credit hour reimbursed by the state would not be received until the end of the semester. What would happen in the meantime? How would faculty members be assigned, especially those that taught both high school and college classes with split loads? Would the College Board of Trustees recognize the faculty union and honor the contract negotiated with High School District 204?

As weeks passed, the High School Board began pressing college trustees to legally assume responsibility for operating District 525. On June 12, 1967, the College Board hired consultants to screen applicants for president. Elmer Rowley, who had served as college dean for twenty years, retired on June 30 and did not apply for the job. Ten days later, the Board named Rowley's assistant, Susan Wood, to serve as Temporary Chief Administrator until a college president could be hired. She was authorized to order supplies and make preparations for the fall semester. When the Board met on August 14, 1967, several important decisions were announced. The Board of Trustees would officially assume responsibility for college operations on August 28; the college would rent space in the high school building for the 1967-68 academic year at a cost of $140,000, and Elmer W. Rowley would serve as the first president of District 525. Although Rowley had already received his first retirement check, the consultants persuaded him and the Board that Rowley's knowledge and experience gained during twenty years as college dean were just what JJC needed at this critical point in the history of the college.[2]

The 1967-68 school year opened with a limited staff and an unlimited sense of anticipation. Numerous, important decisions had to be made regarding the future of the institution. Early in 1968, the American Association of Junior Colleges offered consulting services to address such matters as college administration, finance, and curriculum. Following the recommendation of three consultants, the Board fleshed out the administration with several appointments. Joining President Rowley and Administrative Assistant Susan Wood were Dr. Joseph C. Piland, Dean of College Parallel and General Studies; Joseph A. Borgen, Dean of Occupational and Technical Studies; Walter F. Zaida, Dean of Student Personnel Services; Maynard Boudreau, Dean of the Evening and Summer College; Vera Smith, Director of Admissions and Records;

James J. Hines, Director of Business Affairs; Robert Glenn, Assistant Director of Business Affairs; Douglas Graham, Director of Research, Development, and Federal Aids; Everett Nelsen, Director of Student Financial Aids; Helen M. Tea, Director of Nursing Education; Henry Pillard, Dean of Men; Dulce Hornvale, Dean of Women (part-time); and three counselors: Dorothy Black, Carolyn Engers, and Roger Gordon.

Having participated in a bitter strike a few years earlier to secure collective bargaining rights with High School District 204, union faculty members were anxious for the new College Board to recognize the American Federation of Teachers as the sole collective bargaining agent for JJC instructors. Some members of the new College Board "did not believe in teachers' unions," and a stalemate ensued. For nine months, the Board deflected requests for union recognition and offered, instead, to discuss salaries and fringe benefits with elected representatives of the entire faculty. Union members en masse attended Board meetings, sometimes held in outlying areas of the district, and repeatedly requested that an election be held to determine bargaining agency. Finally, the Board of Trustees agreed to permit the faculty to vote on the matter. On April 26, 1968, in a special election supervised by the Will County Bar Association and the Grundy County Bar Association, 86 percent of the college faculty voted to be represented by the JJC Council of AFT Local 604. With one dissenting vote, the Board of Trustees ratified the election results and scheduled bargaining sessions with the union representatives.[3]

The consultants provided by AAJC also recommended a complete review of the curriculum with as much community involvement as possible. Deans Piland and Borgen assembled advisory committees of business, educational, and community leaders to survey the needs of the college district and assist in the development of new courses and curricula. Over the next three years, twenty-eight new programs were introduced, primarily in occupational and technical studies. However, space restrictions in the high school building delayed the implementation of most new courses of study. Only the Law Enforcement and Nursing Education programs were started prior to JJC's move to its new campus.

During the fall of 1967, the Board of Trustees began interviewing architectural firms specializing in school construction. From the twelve companies that presented proposals, the Board on January 8, 1968, selected the Texas firm of Caudill, Rowlett, and Scott to design a permanent campus for District 525. Next, the Board would have to choose a site strategically located in the sprawling new district. It was determined that the geographic center was one mile east of Channahon, and the population center was near Six Corners where Plainfield Road intersects Raynor Avenue and Black Road in Joliet. However, the area of greatest growth in District 525 was projected to be north and west of the city. Board President William Glasscock drove throughout the district searching for the ideal location, as did attorney Kenneth Timm and Agriculture Department Chair Max Kuster. Timm and Kuster often rode together during their lunch hour and talked to farmers who might be willing to sell land for a college campus.[4]

At a Board meeting on February 6, 1968, President Rowley announced that the Richards farm on Airport Road (now Houbolt Road) southwest of Joliet had been selected as the site for the new campus. Located near the intersection of I-55 and I-80, the 368-acre parcel held potential for excellent access by commuting students. Furthermore, situated on the property away from the road was a wooded area that sloped toward a small lake, a setting that captured the imagination of the architects. They envisioned buildings on both sides of the water and began preparing a master plan that included an enclosed bridge with glass walls. Several administrators, department chairs, and Board members visited community colleges in nearby states to gather design ideas to share with the architects.[5]

The college master plan steadily took shape, but before it could be submitted to the Illinois Junior College Board for final acceptance, District 525 voters would first have to approve a $10.5 million bond referendum and a three-cent increase in the building fund rate. Publicized as "The Educational Bargain of a Lifetime," proponents of the referendum pointed out that local taxpayers were required to pay only 25 percent of the cost of the new campus plus the expense of equipping the buildings. The state would pay 75 percent of site acquisition and campus construction costs. District voters apparently recognized a bargain when they saw it; the bond referendum and building fund increase were overwhelmingly approved on March 30, 1968.[6]

Renting facilities from Joliet Township High School District 204 severely restricted junior college growth. There simply was not enough room for new students and programs. Dean Piland visited other Illinois community colleges that occupied temporary buildings on interim campuses. He also interviewed JJC students, faculty, and staff members regarding a possible move into prefabricated structures and found significant support for such a plan. When District 204 increased rental costs for the 1968-69 school year from $140,000 to $275,000 and, at the same time, decreased the college's space, the prospect of moving to an interim campus became even more attractive. JJC was also renting the Boys' Club across from the high school as a student center for $3,000 a month. After weighing the advantages and disadvantages and considering the comparative costs, the Board of Trustees decided at its April 3, 1969, meeting that the college would move into temporary buildings on its new campus in the fall of 1969. John Rogers from the Association of Commerce spoke in opposition to the plan, as did Frank Turk, who represented the Boys' Club. Indeed, many business, civic, and political leaders were not pleased that JJC was leaving the downtown area and relocating on the western outskirts of Joliet. Also in the audience that night were students, parents, and school leaders who applauded the Board's decision. For example, Arthur Meadors, Superintendent of Grundy County Schools, noted that the creation of a Class I college district "was sold in our area on the basis of a new college with proper facilities and one offering new courses."[7]

The Board of Trustees employed Becker Brothers, a company experienced in building temporary campuses, to construct seventeen prefabricated buildings at a cost of $744,000. With payments spread over five years, the annual cost for the interim structures was $163,902.[8] Students were generally excited by the planned move and looked forward to larger parking lots with ample spaces. With classes scheduled to begin in five months, Becker Brothers immediately began to transform a country cornfield into a college campus. However, work was abruptly halted on July 25 when Will County Building Inspector John Ferguson posted signs on the buildings that read:

Not built to county code. Not safe construction. Do no further work on this building. A violation of Will County zoning and building ordinances exists on this property.[9]

Among the concerns expressed by Ferguson was the use of quarter-inch plywood instead of plasterboard on interior walls. He also cited the need for wider hallways and more fire exits.

The Board of Trustees and its attorney disputed the inspector's findings and even questioned his jurisdiction over the project. The college insisted that the Illinois Junior College Board should have final authority to approve the buildings.[10] An editorial in the Joliet *Herald-News* detected political overtones in the controversy.

If these buildings are unsafe, then the state should vacate temporary buildings at SIU, U of I, and other colleges. There has been too much harassment. There must be an end to it.[11]

With the fall semester quickly approaching, there was no time for litigation or protracted negotiations. Becker Brothers agreed to work with the county inspector and make all changes deemed necessary. With minimal delay, the project quickly moved forward in a race to meet the fall deadline. On August 5, 1969, a new player entered the picture when the City of Joliet formally annexed the college property. Although provisions had already been made for temporary sewage disposal and water supply, the city would eventually assume responsibility for these and other services.[12]

The college's new home on Houbolt Road was barely ready for occupancy when students arrived on September 22, 1969. Registration and other preliminary activities had taken place at Inwood Recreation Center nearby. On the first morning of classes, it seemed like all 2,000 students reached Houbolt Road at the same time. The traffic jam on this narrow country road extended some two miles from Jefferson Street to the college entrance. The extension of Houbolt Road south of the campus was known as Bush Road and led to Route 6. There was not yet an interchange at I-80, and the poor condition of Bush Road discouraged drivers from using it. When students finally reached campus, they discovered that wet weather had delayed landscaping the grounds and pouring some sidewalks. Cardboard walkways through the mud provided the only dry access to a few of the buildings. Someone with a sense of humor stuck a crude sign in the mud reading "Keep Off The Grass."[13]

Inside the buildings, most furnishings were new. A state ruling had determined that almost everything used by the college before severance from the high school belonged to District 204. Although JJC did purchase the college library and some equipment for about a million dollars, most offices and classrooms were newly furnished with colors and styles selected by the Joan Hilliers Company. Unfortunately, some furniture had not yet arrived. Finding no tables and chairs in the library, students improvised by sitting on the carpeted floor and using empty moving boxes as table tops.[14]

The new campus had a character and style uniquely its own. Each of the temporary buildings was named for an Illinois community college already in existence. Some of them were dry and had no restrooms or drinking fountains. Two L-shaped buildings facing each other formed a quadrangle in the center of campus. One of these, called the Kishwaukee Building, housed the library and media center. Across from it, the Waubonsee Building contained a student lounge, cafeteria, Culinary Arts Department, and various offices for counseling and student services. In the quadrangle stood a flagpole donated by the Veteran's Club and a rustic bell tower, a gift from the Alumni Association. The historic bell that tolled on the quarter-hour once hung in the old Will County courthouse in downtown Joliet. The quadrangle was a convenient gathering place in the center of campus for numerous activities ranging from pep rallies to anti-war demonstrations to students protesting the condition of Houbolt Road.

On September 18, 1969, four days before the new campus opened, the City of Joliet celebrated John Houbolt Day and renamed Airport Road in Houbolt's honor. Houbolt was an alumnus of JJC who won worldwide acclaim as the developer of the Lunar Excursion Module (LEM), which was responsible for putting a man on the moon two months earlier.[15] When Houbolt Road experienced heavy student traffic, it rapidly deteriorated and, at times, became almost impassable. Students likened the road to the moon's surface and suggested that Dr. Houbolt should consider inventing a vehicle capable of maneuvering through the potholes and ruts in the road bearing his name. Others referred to the roadway as "The Ho Chi Minh Trail" and demanded that the city stop stalling and immediately begin to widen and resurface it. Year after year, students held rallies, wrote letters, formed committees, and insisted that their cars be spared the torture of driving on Houbolt Road. In October 1980, the project was final-

ly completed, eleven years after the campus opened. Fourteen years later, the interchange at Houbolt and I-80 was completed, giving college commuters a second access route from an interstate highway.[16]

During the 1970s, students often formed college clubs to actively promote their views and interests. Students for Political Involvement was organized in 1969 and rallied against the Vietnam War. SPI also held seminars and "teach-ins" on the draft, birth control, pollution, and drugs. Demonstrations on the campus quadrangle sometimes attracted large crowds of participants and onlookers, but they always remained nonviolent and peaceful. Although the Cultural Cinema Club published an unauthorized newspaper called the *Subterranean Side Show,* it never stretched the boundaries of free speech to the extent that underground newspapers did on university campuses. Also organized in 1969, the Black Student Union addressed a variety of issues, including the need for African American faculty and staff members. The BSU demanded that at least one black faculty member and counselor be hired immediately. At that time, there were none. A number of leading African American speakers were brought to campus, especially during Black History Week. In an effort to open and maintain communication with students, President Rowley established the President's Round Table to provide a campus forum for asking questions and voicing concerns.[17]

Some students recommended that the college name be changed now that the district encompassed a much broader region than Joliet Township. Others believed that for the sake of tradition, the word "Joliet" should not be removed from the college name. In fact, student leaders presented a petition with 3,382 signatures requesting that "Joliet" be retained in the name. The Board of Trustees invited community input, and the Joliet *Herald-News* solicited the public's help in selecting a name from several possibilities: Five Rivers, Joliet Dresden, Louis Joliet, Pioneer, J. Stanley Brown, Joliet Community College, and Joliet Junior College. Few readers responded to the newspaper's request for public opinion. Finally, at the January 12, 1970, Board meeting, President Rowley encouraged trustees to settle the matter. William Glasscock made a motion to leave the name unchanged. When a few members suggested that it did not accurately reflect the expanded district and that, at least, the word "Community" should be substituted for "Junior," Glasscock observed that there never would be a perfect name. Furthermore, he said, "When Junior grows up and has gray hair, the neighbors still call him Junior." The motion passed with Ronald Whitaker and Daniel Kennedy voting "no." Five years later, the district's name was officially changed by the state legislature to *Community College District 525*. Official publications now refer to the college as "Joliet Junior College, Illinois Community College District 525."[18]

In 1970, President Elmer Rowley retired, and Douglas Graham was appointed Acting President by the Board. He had the honor of presiding when ground was broken on November 15, 1970, for construction of Phase I of the permanent campus. Included in the first phase were Buildings A through G that housed agriculture, technical, nursing, public service, English, foreign language, math, science, social science, physical education, a planetarium, and a gymnasium. Dr. John C. Houbolt, celebrated space engineer and JJC alumnus, was the principal speaker at the dedication ceremony on October 22, 1972. The second phase of construction included a five-story structure across the lake from Phase I with an enclosed connecting bridge that served as a student center. When Phase II was completed in the fall of 1974, the new building was occupied by social science, business education, data processing, culinary arts, the cafeteria, bookstore, post office, administrative offices, and the Learning Resource Center/Library. The construction of a Fine Arts Center in Phase III was delayed for several years when the state ran out of funds for community college building projects.[19]

During the decade of the seventies, JJC embarked on a course of dramatic expansion in academic programs, student services, and facilities. In 1970, the college began tapping one of its most valuable resources when the Joliet Junior College Alumni Association was founded. William Glasscock, who had served as the first Board president and was himself an alumnus, approached Administrative Assistant Susan Wood upon her retirement and enlisted her help in forming an alumni association. Her long tenure with the college in a highly visible role made Ms. Wood the ideal person to organize and energize the many graduates of JJC. At its inaugural meeting on October 13, 1970, a constitution was adopted, and Dr. Tom Streitz was elected president;

Robert Laraway, vice president; Tessie Heuback Heath, secretary; and Ronald M. Whitaker, treasurer. Over the years, the Alumni Association has been very active in sponsoring annual reunions, honoring distinguished alumni, and raising funds for student scholarships and other worthy causes.[20]

In August 1973, the Joliet Junior College Foundation was incorporated to foster, encourage, and promote the purposes of the college by providing financial assistance in support of its academic and public service programs. Former Joliet mayor Maurice Berlinsky served as the Foundation's first president, and Dr. Harold W. "Woody" Phend was appointed the first executive secretary in 1975. Working with the Alumni Association, numerous scholarships have been established and awarded to JJC students. Foundation grants have also enhanced instruction, improved facilities, and provided seed money to conduct feasibility studies for such projects as the Fine Arts Building, the Louis Joliet Renaissance Center, the Dr. William M. Zales Arboretum, and many more. The Foundation's assets currently exceed $6 million.[21]

In an effort to better serve one of the fastest growing segments of District 525, the college established a North Campus in Bolingbrook in 1975. Originally located in the lower level of the Fountaindale Library, the extension campus was well received by residents of the area. Five years later, services were doubled when additional space was leased in the new Bolingbrook Town Center. In 1982, programming was discontinued at Fountaindale Library and moved to the Romeoville Center at Valley View School. In order to expand and consolidate North Campus operations and to establish a more permanent presence in the region, the college acquired a 40-acre site on 135th Street just east of Weber Road and opened a new 35,000 square-foot facility in 1993. North Campus mirrors Main Campus in many respects with a full array of courses, programs, and student services.[22]

A second extension campus known as the Louis Joliet Renaissance Center was established in 1980 in downtown Joliet. Despite objections from those who questioned the nature and cost of the arrangement and a petition presented in opposition by economics instructor William Brinkman, the Board of Trustees voted to acquire the Sheraton Joliet Motor Inn at 214 North Ottawa Street. The JJC Foundation actually purchased the motel/restaurant on behalf of the college for $1 million and borrowed an additional $500,000 to renovate the complex. The College Board agreed to pay the Foundation $120,000 a year for two years, an amount equal to 8 percent interest on the Foundation's $1.5 million investment in the property. At the end of two years, the college could evaluate the project and decide whether to continue leasing the facility. In addition to offering a variety of courses and programs to people who lived and worked in the downtown area, the Renaissance Center's restaurant and banquet room provided JJC culinary arts students with realistic hands-on experiences in preparing and serving food in a variety of settings. A grant of $205,530 from the Illinois Board of Higher Education assisted the Culinary Arts Department in developing a Hotel, Restaurant, and Food Service Management program that would be based primarily at the new downtown campus.[23]

The lease arrangement for the Louis Joliet Renaissance Center got much more complicated in 1983 when the JJC Foundation joined the Pact for Progress to help revitalize the downtown area. Working with the Will County Metropolitan Exposition and Auditorium Authority (also known as the Rialto Authority) in its effort to win a $6 million state grant to renovate Rialto office buildings, the Foundation sold the Renaissance Center to the Rialto Authority. The Foundation received $1.6 million to cover the original mortgage plus $100,000 for a new roof. The Rialto Authority now possessed sufficient assets necessary to meet the local matching requirement to qualify for the state grant. The college then entered a new lease agreement with the Rialto Authority for annual payments of $100,000 for three years followed by payments of $139,544 for the next twenty years. At the end of twenty-three years, the college would receive ownership of the Louis Joliet Renaissance Center. Known today as the City Center Campus, the facility still provides culinary arts students with experiential training, although few other general education courses are taught there. It also houses the college's Division of Adult and Family Services as well as the Institute of Economic Technology.[24]

The present-day Institute of Economic Technology is an outgrowth of the Industry/Business Institute, which was organized in 1976 under a contractual agreement with the JJC Foundation. The IBI provid-ed educational services and training for business and industry in the college district. It offered tailor-made courses, seminars, and workshops to meet the specific needs of companies. Flexible scheduling assisted employees in dovetailing work responsibilities with training opportunities. Courses and seminars ranged from college credit classes to certificates of attendance workshops. In short, the IBI attempted to serve the diverse economic training needs of District 525.[25]

Although the college retained the word "Junior" in its name, its outreach efforts in the past twenty-five years suggest that it is, indeed, dedicated to being a comprehensive "community" college that offers services and educational opportunities to all residents of the district. For example, activities and classes are held on campus for people of all ages, ranging from the Early Childhood Center and Youth College to Emeritus College and Lifelong Learning programs. For academically gifted students, the college offers an Honors Program, College Bowl teams, and membership in Phi Theta Kappa, the national junior college honor society; and for students that need individual assistance, peer tutoring and Project Achieve/Student Support Services are available. The Student Accommodations and Resources office supports students with documented disabilities, health concerns, limited English proficiency, and those enrolled in non-traditional majors. The college offers a Holistic Wellness Program, a Student Assistance Program, a Multicultural Transfer Center, and a Women's Center. Also, through its Division of Adult and Family Services, JJC provides GED preparation for earning a high school diploma, English as a Second Language (ESL) classes, Welfare to Work assistance, and a full range of services in the Family Support and Self-Sufficiency Center designed to provide families with educational skills, job training, and a support network necessary to achieve self-sufficiency.

Not only has the college expanded its programs and services, but its facilities on Main Campus have continued to expand as well. In September 1981, the long-awaited Fine Arts Center was opened without state assistance. With a budget of $2.2 million left in local matching funds from the original building referendum in 1968, Acting President Tim Helton worked with Joliet architects Healy, Snyder, DeYoung and Associates to design a very practical structure of 50,000 square feet. The three-story building adjoins J Building and houses music, art, speech and drama programs. The facility includes a 405-seat theatre, dressing rooms, music rehearsal and practice rooms, art studios and labs, faculty offices, and general classrooms. Further, in the early 1990's, the state made funds available to cover 75 percent of construction costs to erect buildings designed to provide students with technical skills and training. However, the college had depleted its building fund on the Fine Arts Center.[26] A generous gift from Arthur and Vera Smith made possible the local match and subsequent construction of a new technology building. In 1996, the Arthur G. and Vera C. Smith Business and Technology Center was opened with state-of-the-art facilities in business education, computer information, office systems, and technical training. The most recent addition to Main Campus is the Veterinary Technology/Industrial Training Center. Completed in the spring of 2000, the facility houses the "Vet Tech" program, one of only two such programs in the state. The college's Institute of Economic Technology also uses part of the building for custom-designed training programs offered to area businesses.[27]

Joliet Junior College has historically recognized the value of student clubs, social activities, and athletic competition in the overall educational experience of students. Men and women's athletic teams have won conference, state, and national championships, and numerous individuals have been named to all-star teams. The list of clubs and social activities available to students is long and impressive and covers a wide variety of interests. The list includes the Art Alliance, Automated Systems Club, Gamers Club, Gay Alliance, Holistic Wellness Club, Intervarsity Christian Fellowship, Judo Club, Latinos Unidos, Parapsychology Club, Soccer Club, Unity, and many more. There are also national honor societies in foreign languages, Hispanic studies, and drama and theatre. Publications such as the *Blazer* and *Wordeater* offer students opportunities to creatively express themselves in writing. For those who prefer oral communication, the Forensics Team welcomes participants. Instrumental and vocal groups are available for those with musical talent while students who prefer theatrical performance are encouraged to join the JC Players. In short, whatever students' interests, abilities, or talents might be, they are almost certain to find a club or activity to their liking.[28]

The years from 1969 to 2000 witnessed remarkable changes in the history of the college. JJC left its original home in an urban high school and carved a modern campus out of cornfields and pastureland. In its quest to provide District 525 residents with affordable, quality education, the college's programs and support services have continually evolved to meet the diverse and changing needs of students. Also, in fulfilling its commitment to lifelong learning, JJC has implemented a broad spectrum of adult, transitional, continuing, and workforce education. With three campuses and numerous other instructional sites, the college has attempted to make its programs and services accessible to residents. Computer technology even makes it possible for today's students to take courses online; their living rooms have virtually become their learning rooms. JJC has demonstrated the determination and ability to remain a flexible and responsive institution. It is well positioned at the outset of the new millennium for a second century of service as a comprehensive community college.

Susan H. Wood, Temporary Chief
Administrator, July 1967-August 1967

Douglas Graham, Acting President,
1970-71

Elmer W. Rowley, President, 1967-1970

Harold McAninch, President, 1971-79

Tim Helton, Interim President,
January 1979-March 1979

Derek Nunney, President, 1979-84

Raymond Pietak, President, 1985-95

Walter Zaida, Interim President,
July 1984-July 1985

Thomas E. Gamble, President, 1995-98

J. D. Ross, President, 1998-

The men pictured here were elected in 1967 to serve as the first Board of Trustees of District 525, the new Class I junior college district. **Front:** Samuel Saxon, Daniel L. Kennedy, Dr. Cecil W. Ingmire, H. Allen Holler. **Back:** Ronald M. Whitaker, William Glasscock, Victor Scott.

Although he had been retired for six weeks and did not apply for the job, Elmer W. Rowley was appointed by the Board to serve as the first president of Joliet Junior College.

In July 1967, Susan H. Wood served as Temporary Chief Administrator until the first college president was hired.

In a mock election in the fall of 1968, students selected Richard Nixon as their presidential choice. JJC student Robert Hewlett is pictured with a cutout of the college mascot announcing the election.

After achieving Class I legal status in 1967, JJC rented space in the high school for two years before moving into temporary buildings on its new campus. During this time, the college supplemented its limited space in the high school by renting facilities in the nearby Boys' Club, where a student center was established with such activities as Ping-Pong and pool.

138

With no community college either in their high school district or within commuting distance, seven students from Blue Mound, Illinois, decided to attend Joliet Junior College in 1968. Attracted primarily by the reputation of JJC's agriculture program, the "Blue Mound Bachelors" lived in rented rooms and apartments during the week and drove some 160 miles back to their hometown on most weekends. **Front:** Ken Huffman, Joe Zeeb. **Back:** Ross Nelson, Bill Brown, Bob Willis, Phil Brown, John Brown.

Although John Brown is pictured with a pan at the kitchen stove, the "Blue Mound Bachelors" usually ate fast food or TV dinners.

Phil Brown and Ross Nelson are seen tidying up the kitchen.

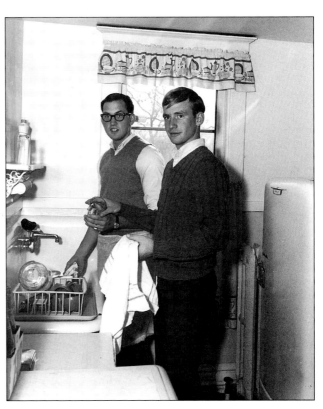

Pictured here are the farmhouse and other buildings on the property purchased by the college for its new campus on Airport Road.

A sign was erected along the gravel road fronting the 368 acres of farm-land purchased by JJC for its new campus on the far west side of Joliet

In March 1968, Board President William Glasscock visited the newly acquired campus site and pointed to the place where a building would one-day bridge the small lake on the property.

At a meeting of the Board of Trustees on February 6, 1968, President Elmer Rowley (right) and Board President William Glasscock announced the location of the new campus. Rowley is seen pointing to the Richards' farm on Airport Road, some six miles southwest of downtown Joliet.

On January 8, 1968, the Board of Trustees selected Caudill, Rowlett, and Scott, a Texas architectural firm, to design a permanent campus for District 525. As seen in the model pictured here, the small lake and wooded area on the property were aesthetically incorporated into the architects' plan.

Northern Illinois Gas Company sponsored a trip for college administrators and Board members to visit other college campuses that utilized natural gas. About to board the chartered bus are Administrative Assistant Susan Wood, Trustee Ronald Whitaker, President Elmer Rowley, Trustee William Glasscock, Trustee Cecil Ingmire, and two gas company representatives.

At the 1969 graduation ceremony, President Elmer Rowley noted the historical significance of the occasion, the last time college students would receive diplomas in the high school building. JJC was scheduled to open its new campus in September 1969 and to formally sever its sixty-eight year relationship with the Joliet Township High School. Speakers at the 1969 graduation included faculty member Robert E. Sterling and student Sandra Perrine.

THE EDUCATIONAL BARGAIN OF A LIFETIME

PROPOSED CONSTRUCTION PROGRAM FOR JUNIOR COLLEGE DISTRICT NO. 525

From left to right in the upper tier of buildings: Divisions of Business, Science-Mathematics, Fine Arts, Little Theatre, Library and Auditorium. The building connecting the two tiers and spanning the lake is the proposed Student Center including cafeteria, a number of classrooms and the passageway across the lake. The lower tier of buildings, from left to right, includes: Building Services, Technical-Vocational, Agriculture, and Physical Education Divisions. Large areas in white at the top and right side indicate parking lots fed by two driveways. All buildings to be connected with an enclosed walkway.

THE $22 MILLION DOLLAR BARGAIN

(See full explanation on reverse side)

STATE PAYS $22 MILLION

WE PAY 3.2 MILLION

7.3 MILLION

MOVEABLE EQUIPMENT NOT MATCHED BY STATE

¼ TOTAL BUILDING COST

¾ TOTAL BUILDING COST

VOTE YES ☒ ON BOTH ISSUES MARCH 30th

Publicized by proponents as "The Educational Bargain of a Lifetime," voters approved a $10.5 million bond referendum and a three-cent increase in the building fund. Approval of both propositions on March 30, 1968, was necessary to secure $22 million in state funds for site acquisition and campus construction.

141

Will County Building Inspector John Ferguson red-tagged the seventeen buildings and halted construction on the temporary campus. He described the buildings as "fire traps" and said that they did not meet the county's building code. Others disagreed, including the Joliet *Herald-News,* and characterized the action as a form of harassment by those who opposed the construction of the new campus so far away from the downtown district.

NOTICE

DO NO FURTHER WORK ON THIS BUILDING

A Violation of the Will County Zoning and or Building Ordinances Exists On This Property

In this aerial view, the temporary buildings on JJC's new campus are under construction in the summer of 1969. Beyond the buildings to the right appears the small lake that would become the centerpiece of the permanent campus.

With construction delays caused by rainy weather and a building code controversy, the new campus was barely ready for occupancy when classes began on September 22, 1969. Traffic was backed up for more than two miles on Houbolt Road, which at that time was little more than an unpaved country lane. Once on campus, students circled the crowded lots to find a place to park.

Remnants of the last-minute move were strewn and stacked outside the buildings, which were named for other community colleges in the state. Two L-shaped buildings in the center of the complex — Kishwaukee and Waubonsee — created a campus quadrangle.

Since library furniture was late in arriving, students often sat on the carpeted floor and used makeshift surfaces for writing and studying. The library was eventually furnished with comfortable chairs and tables.

Although conditions were less than ideal when the campus opened, most students were happy to have a place of their own away from the congested high school. One person with a sense of humor stuck a crude sign in the mud that read "Keep Off The Grass."

When JJC moved to its new campus in 1969, a Safety Office was established; the following year, Lou Korilko (pictured here) was named Security Chief. As enrollment increased and the campus developed, security personnel found it increasingly necessary to perform police functions. Investigating thefts and assaults, dealing with drug and alcohol incidents, and enforcing parking regulations became more commonplace. Therefore, in 1981, the JJC Safety Office became an official Campus Police Department with power to arrest and enforce the laws.

Pictured here in 1974 in Safety Office attire, Chuck Kramer has been an officer on campus since 1971.

Gerald Zeborowski served as Chief of the Campus Police Department from 1983 to 1998.

144

On September 18, 1969, the City of Joliet celebrated John Houbolt Day in honor of the former resident and JJC graduate who developed the LOR (Lunar Orbit Rendezvous) and LEM (Lunar Excursion Module) plans, which were responsible for putting a man on the moon in July 1969. The day began when Dr. Houbolt addressed students at Hufford Junior High School and explained that other scientists had been committed to the concept of a direct flight to the moon with no rendezvous mission. He told the audience that he had had a very difficult time convincing others of the merit of his concept of designing a separate landing module. Houbolt estimated that his plan saved the United States about $20 billion and accelerated the moon landing by about three years.

The Houbolt family was paraded through the streets of downtown Joliet and honored at a special luncheon at D'Amico's 214, now the site of JJC's City Center Campus. Riding in a lead convertible, Dr. Houbolt waved to the cheering crowd. A red, white, and blue stripe had been painted down the center of Chicago Street, and flags decorated the light poles. Several bands marched while playing patriotic songs, and two Model A Fords carried signs reading "Thank you, John" and "The Eagle Has Landed."[33]

Over 600 people attended a luncheon in Dr. John Houbolt's honor and watched as Harry Atkinson presented the highly acclaimed scientist (left) with a plaque. Atkinson had been one of Houbolt's instructors at Joliet Junior College and expressed tremendous pride in the accomplishments of his former student. Mayor Maurice Berlinsky also addressed the gathering and stressed the significance of renaming Airport Road in Houbolt's honor. The road fronted the new college campus, and Berlinsky noted that it was "fitting that our young people for years to come will travel Houbolt Avenue to the new junior college." The mayor also said "it is a tribute to our educational system that our junior college is where John Houbolt began his higher education career." John Houbolt Day ended with an evening tribute at the stadium where 5,000 people cheered the hometown scientist who had played a key role in the successful Apollo 11 mission to the moon.[34]

The Alumni Bell Tower

The JJC Alumni Association spearheaded the effort to acquire the bell from the old Will County courthouse and install it in a permanent tower on the new campus. The ten-year project took some interesting twists and turns along the way. For more that fifty years, the bell had chimed the hour from the clock tower high atop the courthouse in Joliet. When the clock and bell were installed in the late 1880s, county employees took turns once a week climbing several ladders in the tower to wind the clock. A 400-pound weight controlled the clock while an 800-pound weight operated the bell. Each was wound separately; the clock required 125 winds and the bell 225 winds. The mechanism was electrified in the 1940s, but age and weather took their toll, and soon the bell ceased to chime.[29]

When the courthouse was razed in 1969 to make way for its modern replacement, William Glasscock and other alumni remembered the bell and decided to acquire it for the new college campus on the far west side of town. Glasscock was a member of the JJC class of 1937 and served as Chair of the first Board of Trustees when the college achieved Class I status. Joined by a few other alumni, Glasscock took the lead in purchasing the bronze bell for $1,500 from the company that demolished the courthouse. Cast in 1872 in Troy, New York, the bell weighed 1,500 pounds with a 50-pound clapper.[30]

Unable to clean their tarnished prize, the JJC graduates shipped the bell to specialists in Cincinnati, Ohio, to be restored and equipped to operate both as an hourly chime and a victory

In December 1969, the bell was mounted on a rustic tower overlooking the temporary buildings.

The bronze bell in the Alumni Bell Tower once chimed the hours from the clock tower of the Will County courthouse pictured here.

bell. Until the permanent campus was completed with a modern bell tower, it was decided to mount the bell on a rustic pole platform in the quadrangle of the temporary campus. While funds were being raised to defray the expense of purchasing and refurbishing the bell, a story appeared on the front page of the Joliet *Herald-News* purporting to describe in great detail the bizarre history of the bell. The account was completely false. The embarrassed editor apologized for not checking the accuracy of the story or the reliability of the source. The writer, Richard Martin, explained that he had perpetrated the hoax to prove a point. For years he had tried to get letters and articles published, but they were either rejected or buried in some obscure part of the paper. However, said Martin, when he submitted an outlandish lie, it was given front-page coverage.[31]

In the mid-1970s, the Alumni Association began soliciting contributions to move the bell to a modern tower centrally located near the new buildings. The project was delayed first by sluggish fund-raising results and then by a lively controversy surrounding the structural soundness of the supporting tower. College employees, alumni officers, school trustees, and building engineers discussed and debated whether a strong wind would topple the tower. Work on the project was suspended until it was determined that the structure was safe. Finally, on October 10, 1979, the Joliet Junior College Alumni Association held a ceremony and officially dedicated the new bell tower. "Let it ring forever," proclaimed one of the speakers, echoing the theme of the day. Alumni Director Sheila Sasso sighed, "It's finally over."[32]

The bell remained in the quadrangle of the temporary campus until the new tower was erected.

A ribbon was cut at the dedication ceremony on October 10, 1979. Participants were Chris Dragatsis, Vice President of the Alumni Association; Robert Kiep, Chair of the Board of Trustees; Dr. Derek Nunney, JJC President; and Jay Bergman, President of the Alumni Association.

The new Alumni Bell Tower is seen here with J Building in the background.

Those Roads??!!

The condition of roads leading to the college – Houbolt, McDonough, and Bush Roads – and the prolonged struggle to have them widened and resurfaced remained a controversial issue for more than a decade. When the new campus opened in 1969, access roads were little more than rural lanes, ill-suited for the high volume of student traffic and construction vehicles. To complicate matters, there were jurisdictional issues involving the city, county, and township. As potholes deepened and rattles worsened, students and staff became increasingly frustrated with the endless delays in solving the problem. Signs reading "Welcome To The Ho Chi Min Trail" and "Yes Mr. Taxpayer, This Is The Road? To Your New Multi-Million Dollar College, Shamefull Isn't It?" appeared along Houbolt Road, which fronted the campus. College Trustee Robert Kiep echoed the frustrations and sentiments of students and employees when he said, "I can't see building a $32 million campus with a nickel road. . . . The city and county are willing to jump for industry," said Kiep. "There is a four-lane highway to the Caterpillar plant [on McDonough Street] and a short distance west it turns into a nickel road."[35]

The controversy involving road conditions first came to a head in March 1972 when Joliet Mayor Maurice Berlinsky, accompanied by various city officials and college trustees, met with protesting students at an outdoor rally on campus. Student leader Ed Bruske outlined students' demands and presented the mayor with petitions containing 1,500 signatures. Bruske asserted that government officials obviously had decided that JJC was not going to have a good road. Dumping loose gravel into potholes doesn't really help, stated Bruske. "The next time they come out here with gravel, we're going to throw it back at them." Mayor Berlinsky and Councilman Robert Hacker received cool receptions from disgusted students, but the assurances of city officials that the roads would be fixed by May 1 caused Bruske and other leaders to call off the scheduled car caravan and protest rally in downtown Joliet.[36]

Weeks became months, months became years, and still the roads remained a mess. In 1973, a group of students followed the mayor's suggestion and formed a committee to address the problem. In a *Blazer* article, Bruske chided his fellow students for permitting the establishment to mute their protest. "So let's get organized and do it right this time," he stated. "Let's see if we can't get the mayor and his friends in the City Council to sing an octave higher this spring." City officials and college trustees continued to meet and issue statements that progress was being made. In April 1973, Regional Transportation Engineer Sigmund C. Ziejewski attended a meeting and raised

Student leader Ed Bruske presents petitions and demands to city officials at a protest rally on March 17, 1972.

148

hopes that Houbolt Road would soon be a four-lane highway with a new interchange at I-80. But the road got worse. In a letter to the *Blazer*, one student wrote, "I had a rough time finding my way out of one big mudhole and just about lost parts of my car in another one. They're impossible to avoid because the entire road is full of holes."[37]

The opening of College Park Subdivision across from the college in 1975 and a new YMCA two years later increased the

Looking north on Houbolt Road near the McDonough Street intersection in 1971.

volume of traffic and the number of potholes. In 1978, City Director of Public Works Bernard Prola presented a "progress report" to college trustees. He said that the planned widening and rebuilding of the road was now being stalled by negotiations between the city and property owners along Houbolt Road. Condemnation suits, if necessary, would further delay the work. Each year, new student reporters writing for the *Blazer* expressed the same frustrations as

their predecessors. For example, in 1978 Karen Riel wrote, "Well, gang, here we go again with all the junk about Houbolt Road. . . . And I won't even begin to count how many times aspiring young journalists have pounded the typewriters explaining, arguing, and protesting the road."[38]

In May 1979, the city acquired the last piece of property needed to begin the Houbolt project. "Hallelujah—is the strife over?" asked a *Blazer* editorial. Many students and employees remained skeptical until they witnessed the beginning of construction in the fall of 1979. Although work was suspended during the winter months, the widening and resurfacing of access roads were completed in October 1980, more than eleven years after the new campus opened. The I-80 interchange at Houbolt Road was completed twenty-one years after it was first unveiled and discussed in 1973. Thus, in 1994, Joliet Junior College's Main Campus was finally accessible from both I-55 and I-80 on well-paved, four-lane roads.[39]

Mayor Maurice Berlinsky assured students that the roads would be fixed within six weeks.

149

In April 1973, College President Harold McAninch (left) and Trustee Aubrey A. "Fizz" Wills listen to Regional Transportation Engineer Sigmund Ziejewski describe plans for reconstructing Houbolt Road and building a new interchange at I-80.

In March 1979, ten years after the new campus opened, Houbolt Road was still filled with potholes and littered with hubcaps and mufflers. Though the road was no laughing matter, students sometimes joked that college jackets and shirts were really unnecessary. People could easily identify JJC students by the pitiful condition of their cars.

In 1974, a crew fills potholes in Houbolt Road just south of the Jefferson Street intersection.

With College Park Subdivision on the right and the YMCA on the left, students wound their way past the new roadbed being laid. Widened to four lanes and totally resurfaced, Houbolt Road was finally completed in October 1980.

Political Involvement

During the 1960s and '70s, campus clubs provided students an opportunity to address many of their social concerns and special interests. Organized in 1969, Students for Political Involvement (SPI) held seminars on such topics as the draft, birth control, pollution, drugs, and Vietnam. The club planned a "Freeze Nixon" march and sponsored Moratoriums for Peace at which students, faculty, clergy, and other activists spoke. Although JJC students participated in the protest movements that swept college campuses across the nation, activities and demonstrations locally remained nonviolent and peaceful. Members of SPI are pictured here in 1970. **Front:** Jackie Etcher, Peggy Macko, Sylvia Mejia, Kathy Scarboro, Michele Burns, Mary Hassert, Ruth Swanson, Dick Jenkins. **Back:** Rick Tozzi, Diane Colaric, Fred Gutierrez, Bob Coleman, Jerry Kinney, Dave Robertson, Rick Barr, Mike Esposito.

Students were extremely anxious about the draft and their exposure to compulsory military service under the lottery system.

JJC English instructor John Stobart is seen speaking at a Moratorium for Peace rally while students with signs convey their own sentiments.

Above: Kim Morris, Pat Horrigan, and Bonnie Jones, all wearing "Peace" armbands, are pictured registering voters in the college quadrangle during a 1971 Drug Symposium on campus.

The Cultural Cinema Club studied cinema as an art form and examined its relevance to timely issues and social change in the 1960s and '70s. Club programs included presentations ranging from student-made films to major award-winning commercial productions. The CCC also published an underground or unauthorized student newspaper, the *Subterranean Side Show*. Club members are pictured here in 1970. **Sitting:** Sandy Bennington, Frank Cernugel, Joe Boyle, Barbara Lorenz, Bob Newsome, George Henze, Barry Roberts, Ellen Hooks, John Stobart (faculty sponsor), Debbie Trotter, Saul Brass, Karen Lavazza, Ruth Swanson, Jim Ridings. **Standing:** Steve Kasak, John Carli, Angelo Sallese, Larry Herrod, Delores Welch, Peter Neff (faculty sponsor).

The *Subterranean Side Show* was produced largely by the CCC members pictured here, John Goodwin, Ruth Swanson, Jim Ridings, and John Shields.

For a different slant on campus news, students read the *Side Show*.

Women's Activities and Programs

In 1975, proponents of the Equal Rights Amendment participated in the "ERA Yes" campaign on campus by collecting signatures on petitions to lobby legislators in Springfield.

On March 4, 1975, several JJC students joined other members of the Joliet ERA Coalition in traveling to Springfield to support the Equal Rights Amendment. Two students are seen here being interviewed by a Channel 2 TV News reporter. Despite the efforts of ERA proponents, Illinois lawmakers refused to ratify the amendment.

In 1972, JJC received a Public Services Grant from the Illinois Community College Board to establish a Women's Studies Program on campus. Directed by Alice Herron, the program "New Horizons for You" provided workshops and noncredit mini-courses designed to help women explore their self-image and identity and to establish new personal, educational, and career goals. In 1975, JJC's Women's Program joined the College of St. Francis Women's Studies Program and the American Association of University Women in sponsoring a conference to celebrate International Women's Day. Featured speaker Dr. June Sochen (pictured here) challenged her predominantly female audience to actively support the conference theme, "Stop the World – We Want to Get On."

The Women's College within Joliet Junior College was established in July 1997 with grant funding from the Illinois Board of Higher Education. Dr. Roya Falahi (right) and Suzanne Pryga were instrumental in securing the grant to establish the Women's College, the first community college in the state and the second in the nation to establish a women's college within a college. Falahi and Pryga serve as co-directors of the college, whose mission is to integrate gender equity into all aspects of the educational process, from college policies and student services to classroom methods and materials. The Women's College offers an array of educational programs and outreach activities designed to promote gender equity. In addition, it is supportive of single parents, displaced homemakers, returning adult and nontraditional students, and victims of sexual harassment and domestic abuse.

Beginning in February 1998, the Women's College began sponsoring an annual Empowerment Conference with a keynote speaker, breakout sessions, and display booths. Featured at the first conference was noted *Chicago Tribune* columnist, author, and women's rights advocate Carol Kleiman, who spoke on the subject of gender equity in the workplace. She encouraged women to take individual responsibility to advance their own careers, including nontraditional careers. A nontraditional career for women, said Kleiman, is one in which she is well paid.

153

Black Student Union

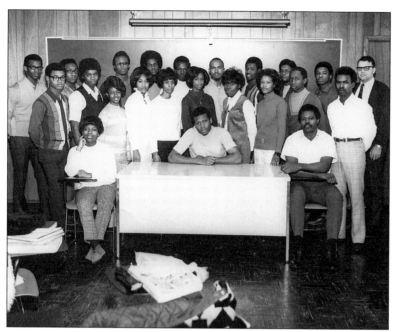

Pictured with some of the canned goods collected in their 1969 Christmas Food Drive are Black Student Union members Glenda Malone, Clyde Winters, Greg Harris, and Arnell Shinault.

The Black Student Union was organized in 1969 and quickly made its presence felt on campus. It sponsored many prominent speakers and programs dealing with African American history and culture. Food drives were held at Thanksgiving and Christmas to assist needy families during the holidays. The BSU also addressed the issue of faculty and staff diversity. Since there were no black instructors or counselors on staff, the Black Student Union demanded that at least one African American faculty member and one African American counselor be hired immediately. Members of the BSU are pictured in 1970. **Front:** Barbara Edwards, Clyde Winters, Warren Wallace. **Middle:** Ronnie Banner, Saul Brass, Char Palmer, Gladys Johnson, Shirley Nicholson, Char Dorris, Barb Singleton, Louise Carr, Alvin Edwards, Carleton Bates. **Back:** Robert Walker, Leslie Beavers, Carlton Quarells, Willie Smith, Cliff Shoemaker, Steve Simpson, Charles Betts, Norman Tate, Leonard Gavin, Robert Sterling (faculty sponsor).

In 1971, Jeffery King was the first African American student selected to speak at college commencement exercises. After graduating from Illinois Weslyan University, King returned to JJC to serve as Director of Veterans' Affairs and Assistant Director of Admissions.

Julian Bond (pictured here), a Georgia legislator and rising black leader, spoke to a packed house in November 1970. The Black Student Union also helped bring many other prominent African American speakers to campus, including U. S. Congresswoman Shirley Chisholm, activist comedian Dick Gregory, author Louis Lomax, and JJC graduate Katherine Dunham, a nationally known anthropologist, writer, choreographer, and dancer.

Mrs. Juliet King, world-traveled soprano and renowned musician, presented a concert at Joliet Junior College in December 1972. Mrs. King is a Joliet resident and mother of JJC student Jeffery King, president of the Black Student Union in 1970.

During Black History Week in 1971, the BSU hosted an art show featuring the work of inmates from Stateville Penitentiary. Viewing some of the pieces are Robert Sterling (left), Jo Ann Sterling, and Charles Kennedy (center), new political science instructor and popular advocate of racial diversity on campus.

Phase I of the Permanent Campus

On November 15, 1970, ground was broken on JJC's 368-acre site for construction of its new $32 million campus. The first phase of construction included buildings that housed agriculture, technical programs, nursing, public service, English, foreign language, math, science, social science, physical education, a planetarium, and gymnasium. Manning shovels in the groundbreaking ceremony were the seven college trustees and Acting President Douglas Graham. **L-R:** Daniel Kennedy, Robert Kiep, Dr. Cecil Ingmire, H. Allen Holler, A. A. "Fizz" Wills, Victor Scott, William Glasscock, and Acting President Douglas Graham. **Above:** With the temporary campus in the foreground, this 1971 aerial view shows Phase I of the permanent campus under construction.

On October 22, 1972, Phase I of the permanent campus was dedicated. The new buildings were nestled alongside the small lake in a wooded area. Architects explained that the extensive use of glass in the two-story concourse was reminiscent of Frank Lloyd Wright's concept of integrating natural environment and building design. Dr. John C. Houbolt, celebrated space engineer and JJC graduate, was the principal speaker at the dedication ceremony, which was followed by an Open House with guided tours. The curvature of the planetarium pictured here softened the effect of the predominantly cube construction.

Construction view of the concourse connecting Buildings C through G.

155

Phase II of the Permanent Campus

Beyond the glass walls of the bridge, the J Building is seen taking shape in the summer of 1973. The new five-story structure would house the cafeteria, bookstore, post office, Learning Resource Center/Library, administrative offices, data processing, Culinary Arts Department, Business Education Department, and the Social Science Department.

The JJC Board of Trustees is seen in 1974 holding one of its last meetings on the temporary campus before moving into the new Board Room in J Building.

The second phase of the permanent campus included a bridge, seen here under construction, and a large five-story structure. Known as the H Building, the enclosed bridge was designed to be a comfortable area where students could relax or study.

The college library moved into the Learning Resource Center on the third floor of J Building when Phase II of the permanent campus was completed. In the mid-1970's, students used the card catalog to locate print material on the shelves. An exterior wall of glass provided natural light and a pleasant view for students reading and studying in the library.

Phase II of the permanent campus is seen here after its recent completion in the fall of 1974. No formal ceremonies were held to mark the opening of the bridge and J Building. District residents were invited to visit campus and tour the new facilities at their convenience. Guides were available on Sunday afternoons during the months of September and October.

156

Secretarial Staff

In 1972, college administrative offices were located in Harper Building on the interim campus. Secretaries and clerks that worked in Harper are pictured here. **Front**: Mary Ullrich, Sheila Short, Betty Yentz, Margaret Webster, Ramona Sanchez, Vi Starmann, Nancy Meinert, Sue Taylor, Karen Erickson, Betty Bass, Lupe Ferreira. **Back**: Gertrude Shroba, Kay Vreuls, Sondra Flint, Opal Moore, Marie Speckman, Vivian Tinley, Carol Tatro, Donna Newkirk, Cheryl Eliason.

Secretaries in the Social Science Department in 1971 were Darryl Sieger and Regina McKenzie.

The library staff in 1972 included Ruth Kuchta, Mary Lou Newell, and Joan Slabozeski (standing).

The JJC Board Room is often used for receptions and social gatherings. In 1990, Karen Erb, Carolyn Engers, and Gertrude Shroba are seen dressed in interesting attire for a staff Halloween party.

Administrative Staff

As college facilities and programs expanded and grew, administrative staff developed accordingly. The only constant was frequent change; titles changed, people changed, and the institution continually evolved. Pictured here are a few of the college administrators who helped chart the course of JJC during the past twenty-five years.

Joseph Borgen, Dean of Occupational and Technical Studies

Dwight Davis, Vice President for Instruction

Dr. Paul N. Thompson, Vice President for Instructional Services

Walter F. Zaida, Vice President for Planning and Informational Resources

Maynard Boudreau, Dean of Career Education

Dr. Everett Van De Voort, Dean of College Parallel and General Studies

Dr. John M. Peterson, Director of Institutional Research and Planning

Richard R. Brandolino, Dean of Community Services and Continuing Education

Ronald Bleed, Director of Data Processing

Robert Glenn, Assistant Director of Business Affairs and college liaison for campus construction

Associate Dean for Special Programs J. D. Ross and his secretary, Bunnie Hunter.

Members of the President's Cabinet are pictured here in 1996. Thomas Ryan, Vice President for Business and Financial Affairs; Dr. Joelyn Ainley, Vice President for Student Affairs; Dr. Thomas Gamble, President; Fred Bettarelli, Director of Human Resources; Dr. James D. Lepanto, Vice President for Academic Affairs; and Steve Daggers, Director of Community Relations.

159

College President Derek Nunney (left) receives instruction in word processing on a Kaypro II from Glenn Harvey, Director of Data Processing.

Paraprofessional Scott Olsen is seen working at an Apple Computer in the Biological Sciences Department. Olsen later became Supervisor of Academic Computing and, most recently, JJC Webmaster.

Beginning as a reading lab in the corner of the library on the interim campus, the facility evolved into a Reading-Writing Lab in B Building and then into an Academic Skills Center in J Building with a wide array of student services. During its early years of development, Dr. Robert Burke, Chair of the English Department, served as director of the lab with Natalie Miller serving as reading specialist and Myra Linden (standing here) as writing specialist. In addition to reading and writing assistance, students were provided courses, workshops, and self-paced individual programs on effective note-taking, study methods, research techniques, vocabulary improvement, test-taking, and various other academic enhancement aids. Peer tutoring proved to be a popular addition to the menu of services offered by the Skills Center.

With the opening of Phase I of the permanent campus in 1972, the college established a Child Care Center in the Home Economics Building. Intended primarily for children of JJC students, the center made it easier for parents of preschoolers to attend college. The Center served the dual purpose of freeing parents to attend classes while, at the same time, allowing education, psychology, and nursing students to observe child behavior through the use of one-way glass. In addition to planned activities, the children had plenty of free time for play.

Often juggling jobs and family responsibilities with attending college, students consult advisors or counselors, like Roger Gordon pictured here, to develop a schedule of classes best suited for them.

Even though touch-tone phone registration was introduced in the early 1980s for part-time students, lines remained long on the first days of registration as full-time students tried to arrange desirable class schedules. If classes were full when students reached the window, the next stop was often an instructor's office to plead for admission by raising class limits.

Agricultural/Horticultural Sciences

The agriculture and horticulture programs have enjoyed a long, successful, and unique history at Joliet Junior College. The roots of the agriculture program can be traced back to the early 1940s when the college and high school shared facilities and faculty. In June 1941, the Board hired Gordon K. Grose to teach courses in the newly approved high school agriculture curriculum. A year later, Grose resigned, and Elmer W. Rowley was employed to teach both day and evening classes. During World War II, the school participated in the government's food production program and designated Rowley as the supervisor of canning centers and coordinator of victory garden seminars and classes.

When Rowley became the first full-time dean of the junior college in 1947, Max Kuster was hired as his replacement in the high school agriculture program. Kuster also took over the Farmer's Short Course that Rowley had been conducting. The Agriculture Department was located in an old frame building south of the high school on Jefferson Street. The structure was in such poor repair that when students began raising chickens on the third floor, feed and other material sifted through the flooring into classrooms and offices below. In 1952, the department moved to leased space nearby, and the original agriculture building was razed and replaced with tennis courts.

In 1954, Kuster was concerned that the new Lincoln-Way High School District east of Joliet would drain students from the program, and he suggested that an agriculture curriculum be developed for the junior college. The plan was approved, and courses were offered in agriculture economics, dairy science, principles of feeding, and crop production, all of which are still taught fifty years later. Walter Zaida was hired as the second instructor in the Agriculture Department; however, he soon moved into an administrative position as an assistant to Dean Rowley.

The first two graduates of the agriculture program were John Findlay and John Richards. Interestingly, the Richards' family farm was purchased by JJC in 1967 and developed into the current college campus. When Findlay and Richards transferred to the University of Illinois, the Assistant Dean of Agriculture decided that they would have to take proficiency tests to receive credit for their JJC courses. Following an exchange of letters between Kuster and the U of I, a team of university officials visited Joliet and examined the content and structure of the program. They were impressed with the agriculture curriculum and immediately ended proficiency testing.

The Vocational Education Act of 1963 produced a major change in agriculture education at JJC. Department Chair Max Kuster was contacted by the University of Illinois and the Agriculture Department of the State of Illinois to see if Joliet Junior College would be interested in developing a pilot program in agriculture supply and business. Grant monies were available to design a two-year occupational curriculum, the first of its kind in the state and one of the first in the nation. Since JJC was the only community college offering a full two-year transfer program in agriculture, it seemed logical that Joliet should develop the new non-transfer program. Superintendent William French approved the pilot program on the condition that a minimum of six students could be recruited for the new courses. Robert Jurgens, the agriculture instructor at Serena High School, was hired for the new vocational program. When the semester began in the fall of 1964, there were forty-four students enrolled. The following year, Maynard

The Farmers' Short Course annually attracted numerous participants during the winter months. For a registration fee of $1, the lecture-discussion course introduced farmers to the latest research and newest techniques in agriculture. There were usually nine weekly classroom sessions and a final dinner meeting to which spouses and guests were invited. Max Kuster was the organizer and instructor when the Short Course pictured here was conducted in the late 1960s.

Boudreau and Ronald Seibel were employed to teach agribusiness courses, which soon attracted more than one hundred students. The first graduating class in 1966 had forty-two students; all but one were males.

When the college moved to the new campus on Houbolt Road, the Agriculture Department had additional room to grow. William Johnson was hired in 1968 to help develop and coordinate a new program in agriculture production, and Robert Cottingham was employed the following year to develop a program in horticulture. In 1972, the department moved into a large, new building, a facility made possible by a federal grant secured through the efforts of JJC administrator Douglas Graham and college Trustee William Glasscock. Designed largely by Max Kuster, Robert Jurgens, Stan Kosiba, and Maynard Boudreau, the new classrooms and labs provided the department even more space to expand. The horticulture program blossomed in the 1970s and '80s, benefiting greatly by the construction of a greenhouse in 1973. Student organizations and activities also flourished on the permanent campus. For example, Dave Cattron organized and coached the first livestock judging team in 1972, and the Student Agriculture Association sponsored such events as the Spring Fling and Sadie Hawkins Days, complete with chicken chases, greased pig contests, and bikini competitions.

A long-range goal of the agriculture faculty was realized in 1983 when operation of the 143-acre farm on college property was turned over to the department. Designated as the J. F. Richards Land Laboratory in honor of the family that sold the property to the college, the farm supplements classroom instruction. It is used extensively by instructors and students for agricultural research and agronomy demonstrations. Also, when the farm was acquired, a swine confinement option was added to the agriculture production program. Not only have faculty members made use of practical, hands-on learning experiences and internships, but also in 1980, a few

Pictured here is the panel convened to discuss the proposed two-year vocational program in agriculture supply and business. **L-R:** Dr. Lloyd Phipps, Chair of the Agricultural Education Department at the University of Illinois; Walter Zaida, Assistant to the Dean; Elmer Rowley, Dean of Joliet Junior College; Allen Utech, Local State Supervisor; Ralph Guthrie, Chief State Supervisor of Agricultural Education.

instructors introduced computers into their classrooms. Twenty years later, faculty routinely use computers in classroom instruction, and students spend considerable time in the department's computer lab. In 1993, Dave Cattron developed a course devoted entirely to agricultural computing. Furthermore, a computer is used to control the temperature in the two new state-of-the-art greenhouses built in 1994.

In the fall of 1999, the department added a Veterinary Medical Technology Program to its long list of degrees and certificates and hired Dr. Scott Keller to coordinate the curriculum. A new building to house the program was opened in January 2000. Also in 1999, John Weitendorf donated 30.7 acres of land on Laraway Road to be used by the Agricultural/Horticultural Sciences Department as an off-campus educational center. Beginning in 1954 with four agriculture classes, the department now offers almost a hundred courses, ranging from the operation and adjustment of farm machinery to surgery technology, and from artificial insemination of cattle and swine to videoscape design. Indeed, JJC's programs have been in the forefront throughout the state for almost fifty years.

Robert Jurgens was hired in August 1964 to implement and guide the new two-year curriculum in agriculture supply and business, the first occupational program of its kind in the state. He is seen here teaching one of the courses in the program.

Organized in 1964, the Student Agriculture Association has been one of the largest and most active clubs since its inception. Seen here in 1966 are sophomore members of the S.A.A. **Front:** Dave Phillips, Jim Ramseyer, Dick Tindall, Dallas Good, Bob Thompson, Dave Kinsella, Scott Buck, John Nienhuis, Don Carlson. **Middle:** Bob Kampe, Mike Kleen, Roger Cook, Rodney Block, Stan Yordy, Bob Jarboc, Bill Grimes, Tom Wilkey. **Back:** Maynard Boudreau (faculty), Max Kuster (department chair), Bill Barr, Dave Westphal, Steve Peters, Bob Christian, Mike Stogan, Dan Olson, John Rowley, Doug Miles, unidentified, Ronald Seibel (faculty), Robert Jurgens (faculty).

In 1983, the college turned over to the Agriculture Department 143 acres of land to be used for research and demonstrations. Designated as the J. F. Richards Land Laboratory, the acreage is used extensively by students in all agriculture programs. In 1985, the former owner of the property, Mrs. Virginia Richards, presented a framed picture of the farm as it looked before being purchased by JJC and developed into the college campus. Mrs. Richards has been a friend to the school. She sold her farm at a favorable price and, for many years, has annually donated two agriculture scholarships to JJC students in memory of her husband and son, both named John F. Richards. Pictured here at the presentation ceremony on Agriculture Day are Department Chair James Ethridge, Vice President Walter Zaida, Mrs. Virginia Richards, Dean J. D. Ross, President Raymond Pietak, and guest speaker Orien Samuelson.

James Ethridge conducts a horticulture program in the concourse of A Building in February 1976. Dr. Ethridge joined the staff in 1973 and has served as Chair of the Agricultural/Horticultural Sciences Department from 1984 to the present.

Horticulture instructor Roger Ross is seen with students walking the campus and providing practical hands-on instruction. Ross sponsored the Student Horticulture Association when it was chartered in October 1976.

The JJC Livestock Judging Team won first place in the National Agriculture College Teachers Association Livestock Judging Contest at Eastern Oklahoma State College in 1994. The competition included ten classes of cattle, swine, and sheep and six sets of oral reasons. The team was the overall winner by placing first in beef and sheep, second in oral reasons, and third in swine. Tammy Kurtenbach, now a faculty member at JJC, was the contest's overall individual winner. Members of the championship team are pictured here. **L-R:** Chad Martin, Dan Hamilton, Jessica Murray, Mike Taylor, Matt Taylor, Suzy Martin, Tammy Kurtenbach, Beau Byington, Rodney Knittel, and Coach Dale Hummel.

In 1987, an historic one-room country school was donated to the Joliet Junior College Foundation by the Ed Larkin family and moved five miles to campus for use as a living educational history museum. Jim Shinn and Dave Cattron, members of the Agricultural/Horticultural Sciences Department, spearheaded the effort to acquire and restore the building. Known as the Cronin School, the small structure was built in 1863 and served the students of Troy Township until January of 1950. In 1935, the original building was remodeled and equipped with electricity. When the school district no longer needed the building, it was sold at auction in 1952 and later acquired by Ed Larkin. The structure was converted into a home and used as a residence until about 1970. When the college acquired the building, it was being used for storage.

The building has been restored to its pre-1935 condition with furnishings, fixtures, and materials replicating, as closely as possible, that era in the school's history. Today, children enjoy visiting the one-room country school and discovering what it was like to attend school seventy-five years ago. They enjoy operating the pump outside in the yard and wondering about the restrooms. They are also amused by the old desks and amazed that one teacher taught eight grades in a single room.

Pictured here are students attending Cronin School in December 1946.

In the fall of 1969, when JJC moved to the campus on Houbolt Road, the college admitted the first class of nursing students into its new RN preparatory program. For several years, the college had partnered with Silver Cross Hospital School of Nursing, and JJC faculty had taught science and related courses to Silver Cross nursing students. However, in the early 1960s, Illinois nursing leaders began pushing a state plan to move RN preparatory programs from hospital-owned diploma schools to college campuses. The new approach envisioned students training in a broader educational setting with a wide range of supplementary courses and academic enhancement programs. Locally, this meant phasing out the Silver Cross school and developing an associate degree nursing program at Joliet Junior College.

In keeping with state guidelines, Helen Tea was hired as program director a year prior to enrolling students. Tea was an experienced nursing administrator, having supervised the school at Silver Cross Hospital. She planned the overall program, contacted prospective clinical agencies, and obtained state approval. In the spring of 1969, Emily Zabrocki joined Ms. Tea as an instructor and began designing courses, preparing syllabi, and securing agreements with clinical sites. By the fall of 1969, Mabel Robinson, Therese Czichon, and Irma June Simmons, all of whom had been nursing instructors in the Silver Cross diploma program, joined Zabrocki as faculty members. As recommended by the state, an orderly transition was made from a hospital-based diploma program to an associate degree curriculum on the junior college campus. Silver Cross School of Nursing graduated its last class in 1970, and JJC awarded degrees to its first graduates in 1971.

Since its first eleven graduates in 1971, the program has grown to about one hundred graduates annually. Students who complete the two-year Associate Degree Nursing (ADN) curriculum are eligible to write the Registered Nurse National Council Licensure Examination for Nurses. They may also continue their education by transferring into a baccalaureate nursing program. A spin-off option is available at the end of the first year of nursing classes that permits students to take the practical nurse (LPN) licensure exam. The nursing program has remained flexible to meet society's ever-changing health care needs. Instructional methods have, likewise, changed and now include the use of computers and the World Wide Web.

Helen Tea was hired in October 1968 to serve as Director of Nursing Education at Joliet Junior College. Working with an advisory committee of twenty-nine members, Tea won state approval for a two-year associate degree program with strong classroom and clinical components. The first nursing classes were offered in the fall of 1969.

For health reasons, Helen Tea resigned in 1970, and Emily Zabrocki became program director and department chair, a position she held for some fifteen years before retiring in 2000. Zabrocki is seen here at her desk in the department office.

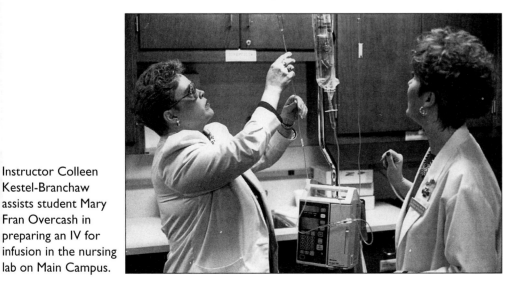

Instructor Colleen Kestel-Branchaw assists student Mary Fran Overcash in preparing an IV for infusion in the nursing lab on Main Campus.

Pictured here in 1971 are the first graduates of JJC's nursing program.

SHARON HOPPLER   MARGARET GLENNEY   JOYCE GLENN   JO ANNE ST. GERMAIN

JOLIET JUNIOR COLLEGE
ASSOCIATE DEGREE IN NURSING
Graduates 1971

JULIENNE NEMCEVIC   JO SIMPSON   DOROTHY HOOPER   KAY MERTZ

JANE BLACKWELL   DANIEL JACKSON   THERESA FICK

Photos by... MATTHEWS

Vice President for Instruction Dwight Davis welcomes graduates and guests to the pinning ceremony in 1976. Seated on the platform are nursing instructors Sally Monken, Lora McDonald, Laura Cato, and Ellen Holmgren; Rev. Kay Collins, Chaplain of Silver Cross Hospital; and nursing instructor Eileen Massura. Department Chair Emily Zabrocki is seated to the right of the podium.

Instructor Mabel Robinson is seen with her students in the Physical Therapy Department at Saint Joseph Hospital (today Provena Saint Joseph Medical Center) in Joliet. **Front:** Bette Ristinen, Cecelia Peacock, Mabel Robinson (instructor), Bridget Rubocki, Betty Wilker. **Back:** Carol Paetle, Judy Balos, Eileen Caudill, Peggy Williamson, Janet Barfield, June Sullivan, Linda Rothlesberger, Hilda Warlick.

Law Enforcement/Criminal Justice Studies

In response to inquiries and requests by area police agencies, Technical Department Chair Al Racchini formed an advisory committee in 1967 to assist the college in developing a law enforcement program. A two-year curriculum was designed and subsequently gained state approval in July 1968. The first classes were taught by adjunct instructors in the spring of 1969. The following summer, Frank Alberico was hired to teach law enforcement classes and to provide program leadership. Increasing enrollments necessitated the employment of Patrick O'Connell as an additional staff member in 1973. When he resigned the following year, Donald Ernst was hired in August 1974 to teach in the law enforcement program. For the past twenty-seven years, Alberico and Ernst have been the full-time faculty responsible for law enforcement and related programs.

In the spring of 1972, a two-year degree program in corrections was added to the curriculum, the first of its kind in the state. The Illinois Board of Higher Education provided the college with a $30,000 grant to design and pilot the corrections program. Since the Joliet region has more correctional agencies than any other area in the state, JJC was deemed the ideal location for such an initiative. Frank Alberico, who had written the proposal, formed an advisory committee to develop the program. Dr. Salim Abdul Haaq was hired to coordinate and refine the curriculum and to teach the new corrections classes. However, the program failed to generate sufficient hours to justify a full-time instructor and coordinator, and Haaq left the college. Law enforcement instructor Donald Ernst eventually provided program leadership and assumed responsibility for staffing corrections classes, most of them with adjunct faculty.

With the assistance of a committee of professionals in the field, Ernst developed a broad-based Criminal Justice Studies Program in 1991 to replace the corrections curriculum. While the program continues to provide course work for uniformed officers, it also serves the educational needs of students interested in the diverse opportunities available in the field of criminal justice. The curriculum is interdisciplinary and flexible and can be individualized for students pursuing careers in law enforcement, the courts, corrections, forensic science, and private security. It blends theory and real-world experiences by utilizing classroom lecture and discussion, independent research, guest speakers, field trips, and internships. Based on personal and professional goals, students can select a course of study designed either for immediate employment or for transfer into a university baccalaureate program.

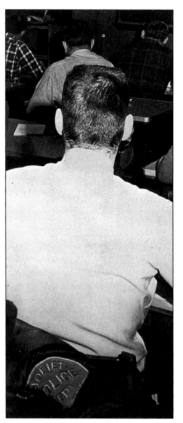

Since the program began in the spring of 1969, numerous members of regional law enforcement agencies have received training at Joliet Junior College. In fact, the current Sheriff of Will County, Brendan Ward, is a former JJC student.

Each year students serve internships with numerous law enforcement and criminal justice agencies in the area. At an annual spring banquet, representatives of participating agencies are honored and thanked for their role in providing interns with real-life learning experiences. The banquet also serves as a forum for professors Frank Alberico and Donald Ernst to recognize the accomplishments of outstanding students by presenting them with various awards and scholarships. Pictured here at a banquet in the mid-1970s are Public Services Department Chair Dr. William Chase, Dean of Career Education Maynard Boudreau, Frank Alberico, and Don Ernst.

Working with an advisory committee in 1991, Donald Ernst, pictured here, developed a Criminal Justice Studies Program designed to prepare students either for immediate employment or transfer into a baccalaureate degree program.

Organized in 1969 as the Law Enforcement Club, its name was changed in 1978 to the Association for Criminal Justice Students. The ACJS annually sponsors a variety of field trips, programs, and social activities under the direction of faculty sponsors Frank Alberico and Don Ernst. Pictured here are club members in 1975. **Front:** Timothy Tracy, Gene Golden, Richard Strelak, Craig Long, Carol Bickel, James Creed. **Middle:** Richard Whyte, Alfredo Coronado, Bob Kirwin, Jim Hines, Kathleen Purdy, Diane Cramer, Carol Farrero, Mike Elsen. **Back:** Alan Love, Jeff Wix, Delbert Berguson.

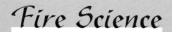

Fire Science

Larry Walsh, Chief of the Joliet Fire Department, coordinated the college Fire Science Program for many years. Walsh helped develop the program in 1970 to meet the demand for firefighter training. The program immediately attracted students from numerous municipal departments as well as from nearby industries with fire fighting units.

In many fire science courses, classroom instruction is supplemented with field experiences, especially in such areas as fire apparatus and equipment and advanced techniques of fire fighting.

Culinary Arts

The culinary arts program at Joliet Junior College began in the spring semester of 1970 with instructors Claude Kern and Siegfried "Mike" Mieland. Swiss-born chef Kern was hired in August 1969 to develop the program and to direct JJC's food services operation. Mieland, a native of Germany, had considerable experience as a professional cook and executive chef in Switzerland, England, and the United States prior to teaming with Kern in implementing the new culinary arts curriculum at JJC. Beginning with eight students in the spring of 1970, the program rapidly expanded, and Chef Siegfried Stober was added to the staff in 1971. Classes were taught to full-time and part-time students in both the day and evening schools. Courses were even offered at Pontiac and Stateville Prisons as part of JJC's Inmate Training Program. A total of 150 students were enrolled in culinary arts by December 1973.

In 1974, the Culinary Arts Department and food services moved from a temporary building on the interim campus to the ground floor of J Building on the permanent campus. The same year, the student Epicurean Club was organized, and the first annual Classical 100 was held. The Classical 100 provides students an opportunity to showcase their talent by preparing and serving gourmet food. Proceeds from the dinner are placed in a scholarship fund for deserving culinary students. From the very beginning, the Culinary Arts Department developed

In February 1970, when the culinary arts program was only a few weeks old, Siegfried "Mike" Mieland and Claude Kern met to discuss the day's menu.

a reputation for producing excellent graduates. During the first ten years of the program's existence, JJC students won first place each year at the National Restaurant Salon of Culinary Arts competition.

Officers of the Illinois Restaurant Association often described the JJC program as the "best in the Midwest."

When the college opened the Louis Joliet Renaissance Center as a downtown instructional site, the Culinary Arts Department expanded its offerings to include a hotel and restaurant management program. The building had housed the Sheraton Hotel and D'Amico's 214 Restaurant and now provided a practical setting for training students. The facility provides students with hands-on experience in planning and preparing food for banquets, parties, wedding receptions, candlelight dinners, and Sunday brunches. In 1986, the department won the coveted Award of Excellence from the National Restaurant Association and the American Vocational Association. The NRA/AVA award recognized the JJC program as the best post-secondary food service education program in the United States.

The art of sculpturing ice into artistic forms has challenged culinary arts students since the inception of the program. The students seen here in 1977 use various cutting and carving tools to shape their block of ice.

Internationally known as an expert in blowing and pulling spun sugar, JJC Chef Charles Wagner is seen demonstrating the art of blowing sugar into artistic and delicate forms. Blown sugar swans and pulled sugar baskets and flowers were a few of Wagner's specialties.

Reflecting the theme of ancient Mexico, culinary arts students showcased their edible creations for an open house in 1979. The seven-tiered ziggurat with its exterior staircase and shrine at the top was formed out of pastillage, a sugar-based modeling paste.

During the holiday season, sophomore students capture the magic of Christmas in their gingerbread creations, displayed annually in the college cafeteria. Each house is uniquely designed with exterior decorations limited only by the imagination of the culinary architect.

Under the watchful eye of Chef Stober, students prepare food in 1977 for the Classical 100 Dinner, an epicurean delight held annually to raise scholarship funds for culinary arts students.

Gene Bogdan, owner of the Joliet Holiday Inn, is seen plating food for students to serve at a Classical 100 Dinner. As a member of the original advisory committee that developed the culinary arts program, Bogdan often served as a Classical 100 table captain.

In October 1997, JJC received a Chef Boiardi grant of $150,000 to create a Hector Boiardi Endowed Memorial Scholarship for culinary arts students at the college. Holding the generous-sized check are JJC Foundation President William Kaplan and Chef Patrick Hegarty, Chair of the Culinary Arts Department.

Opposite page, bottom right: Chef Siegfried Stober, Chair of the Culinary Arts Department, provides instruction and encouragement as Cindy Piket decorates Christmas logs and other holiday pastries in 1985.

Chef John Noe tastes the soup of the day. Noe graduated from the JJC culinary arts program and later returned to serve as an instructor and department chair.

173

For fifteen years, from 1970 to 1985, Joliet Junior College offered a unique educational program to residents of District 525's several correctional facilities. With grant funding from the Illinois Division of Vocational Rehabilitation, Division of Vocational-Technical Education, Illinois Junior College Board, and the Department of Corrections, JJC's Inmate Training Program provided a wide range of educational opportunities at the Pontiac Correctional Center, Stateville Correctional Center, Joliet Correctional Center, Illinois Youth Center at Joliet, and the Dwight Correctional Center for women. Beginning with vocational-technical degree and certificate programs in culinary arts, data processing, automotive services, accounting, mechanical production technology, mechanical design technology, and secretarial science, the program was gradually expanded to include general education courses necessary for earning a transfer degree. The Inmate Training Program was discontinued in 1985 when funding agencies decided to explore less expensive options for providing educational services to residents of correctional facilities. Built in 1858, some of the walls and historic guard towers of the Joliet Correctional Center (pictured here) are reminiscent of nineteenth century penal institutions.

JJC's Electronics/Electricity curriculum has a long history dating back to 1923, when Ira McCoy and Fred Hahn began teaching electricity classes in what was then called the manual training program. A comprehensive list of course offerings in electrical wiring for the building trades was added in 1948 by Lewis Englehardt, a journeyman electrician. When the college split from the high school in 1969, the program was temporarily housed in Room 103 of the Blackhawk Building on the interim campus. In 1972, it moved into permanent facilities when Phase I of the new campus was completed. The courses and programs have evolved over the years and in the 1990s began incorporating robotic equipment, programmable controllers, and other state-of-the-art technology.

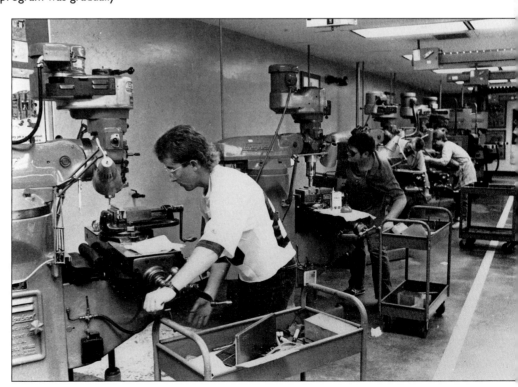

Under the direction of instructor Jim Morris, JJC developed an excellent machine shop that prepares students for employment in regional businesses and industries.

n 1973, Jack Richardson is
een discussing the "Golden
Age" of Greece with his
History 105 class.

Known for his loud sport
coats, world travel, and
student-centered teaching,
Dr. Lloyd Tinkle was a popular business law instructor.

The automotive service curriculum trains students as service technicians for independent garages, dealerships, and service stations.
Students in the program, like the one pictured here in 1979, gain
practical experience working on the automobiles of other students
and college employees.

In August 1980, JJC metalworking student
David Harvey received a toolbox award from
District 55 of the International Association of
Machinists and Aerospace Workers in recognition of hard work and pride in craftsman-
ship. The Machinists' Union annually awarded
a toolbox and tools to an outstanding college
student to provide recognition and encouragement in the field. Harvey was a student in
the Mechanical Production Technology program under the supervision of instructor Jim
Morris. Pictured here at the award ceremony are Ron McCure, President of District 55
of the Machinists' Union; Harold Spreitzer,
President of Local 124 of the Machinists'
Union; David Harvey, award recipient;
Maynard Boudreau, Dean of Career
Education; and JJC instructor Jim Morris.

Instructor Jim Fox examines a
student's work in the drafting
lab in 1990. Computers had
not found their way into
drafting classes, and CAD
(Computer Aided Design)
was not yet being taught.

When typewriters were the mainstay of secretarial positions, JJC's Business Education Department developed an open lab where students used audio and visual aids to work at their own pace. Most courses were offered on an open-entry, open-exit basis with a maximum of sixteen weeks allowed for completion. Instructors monitored the lab and were available to students for individual assistance.

In 1970, instructor Bobby McDowell taught students how to use a key punch machine in his data processing classes.

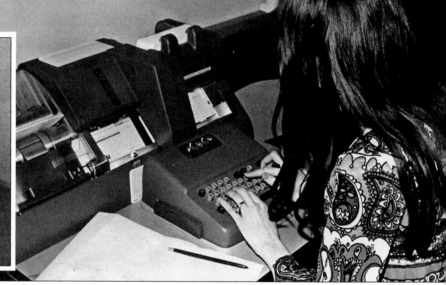

William Burns is pictured at the podium teaching a French class in 1968.

Margaret Cockbill is seen here in 1969 teaching an English class.

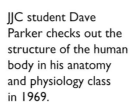
Sociology instructor Phil Piket interacts with a student after teaching a class in marriage and the family.

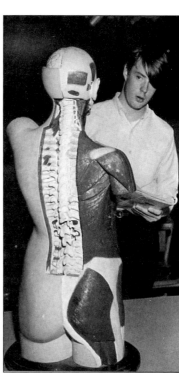

JJC student Dave Parker checks out the structure of the human body in his anatomy and physiology class in 1969.

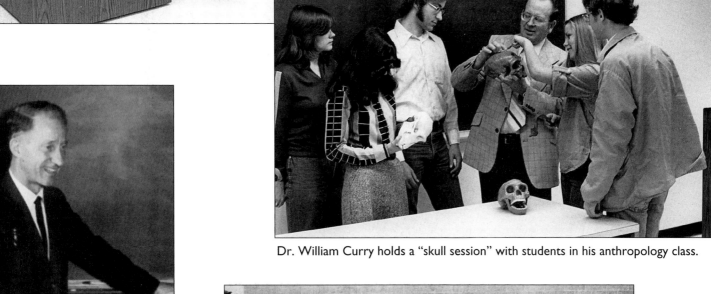
Dr. William Curry holds a "skull session" with students in his anthropology class.

Foreign language instructor Art Walters shares a light moment with students in his German class.

Psychology instructor Ken Warman delivers a lecture in 1974 in one of the few large-group instruction rooms on campus.

History instructor James Hurst emphasizes a point in his western civilization class.

In 1976, Robert Mallary puts students at ease in his speech class.

Chemistry instructor John Hirmer is seen using the blackboard to present course material.

In 1969, Will Miner is seen teaching physics.

In 1979, political science instructor Gale "Flash" Filter conducts a planning session in the college cafeteria with students in the model government program.

Richard Meyers uses the blackboard to explain an algebraic equation to his math class in 1969.

Leonard Hodgman is seen interacting with students in his geography class.

In 1975, JJC's first Annual Invitational Math Contest, the largest of its kind in the state, attracted students from numerous area high schools. The over-all winners were Lincoln-Way in the Class AA division and Beecher in the Class A category. Pictured here are contestants hard at work in the 1976 competition.

An individual winner pumps her fist in the air after receiving an award in the 1995 math contest. Announcing the winners and pre-senting the awards are Math Department Chair Nelson Collins, math instructor Jean McArthur, Vice President for Academic Affairs James Lepanto, and math instructor Linda Padilla.

The JJC Planetarium held its first public showing on February 15, 1973, with Douglas Graham, Director of Research and Planetarium, presenting a program entitled "Stars of the North." Pictured here in 1975, Graham explains to curious school children how the planetarium equipment projects such realistic sights and sounds.

In 1988, Douglas Graham retired, and Edward Eichelberger became the new director of the planetarium. The same year, a generous donation by Herbert Trackman, a 1931 graduate of JJC, made possible the refurbishing of the planetarium and the installation of new state-of-the-art audio and video projection equipment. At a ribbon-cutting ceremony in August 1988, the newly equipped and redecorated facility was reopened as the "Herbert Trackman Planetarium." **L-R:** Dr. Peter Nichols representing the JJC Foundation, Herbert Trackman, and President Raymond Pietak.

In the fall of 1992, JJC began implementing Continuous Quality Improvement (CQI) under the direction of Dr. Robert Hauwiller. Working with a Quality Council of twelve employees representing different groups from within the college, Hauwiller encouraged the formation of Master Planning Teams to address campus problems, concerns, and processes. Using CQI principles and techniques, the teams developed action plans for improving college programs and services. Pictured here in 1994

are several college employees wearing CQI T-shirts that read "We Can't Spell Q ality Without U."

On April 16, 1999, JJC won first place in the statewide College Bowl tournament sponsored by the Illinois Community College Trustees Association and the Illinois Community College Student Activities Association. Sometimes called "the varsity sport of the mind," College Bowl features fast-paced competition with questions drawn from such categories as humanities, history, social science, math, science, literature, and current events. At the state finals, team captain Nick Rakes scored the highest number of points by an individual player and was named to the tournament's All-Star Team. Each member of the winning team received a $300 cash stipend to apply toward educational expenses. Bill Yarrow, a member of the English Department, served as team coach. JJC repeated as the state College Bowl champion in April 2000. Pictured here are members of the 1999 team: Bill Yarrow (coach), A. J. Orosco, Karen Olvera, Nick Rakes (captain), Jeff O'Malley, Michael Fletcher.

In 1975, Dr. William Zales originated the concept of a college arboretum as part of the College Use Plan. With financial assistance from the JJC Foundation, an 11-acre tract between the entrance and exit roads of the Main Campus has been planted with more than two hundred species of trees, shrubs, and vines. Designed as an area for both exhibition and study, the arboretum has become more attractive and useful each year. Zales is seen here in 1977 discussing the first plantings and explaining the concept of arranging specimens in an evolutionary sequence beginning at the east end with the most primitive plants.
L-R: Foundation Directors Kenneth Pritz, Helen Harshbarger, Gary Lichtenwalter, and Earl Meisinger; Dr. Zales; and Steve Flanagan, Buildings and Grounds Department. In May 1999, Dr. Zales was honored for the central role he played in establishing the arboretum; it was officially named the "Dr. William M. Zales Arboretum."

Under the direction of Dr. William Zales, biology faculty members sponsored and supported the development of a nature trail on campus. In recognition of the role Zales played in establishing and maintaining the trail, he was honored in May 1999 at a ceremony officially designating the trail as the "Dr. William M. Zales Nature Trail." Unveiling the new sign is Andrew Neill of the Natural Sciences/Physical Education Department.

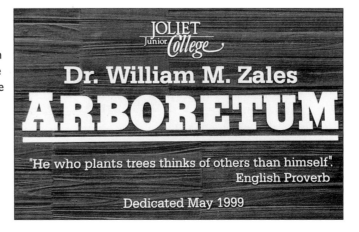

JOLIET Junior College
Dr. William M. Zales
ARBORETUM
"He who plants trees thinks of others than himself".
English Proverb
Dedicated May 1999

In February 1980, a truck from the Buildings and Grounds Department broke through the ice on the college lake while clearing snow for skaters. The truck was pulled from the lake, dried out, and put back into service plowing snow. A week later, the same truck ventured onto the lake to continue making the rink, but it created a spectacle instead: it broke through the ice a second time. With little more than its cab protruding above the frigid water, the truck was once again fished from the lake. Students and staff were amused by the incident and willingly offered lighthearted advice. An exasperated college president issued a directive to Buildings and Grounds that forbade the driving of trucks on the lake. All future snow removal for skaters would be done by hand. A cartoonist for the *Blazer* had fun with the story.

On May 10, 1977, Joliet Junior College passed the only tax referendum attempted since it became a Class I college district in 1967. Publicized as "the untax," proponents explained to District 525 voters that the amount of money paid in property taxes for JJC would not increase. As taxes for the college Bond and Interest Fund decreased by 7.5 cents over the next five years, a corresponding 7.5-cent increase in the Education and Building Funds would be phased in. Although some residents did not fully understand the college's declining bonded indebtedness and the concept of offsetting tax rates, they, nonetheless, passed the referendum and placed the college on a firmer financial footing.

Joliet Junior College acknowledges the outstanding contributions and excellent work of its employees with special awards. Recipients of Employee Recognition Awards in 1992 are pictured here holding their plaques. **Front:** Linda Padilla, Marie Wolff. **Back:** Trustee Eleanor McGuan-Boza, Marvin Schumaker, David Buckley, Sunnie Hunter, President Raymond Pietak.

182

On Strike

Over the years, college employees have not always seen eye-to-eye with the administration and Board of Trustees. Occasionally, the inability to reach agreement during contract negotiations has resulted in picketing and work stoppages. The major issues separating the sides usually have been salary, health benefits, and workload. Following prolonged negotiations, the faculty union voted to strike in 1973, 1977, and 1991. The Firemen and Oilers Union, representing physical plant employees and campus security staff, held strikes in 1973 and 1974. Although all the work stoppages were strikingly similar, each

was different in some way. Court orders ended two strikes, and another was suspended when parties agreed to federal mediation. Following the 1977 strike, the Board agreed to establish a student scholarship fund with the $45,000 that faculty members were docked. In recent years, contract agreements have been reached using an approach to negotiating called Interest Based Bargaining. The IBB method encourages the two sides to focus on shared issues and concerns rather than opposing bargaining positions, a strategy designed to produce more amicable talks and mutually agreeable solutions.

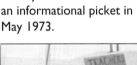

Faculty members conduct an informational picket in May 1973.

Members of the striking Firemen and Oilers Union "walk" the picket line on a warm summer day in 1974. **L-R:** Larry Powell, Ron Tarrant, Dolores Fox, Steve Flanagan.

Braving the bitter cold, faculty picketers warm up to the occasion during a strike in December 1991.

Striking faculty members express their sentiments on various signs along Houbolt Road.

In November 1973, students are met by picketing faculty members at the college entrance.

183

North Campus

In order to better meet the educational needs of the rapidly expanding Romeoville-Bolingbrook area of the college district, JJC established a North Campus administrative and instructional center in 1975 in the Fountaindale Library on Briarcliff Road in Bolingbrook. In addition to several traditional classrooms, the facility included a self-paced business education laboratory and day care services for students with children. In 1980, North Campus doubled in size when the college leased additional space in the new Town Center across the street. Two years later, the college moved out of Fountaindale Library and established an instructional site in the Romeoville Center, located in the Valley View School building. At that time, administrative offices and student services were relocated to the Bolingbrook Town Center.

Having rented facilities in Bolingbrook since 1975 and in Romeoville since 1982, JJC began looking for a permanent North Campus location. In the early 1990s, several areas were considered for developing a new campus to serve students in the northern region of the district. In January 1993, the college opened a new North Campus on a 40-acre site on 135th Street just east of Weber Road in Romeoville. The 35,000-square-foot facility includes twenty classrooms, science and computer labs, a library and media center, conference area, offices for faculty and counselors, child care services, administrative offices, and ample parking. Since the campus opened, the area has experienced an amazing transformation from cornfields and farmhouses to business establishments and housing developments.

North Campus had its beginning in 1975 in the lower level of Bolingbrook's Fountaindale Library pictured here.

In 1980, North Campus operations increased substantially when the college leased space in the new Bolingbrook Town Center pictured here.

In April 1992, ground was broken in a cornfield on 135th Street in Romeoville for JJC's permanent North Campus facility. Participating in the ceremony are Trustee Joyce Heap, Board Chair Eleanor McGuan-Boza, Jeffrey Lanaghan of Industrial Developents International, JJC President Raymond Pietak, Trustees James Wright and Dolores Johnson, Student Trustee Richard Skorupa, Trustee Thomas Smith, Romeoville Mayor John Strobbe, and Trustee David Cryer.

The college moved out of Fountaindale Library in 1982 and established a North Campus instructional site in the Romeoville Center, located in the Valley View School building seen here. At that time, administrative offices and student services were relocated from the library to the Bolingbrook Town Center.

City Center Campus

In the fall of 1980, the college opened the Louis Joliet Renaissance Center at 214 North Ottawa Street in downtown Joliet. Controversy surrounded the Board's decision to acquire the site. Some people questioned the wisdom of investing resources in an aging motel and restaurant in the downtown area, while others were not comfortable with the lease/purchase agreement between the college and the JJC Foundation. However, proponents envisioned the facility as both an instructional site where students could take credit and noncredit courses and a conference center where JJC Culinary Arts and Hotel, Restaurant, and Food Service Management students could acquire valuable hands-on experience. Today, the Louis Joliet Renaissance Center is known as the City Center Campus and serves a variety of purposes in the overall mission of the college.

The City Center Campus presently houses the Division of Adult and Family Services, which provides educational opportunities for students from the literacy level to pre-baccalaureate and vocational training programs. Also located on the downtown campus is the Institute of Economic Technology; IET specializes in work force preparation, employee training, business development, and technology deployment in the college district. Looking to the future, the City Center Campus will soon be linked to a new $9 million historical museum scheduled to open in an adjacent building in 2002.

College President Derek Nunney presided at the grand opening of the Louis Joliet Renaissance Center on May 7, 1981.

Participating in the ribbon-cutting ceremony at the grand opening are Dr. Charles Kennedy, Chair of the JJC Board of Trustees; John Bourg, Mayor of the City of Joliet; and Dr. Derek Nunney, JJC President.

The building pictured here was originally designed as a social center for the 1,500 members of the Joliet Chamber of Commerce. During the 1920s and '30s, members met to play cards and billiards or just to socialize in the dining area. In the early '60s, the building was converted into D'Amico's 214, a popular restaurant and night club featuring headline performers. When a hotel was constructed adjacent to it in 1969, the facility became part of the Sheraton Joliet Motor Inn. In 1980, the college acquired the property through a lease/purchase agreement with the JJC Foundation and converted it into the Louis Joliet Renaissance Center, presently known as the City Center Campus.

The main dining room of the Renaissance Center is pictured here; the stairs in the background lead to the ballroom/banquet facility on the second floor.

185

Fine Arts Building

Construction of the $2.2 million Fine Arts Building began on January 2, 1980, and was completed in August 1981. In addition to a 400 seat theatre, the three-story building houses the classrooms, offices, studios, labs, practice and rehearsal rooms, dressing rooms, and storage areas for the college's music, art, theater, and speech programs. Funding for the 50,000-square foot structure came entirely from the original $10.5 million bond issue passed more than a decade earlier. The building was scaled down and redesigned when the state was unable to contribute its 75 percent share to the project.

Although construction on the Fine Arts Building was well underway, the groundbreaking ceremony was held on April 18, 1980. Presiding at the podium is Robert Kiep, Chair of the Board of Trustees.

Participating in the groundbreaking ceremony were Robert Mallary, speech and theatre instructor; Jerry Lewis, Chair of the Music Department; Michelle Oldham, President of the Student Government Association; and William Fabrycki, Chair of the Art Department.

Until the new Fine Arts Building was constructed, a temporary theatre in C 1007 was used for plays and other performances. Students are seen here rehearsing a play in 1976.

On November 5, 1981, a grand opening and open house were held for the new Fine Arts Building. Participating in the ribbon-cutting ceremony are Earl Meisinger, President of the JJC Foundation; Rabbi Hershman; unidentified; Dr. Charles Kennedy, Chair of the Board of Trustees; Mayor John Bourg, City of Joliet; Chris Dragatsis, President of the JJC Alumni Association; and JJC President Derek Nunney.

An aerial view of Main Campus in the mid-1980s shows the new Fine Arts Building adjacent to the J Building on the near side of the lake.

During the open house, visitors were welcomed at the door and taken on guided tours of the new facility. Exhibits and entertainment were provided by art students and college musical groups.

Veterinary Technology/Industrial Training Center

In April 1999, ground was broken for the new Veterinary Technology/Industrial Training Center. The building officially opened its doors in spring 2000 to students in the "Vet Tech" program, one of only two such programs in the state. The facility also houses specialized, custom-designed training programs offered by the college's Institute of Economic Technology for area businesses. Participating in the groundbreaking ceremony are Trustee Joyce Heap, Trustee Eleanor McGuan-Boza, student trustee Rhonda Carlson, President J. D. Ross, Trustee Dr. John Hertko, Trustee Susan Block, Trustee Robert Wunderlich, Trustee Marilyn Hertko, and Trustee David Cryer.

187

Business and Technology Center

Governor Jim Edgar visited campus in February 1993 and announced that the state was making funds available for facilities to provide students with cutting-edge technical skills and training. Although the state would cover 75 percent of the cost to construct a business and technology center, the balance would have to come from local sources. The college's building fund had been depleted several years earlier when the Fine Arts Building was constructed. A gift from Arthur G. and Vera C. Smith made possible the local match, and ground was broken in May 1994 for the new 90,000 square-foot building. **L-R:** Dean J. D. Ross, Dean Richard Brandolino, student trustee Richard Skorupa, Vice President James Lepanto, Trustee Eleanor McGuan–Boza, Vice President Paul Brinkman, unidentified, Governor Jim Edgar.

Arthur and Vera Smith

In 1996, the Arthur G. and Vera C. Smith Business & Technology Center was opened on Main Campus. Commonly known as the T Building, the new facility houses the Business Education and Computer Information and Office Systems Departments, as well as several programs in the Technical Department. The building was made possible, in part, through a generous gift of a former employee. Vera C. Smith joined the JJC staff in 1956 as an English instructor and advisor. In 1968, she was named Director of Admissions and Records, a position she held until her retirement in 1972. Mrs. Smith is pictured here in 1998 unveiling the sculpture *Dublitore Balancia* in front of the building named in honor of her and her husband. Participating in the ceremony are: **Standing** – Helen Harshbarger, Foundation member; Dr. Thomas E. Gamble, College President; Vera Smith, sculpture donor; Michael A. Dunbar, Coordinator of the Illinois Capital Development Board's Art-In-Architecture program. **Seated** – Walter Zaida, President of the Joliet Junior College Foundation; William Carlson, Professor of Art at the University of Illinois and sculptor of *Dublitore Balancia*.

In May 1985, Joliet Junior College dedicated its Vietnam Veterans Memorial on Main Campus. Located on the campus bridge, the memorial consists of four engraved granite slabs encasing the fireplace. An opening ceremony was held in the A. A. Wills Gymnasium. The program then moved to the cafeteria patio where hundreds of black balloons were released signifying the stigma associated with the Vietnam War.

The Young Republican Club seen here in 1968 played an active role in supporting candidates during the fall elections. Members of the club distributed buttons and brochures for presidential nominee Richard Nixon and various other state and local Republican candidates. Members also helped conduct a mock election in which Nixon emerged as the students' choice. A major topic of discussion at several club meetings was the LUV (Let Us Vote) campaign. **L-R:** Phyllis Seno, Mary Ann Stegner, Paul Lester (faculty sponsor), Richard Madison, Rose Fleishauer, Kathy Golden, Vaughn Whitfield.

The JJC students pictured here were selected to appear in the 1969-70 volume of *Who's Who in American Junior Colleges*. **Seated:** Sharon Pierson, Thomas Glenn Kent Heatherwick, Shirley Forbes. **Standing:** Rita Fornelli, Alice Radcliffe, Debra Trotter, Jeffery King, Gregory Hilsabeck, Wendell Stevens, Norman Bradley, Kenneth Krapf, Myrtle Weikum, JoAnn Pellegrini, Connie Frantz, John Dzuryak.

Students interested in Bible study and Christian fellowship organized Love 101. Members are pictured here in 1975. **Front:** Brent Hanson, Jerry Hull, Ben Komar. **Middle:** Ellen Andrews, Jack Taral, Margo Kraske, Linda Fender, Bob Simenson (sponsor), Larinda Johnson, Beth Jahneke. **Back:** Gary Giroux, Jeff Jaskowick, Beth Kurns, Charles W. Moffatt.

With a noticeable absence of male members, the Students of Home Economics (SHE) Club is pictured here in 1969. Among the activities and programs sponsored by the SHE Club were holiday parties and presentations on food preparation, hair care, and beauty tips. 1. Phyllis Coons, 2. Barb Davy, 3. Doris Bonar (faculty sponsor), 4. Kathy Carr, 5. Marsha Bruns, 6. Pam Morgan, 7. Linda Pruss, 8. Faye Mills, 9. Marie Simunovich, 10. Gail Lynes, 11. Sandy Gabel, 12. Shirley Yahnke.

Times have changed since the early 1970s when students over twenty-five years old had their own club. Today in 2001, the average age of JJC students is thirty. Members of the NCO-25 (Nearly, Clearly, and Over 25) Club are seen here in 1971 planning "Bring a Friend to School Week." Under the sponsorship of college counselor Carolyn Engers (right), the club's meetings and activities were designed to encourage "older" residents of the district to further their education at Joliet Junior College.

The Music Department offered students an opportunity to perform in various instrumental and vocal groups, including the Madrigals pictured here in 1970. **Front:** Cheryl Foster, Elaine Lieske, Debbie Gilbert, Sharon Mathre, Joyce Barfield, Terre Houte, Mary Ludwig. **Back:** Gary LaFontaine, Lee Warner, Ray Shroba, Paul Jaeger, Steve Bredesen, John Petrusa, David Miller.

The Motor Sports Club was very active in the 1970s and appealed to students with interests ranging from professional racing to working on engines. Club members held monthly meetings and often sponsored road rallies and gymkhanas, which tested a driver's ability to follow directions and handle a car on a prescribed course. Members of the club in 1970 are pictured here. **Front:** Dave Cline, Bill Ely. **Middle:** Patrick Asher (faculty sponsor), Jeff Carloss, Pete Apostolou, Jurgen Eicholz, Chuck Southcomb, Paul Scholtes, Dave Meditz, Dennis Guardia, Bob Darin. **Back:** Bob Rositch, Jim Erzycke, John Carli, Leon Felus, Dennis Rogers.

Students with an interest in aviation organized a club known as the JC Flyers. With Joliet Municipal Airport only a few miles away, members were able to spend considerable time in the air. One memorable day, a veteran paratrooper jumped from a low-flying plane and landed in the college quadrangle. Club members were subsequently admonished to stay in their planes and land at the airport. However, Debbie Schmidt joined the club to learn about flying and became intrigued with the sport of skydiving. With just two years experience, she won first place in the style event at the national collegiate skydiving competition in 1972. Her impressive victory came over two-hundred other competitors, including an Air Academy senior who won second place, a former paratrooper who claimed third place, and a West Point senior who placed fourth.

In 1991, *Blazer* Editor Jeni Rees met with her 1932 counterpart, Evelyn Anderson Barnes. The two editors compared copies of their publications and discussed the challenges of meeting deadlines and producing a quality college newspaper.

191

Activities, Programs, and Special Events

The new permanent campus provided a venue for a variety of activities, programs, and special events. They ranged from rock and gem shows to public hearings on pornography, from David Frost to Cheech and Chong, and from author Thomas A. Harris with a message of "I'm OK, You're OK" to activist comedian Dick Gregory warning that things in America were not OK, especially in the area of race relations. Also, dances remained popular, occasionally with an ethnic theme, and sometimes celebrities were invited to crown the queen.

Gem and rock show, 1977

David Frost, 1975

In March 1974, students cheered and whistled as several streakers made a mad dash through the college concourse wearing little more than shoes, socks, and a silly grin. Why did they do it? One winded male streaker commented, "I don't know. It was on impulse. Someone called me chicken. I might do it again." A female wearing a red plastic sack on her head and an open shirt explained, "Life is boring. This was an adventure. It was all for kicks." Hundreds of spectators in D Mall got a kick out of watching and dared each other to strip and streak.[40]

Pornography hearing
in D Mall, 1974

Cheech and Chong, 1976

Author Thomas A. Harris, 1973

Black History Week dance, 1969

Activist comedian Dick Gregory, 1975

"Sweetheart Swing" on Valentines Day, 1969

Kris Kemp was crowned "Miss Shield
1970-71" by Actor Bill Bixby, who
quipped, "With this crown, I thee queen."

Ethnic Expo, 1993

Actress Betty Grable attended the Autumn Dinner-Dance in 1969 and crowned Emma Craft "Miss Shield of 1969-70." Betty Grable is pictured here chatting with student Kent Heatherwick.

Professional bowler Jim Stefanich crowned Carol Clennon "Miss Shield of 1968-69" at the Autumn Dinner-Dance at Pheasant Run.

Delegates from China on a trade mission to Will County toured the college campus in 1988. Serving as tour guides and hosts at the dinner that followed were Deans J. D. Ross (left) and Richard Brandolino (second from right).

JJC has often been a stop on the campaign trail for candidates seeking political office. In 1988, Vice President George Bush appeared on campus in his quest for the presidency. Pictured with Bush on the platform are Governor Jim Thompson and several JJC cheerleaders.

JJC President Thomas Gamble introduces Secretary of State George Ryan (right), who visited the college in 1998 to announce the awarding of a Literacy Grant. Appearing with Ryan and sharing in the announcement is John C. "Jack" McGuire, Illinois State Representative.

From time to time, JJC has hosted legislative luncheons in the dining room on Main Campus. Pictured here at the 1985 luncheon are Trustee Joyce Heap, U. S. Congressman Dennis Hastert, Dean J. D. Ross, President Raymond Pietak, U.S. Congressman George Sangmeister, and student trustee David Wharrie.

In June 1982, Emily Lennon Leinenweber, a 1919 JJC alumna, and Harry D. Leinenweber, a retired JJC faculty member, were honored at the annual Alumni Brunch. Pictured with the Leinenwebers is JJC President Derek Nunney.

Joliet Junior College joined Southern Illinois University Edwardsville in presenting the Katherine Dunham Center Performers in a Black History Week program at the magnificent Rialto Theatre in downtown Joliet. A distinguished alumna of JJC, Dunham won international acclaim as an anthropologist, dancer, choreographer, composer, producer, and writer.

Over the years, JJC has celebrated many anniversaries of its historic founding in 1901. Pictured here on February 20, 1986, in the Renaissance Center Ballroom are some of the guests who attended the banquet marking the college's eighty-fifth anniversary.

In 1975, JJC began honoring individuals for their outstanding service to the college community. Presented at the annual graduation ceremony, Distinguished Service Awards have been granted to numerous individuals during the past twenty-five years. Two DSA recipients were Frank Turk, Sr. in 1987 (left) and Dr. Stanley Rousonelos in 1994 (right).

The college often invites distinguished alumni, political leaders, leading educators, or other noteworthy people to serve as graduation speakers. On May 12, 1995, Illinois Poet Laureate Gwendolyn Brooks challenged JJC graduates to pursue their dreams and to find meaning in life beyond preoccupation with an occupation. Remain curious and compassionate, she said, and never stop thirsting for knowledge or caring for others.

Total Fitness Center

The Total Fitness Center was established in the fall of 1984 with an enrollment of 500 students. In the spring of 2001, more than 1,400 people from seventeen to ninety years old work out in the center or participate in spinning, step aerobic, and cardio-kickboxing classes. The original equipment has been replaced with eighty-five pieces of cutting-edge resistance and cardiovascular equipment. Improvement and maintenance of strength, flexibility, cardiovascular endurance, nutrition, and body composition are goals of the center.

In addition to JJC students, other district residents (44 percent of all participants) enroll in the center to maintain or improve their physical fitness. Some are referred by local doctors as part of a rehabilitation regimen. An orientation is provided to acquaint participants with physical fitness concepts, circuit training, and the correct use of the center's equipment. There are also individual fitness evaluations at the beginning and end of each semester to measure progress toward achieving personal goals. Since 1984, JJC Fitness Center personnel have helped some 350 colleges, universities, high schools, hospitals, health clubs, and park districts set up wellness centers.

People who workout in the Fitness Center enjoy an excellent view of the tree-lined campus lake.

JJC spinning classes offer cyclists an opportunity to ride indoors and avoid cars, dogs, heat, cold and other inclement weather.

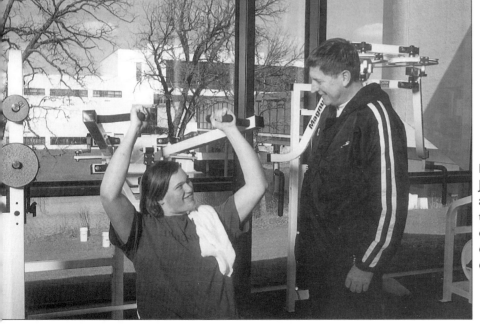

Fitness Center Director John Peterson (standing) and his staff are available to instruct students and other participants on the correct use of the center's equipment.

Spotlight on Sports

During the period from 1967 to 2001, JJC has had a number of outstanding teams and athletes whose performances have reflected well on the institution. The individuals and teams pictured in this section have been selected on the basis of achievement and availability of photographs. To their credit, many of the student athletes highlighted here have excelled in the classroom as well as in athletic competition. Their awards and honors have brought national recognition to the college and have enhanced its image.

JJC cheerleaders won first place at the Carl Sandburg Christmas Tournament in 1975 and then went on to take top honors at the First Annual N4C Conference Cheerleading Competition held at Illinois Valley Community College. Coached by Peg Francisco, the team is pictured here performing one of its athletic routines. **Bottom:** Marsha Kapsch, Vicki Soave, Elvira Warnell, Mary Jo Schmidberger. **Top:** Sue Button, Angie Persico.

Jenny Karges and Coach Tim Vanderwall wait out a rain delay at the national tournament.

Jenny Karges had an outstanding tennis season for JJC in 1991. At the NJCAA Division II Tournament in Tyler, Texas, Karges emerged as the national singles champion.

198

Tracy Kuder was a two-time All-American basketball player for Joliet Junior College from 1992 to 1994. During the two seasons that Kuder played for the Lady Wolves, the team won 38 games. She ranks as JJC's leading women's scorer with 1,240 points and boasts a team-high 40 points in a single game.

Jodi Sievers was an outstanding softball player for the Lady Wolves during the 1996 and 1997 seasons. A slick-fielding performer in center field, Sievers had a .455 batting average in 1996 and established school records with 77 base hits, 58 RBIs, and an incredible 28-game hitting streak. In addition, she hit 25 doubles and 5 home runs. The following year, she was named to the NJCAA Division III All-American Team. Sievers' statistics in 1997 rivaled those of the previous season, except she reduced her strikeouts to a meager 6 in 150 times at bat.

One of the best ball-handling point guards to play basketball at JJC was Kisha Barefield. She holds the school record of 254 assists in a single season as well as the record for career assists with 475. Furthermore, Barefield is fifth on the list of all-time leading scorers at the college with 734 points from 1995-97. She led the Lady Wolves in 1997 to a Region IV Division III title and a berth in the national basketball tournament in Corning, New York, the first time a JJC women's basketball team ever made it that far in post-season play. In the regional championship game, JJC defeated Oakton Community College in a thrilling 1-point game. Barefield scored a team-high 16 points, grabbed a game-high 12 rebounds, and dished out 9 assists in leading the team to its narrow victory. Kisha's outstanding performance during the 1996-97 season earned her Player of the Year honors in the North Central Community College Conference.

In December 1970, two members of the JJC wrestling team were killed in an accident while returning from a tournament at the University of Iowa. Killed in the two-car collision on Interstate 80 were team co-captains Wayne Coleman and Ed Delaney. The team's station wagon was struck by a car that skidded on the icy pavement, crossed the snow-covered median, and crashed head-on into the team vehicle. Four other wrestlers riding in the station wagon suffered injuries. Ken Parker, Chair of the Athletic Department, is pictured speaking at the memorial service for Coleman and Delaney.

Anne Marino was a NJCAA All-American volleyball player for Coach Kym McKay in 2000, a year in which the Lady Wolves finished with a 32-11 record and won the conference championship. An outside hitter, Marino was a two-time All-Conference and All-Region IV Division III player for JJC. She is the only volleyball player in the school's history to win All-American honors.

Dawn Glasscock won NJCAA Division III All-American honors as a softball pitcher in 1998 and then duplicated the feat in 1999. She is the best pitcher who ever played for the JJC Lady Wolves. In 1998, Glasscock pitched 8 shutouts, 2 no-hitters, 1 perfect game, and compiled a 1.91 ERA with 224 strikeouts. During the 1999 season, she won 28 games and led the team to a second place finish in the Division III World Series in Maryland. Dawn won 5 tournament games, 2 of them shutouts. She finished the series with a record 56 tournament strikeouts and established a single game record of 13. During that season, Glasscock threw 14 shutouts, 5 one-hitters and 7 two-hitters. She struck out 329 batters in 270 innings and finished the year with a 1.11 earned run average. Her 553 career strikeouts over two seasons are a NJCAA Division III record.

Led by two-time All-American pitcher Dawn Glasscock, the JJC softball team won a school record thirty-three games in 1999. The team won the National Junior College Athletic Association Region IV Division III Tournament played at the Inwood Softball Complex in Joliet and then went on to win second place in the national tournament in Arnold, Maryland. The team is pictured here proudly displaying its trophy. **Front:** Dawn Glasscock, Beth Schultz, Georgie Szymczak, Tracy Phillips, Tami Valenti, Stephanie Sharp. **Back:** Kendall Swoik (trainer), Jack Smith (head coach), Krystal Himes, Lisa Gierich, Laura Barto, Jenna Pasteris, Lacey Susan, Jill Yaeger, Pam Ethridge (assistant coach), and Sports Information Director Dave Parker.

In 1970, Bill Vail **(left)** capped an outstanding wrestling season by winning the national championship in the 118-pound class. During the tournament in Worthington, Minnesota, Vail defeated six opponents on his way to the national title.

Ken Lewis **(right)** was the only member of the 1976 wrestling team to win a national championship. Competing in the 167-pound class, Lewis won five straight matches at the national tournament to lead the team to a ninth-place finish in the nation. The Wolves also made a strong showing in N4C competition and were crowned co-champions of the conference.

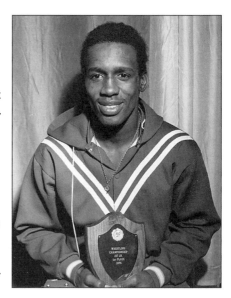

Dillman, Evans win titles

Wrestlers 2nd at nationals

Jeff Dillman
National Champion
State Champion
Conference Champion

Mike Evans
National Champion
State Champion
Second in Nationals in 1978

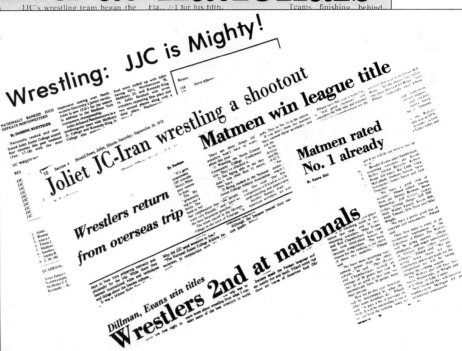

Under Coach Henry Pillard, the Joliet Junior College wrestling program received national and international acclaim. Several JJC wrestlers won national championships and world titles. During the early seventies, Pillard directed five National Clinics for Integrated Wrestling, which introduced high school and college coaches to Olympic wrestling styles. He twice coached the National Junior College Athletic Association qualifiers at the Final Olympic Trials. From 1978 to 1982, Coach Pillard worked with the Joliet Region Chamber of Commerce and Industry to arrange the Joliet International Wresting Tournament, which attracted more than one thousand competitors from a dozen foreign countries and almost every state in the nation. In a unique cultural exchange opportunity, area residents housed many of the foreign wrestlers. A strong advocate of international competition, Pillard accompanied members of his JJC squad on trips to other countries to compete in International Junior World Tournaments. He also served as competitive director for the 1986 World Cup Greco-Roman Wrestling Tournament in Chicago. When Pillard ended his eighteen-year coaching career at JJC in 1985, he had accumulated many awards and honors, including induction into both the National Junior College Athletic Association's Hall of Fame and the Illinois Wrestling Coaches and Official's Hall of Fame.

The JJC golf team won first place in the Illinois State Golf Tournament in 1975. Competing against eleven other teams, Joliet won the tournament by a two-stroke margin. Coach Gil Bell praised the team for its excellent play and balanced scoring. Jack Merriman placed second overall in individual scoring with 154 strokes, and Tony Gerl was fifth in the tournament with a 158.
Front: Dick Hunckler, Doug Behrans, Dwight Anderson.
Back: Jack Merriman, Coach Gil Bell, Tony Gerl.

201

JJC football coach Jerry Yost and his team celebrate moments after soundly defeating top-ranked Rochester (Minnesota) Community College 37-14 on a cold November night in 1976. The Wolves' victory over Rochester was scored at Joliet Memorial Stadium in the Third Annual Midwest Bowl. A tenacious JJC defense recorded seven quarterback sacks and held the opponents to 145 total yards. The team finished the season with a 9-1 overall record, a bowl victory, a conference championship, and a No. 8 national ranking in the final NJCAA football poll. Yost is the winningest football coach in JJC history with 96 victories in 16 seasons.

Harold Brown earned All-American honors as a JJC running back in 1981. One of the best athletes ever to wear a Wolves' uniform, Brown was inducted into the National Junior College Athletic Association Hall of Fame. For many years, the 6'3", 215 lb. runner held the NJCAA single-season rushing record of 2,274 yards. During the 1981 season, Brown scored 20 touchdowns and finished the year with 134 points. He led the team to a conference championship and a berth in the Royal Crown Cola Bowl in Cedar Falls, Iowa. The Wolves lost the bowl game and ended the season with a 9-2 overall record.

During the 1970-71 basketball season, Sylvester Cottrell (No. 54) was the leading junior college rebounder in the nation with a 21.9 average per game. Known as "Chairman of the Boards," he developed his talent under Coach Paul Siron at JJC. As a senior in high school, Cottrell weighed 300 pounds and averaged 7 points and 9 rebounds per game. An amazing transformation occurred during his freshman year in college when the 6'7" center practiced several hours a day and slimmed down to a solid 215 pounds. Cottrell's best single-game performance came during his sophomore year when he scored 32 points and grabbed 30 rebounds.

Following a phenomenal season in 1977-78, Arnette Hallman was voted the number one junior college player in the nation. The National Junior College Athletic Association honored Hallman because of his scoring, rebounding, and amazing shot-blocking ability. During the season, he blocked 111 shots and led the team in scoring and rebounding. Hallman (No. 50) often played above the rim, thrilling fans with power dunks and shot rejections.

The JJC basketball team celebrates its stunning 85-80 victory over two-time NJCAA Division II champs Owens (Ohio) Technical College in the championship game on March 19, 1994. In a game played in downstate Danville, Illinois, the Wolves got 21 points from Craig Brunes, 17 from Kelley Lynch and 18 points and 11 assists from point guard Bobby Krahulik, who was named most valuable player for the tournament. The team was coached by Pat Klingler and finished the season with a 28-8 record. During his four years as the Wolves' coach, Klingler's teams compiled an overall 111-29 record.

Haris Mujezinovic was one of the best basketball players ever to wear the purple and white uniform of Joliet Junior College. Although opposing teams keyed on Haris and usually double-teamed him, he led the Wolves with a 19.6 scoring average and an 11.1 rebounding average during the 1993-94 national championship season. During the first two tournament games, Mujezinovic grabbed 26 rebounds and scored 66 points, making 27 of 33 shots. The following season, he led the team to a 28-4 record and the North Central Community College Conference championship. Haris was named to the NJCAA Division II All-American Team in 1995. He went on to play two years for Bobby Knight at Indiana University and then played professionally in Europe.

The 1994 baseball team finished the season with 46 wins, 11 losses, and a national championship at the NJCAA Division III World Series played in Jamestown, New York. **Front:** John Ward, Jeff Schley, Brian Hobbs, Juan Ceballos, Derek Kopacz, Erik Bialobok, Jim Boyd. **Back:** Jeff Baranoski (assistant coach), Bryan Fonseca, Jim Lukancic, Jason Hafner, Brandy Brenczewski, Jim Tyrrell, Mark Gotts (All-American catcher), Bill White, Mike Fagan (assistant coach), Wayne King (head coach), Mike Chubinski, Mike Alstott, Jason Crockett, Tony Pasch (All-American pitcher), Matt Dunne, David Goes (All-American outfielder), Brian Sullivan, Dave Okrzesik (trainer).

JJC left-handed slugger Dave Goes looks at a pitch in 1994, the year the Wolves won a school-record 46 games en route to winning the NJCAA Division III World Series in Jamestown, New York. Goes had a .359 batting average with 75 base hits, 57 RBIs, 14 doubles, and 6 home runs, two of which were game-winning blows. He was a key player on a team that averaged 10 runs per game and, for his outstanding season, Goes was named an All-American player.

Pitcher Tony Pasch posted an 11-2 record in 1994 in leading the Wolves to the NJCAA Division III World Series championship. The 6' 5" right-handed hurler won the final game against Cedar Valley, Texas, with 10 strikeouts, no walks, and 3 scratch singles. Pasch was voted most valuable player of the tournament and later won first team All-American honors. He holds the school record for pitchers with 11 victories in a single season. During the 1994 season, Pasch recorded a team-high 90 strikeouts in 97 innings pitched, against just 23 walks.

Mark Raciti earned All-American honors as a catcher in 1996. The right-handed power hitter paced the Wolves with a .384 batting average. He belted 3 home runs, 3 triples, 7 doubles and had a team-high 54 RBIs.

Right-handed pitcher Mike Paskvan was named to the 1995 NJCAA Division III All-American first team. He compiled a 2.59 ERA in 94 innings pitched. Paskvan's 9-3 record helped Coach Wayne King's Wolves finish second at the World Series in Batavia, New York.

Left-hander Steve Stamm was 9 and 2 in 1997 and led the team to a third-place finish in the NJCAA Division III World Series in Batavia, New York. His impressive statistics for the year included 64 strikeouts, 19 walks, and an excellent 2.44 ERA. Stamm helped power the team to 44 wins in 1997 and was accorded first team All-American honors.

Coach Wayne King visits the mound to talk to pitcher Juan Ceballos and catcher Mark Gotts. In 1994, JJC won the World Series in its division by winning 4 tournament games in Jamestown, New York. Right-hander Ceballos tossed a 2-hit shutout in posting a victory over Manchester (Connecticut) Community Technical College. Catcher Mark Gotts was a two-time NJCAA Division III All-American player for the Wolves. Gotts hit .383 for the season and led the nation in home runs with 12 and RBIs with 84. The following year, Gotts hit .477 with 8 homers and 69 RBIs. He holds several JJC season records, including 25 doubles, 12 home runs, 84 RBIs, 92 base hits, and a .477 batting average. He is also the career leader with 48 doubles, 20 home runs, and 153 RBIs.

Who's afraid of the big JJC wolf? Most children attending college sporting events enjoy touching and talking to Wily Wolf, the team mascot.

Picture Us Now

Joliet Junior College today bears little resemblance to the institution established a hundred years ago. J. Stanley Brown, C. E. Spicer, and Dr. William Rainey Harper could not have imagined how the educational idea they planted and nurtured in Joliet at the beginning of the twentieth century would totally transform higher education in America and throughout the world. Starting with six students in 1901, the community college movement has developed and grown like no other educational innovation in history. In 2001, there are some 11,000 students taking credit courses at Joliet Junior College and thousands more taking noncredit classes. In the State of Illinois, more than 750,000 students are enrolled in credit courses and another 250,000 in noncredit classes. The state's forty-nine community colleges serve nearly one out of every eleven Illinois residents. In fact, community colleges are the primary provider of higher education in Illinois, accounting for 60 percent of all undergraduates enrolled in college. The pattern is much the same throughout the nation, with some eleven million students enrolled in almost 1,200 community colleges. As Joliet Junior College celebrates its centennial anniversary, it can be rightfully proud of the pioneer role it played in fostering the community college movement.[1]

A snapshot of JJC today reveals students, programs, facilities, and a college district much different than Brown and Spicer ever envisioned. Since the college was originally affiliated with Joliet Township High School, its boundaries were limited to the district boundaries of the local high school. Students who attended from outside the township were required to pay nonresident fees. Today, Illinois Community College District 525 encompasses 1,442 square miles and serves a population of more than 400,000 people in Will, Grundy, Kendall, LaSalle, Kankakee, Livingston, and Cook Counties. Classes are offered at three campuses and more than twenty other instructional sites,

including high schools, libraries, civic centers, and churches. Most off-campus classes are conducted at night as part of the college's extensive evening program.

The profile of students taking classes at JJC has changed dramatically since J. Stanley Brown personally enrolled the first students in 1901. During the early years, junior college students were predominantly recent high school graduates, not yet twenty years old, who registered for classes that closely paralleled freshman and sophomore courses at the University of Illinois. There were very few, if any, minority students, and all classes were taught in the daytime. Today, the average age of JJC students in credit classes is thirty, and they take almost half of their classes in the evening or on weekends. From Youth College to Emeritus College, JJC serves district residents of all ages, from nine to ninety. Furthermore, 58 percent of students are female; 8 percent are African American; 7 percent are Hispanic; 65 percent attend part-time (fewer than twelve credit hours per semester); and 31 percent are enrolled in occupational programs. An ever-increasing number of today's students are in distance education classes and rarely see their instructors face-to-face. Instead, they utilize modern technology to access their Internet classes, telecourses, and interactive TV classes. Computer technology is also used to enhance traditional classes; the college now has 2,100 computers and thirty computer labs spread across its three campuses.[2]

In recent years, the college has renovated buildings and erected new structures to keep pace with student needs, program development, and college growth. A major renovation in 1998 provided new computer labs, a Student Center, and the Cyber Cafe. The latter facility offers students a unique opportunity to use computers in a relaxed and casual setting. Here students can surf the Internet, check their email, or perhaps work on an online class. In 1996, the college opened the Arthur G. and Vera C. Smith Business and Technology Center, which houses the Business, Technical, and Computer Information and Office Systems

Departments. Some of the degree and certificate programs offered in the new technology building are Computer Networking Technologist, Webmaster, Web Design and Administration, Computer Aided Design and Drafting, Electronic Engineering Technology, and Electrical/Electronic Automated Systems Technology. At a ribbon-cutting ceremony in October 2000, the new Veterinary Technology/Industrial Training Center opened its doors to the college's Veterinary Medical Technology program, one of only two such programs in the state. In addition to "Vet Tech," the building is also used by JJC's Institute of Economic Technology to offer specialized training programs custom-designed for area businesses.

Joliet Junior College has developed several recent partnerships with area businesses, agencies, and educational institutions. Through its Institute of Economic Technology, the college has established training partnerships with such companies as Caterpillar, Mobil Oil, ComEd, Dow Chemical, Kemlite, Unocal, Copley Press, and BP-Amoco. The latter won the Illinois Community College Board's Award for Excellence. A partnership with Kankakee Community College and the Kankakee Area Career Center was recently created to offer a program in Fire Science and Safety to train firefighters and paramedics. Finally, JJC has signed formal dual enrollment agreements with the University of St. Francis, Governors State University, Robert Morris College, Northern Illinois University, and Lewis University. Under these joint agreements, dually enrolled students are guaranteed admission into the four-year school after completing the first two years at the junior college. Students work with counselors at both institutions to determine which JJC classes best meet the requirements of the degrees they ultimately hope to earn.[3]

As the college looks to the immediate future, plans are unfolding to expand educational programs, student services, and community enrichment. For example, the John Weitendorf Agricultural Education Center was recently dedicated on Manhattan Road, several miles east of Main Campus, and will be used to enhance the college's highly acclaimed agricultural program. Further, working with a private developer, JJC will soon become one of the few community colleges to offer student housing on campus. It is expected that international students, out-of-district students in occupational programs, student athletes, and those who live on the far edges of the college district will primarily benefit from the new housing scheduled to open on campus in the fall of 2002. The college will share any excess revenue and eventually will be deeded the property at the end of the agreement. JJC is also a partner with the Joliet Area Historical Museum Board in providing the Joliet region with a new state-of-the-art historical museum. A Route 66 Visitors' Center is being constructed to connect the college's historic Renaissance Center with the new multimillion dollar Joliet Area Historical Museum, which will be housed in the renovated church edifice formerly occupied by the Ottawa Street Methodist Church. Museum visitors will have access to meeting rooms at the City Center Campus as well as food service in the Renaissance Center's restaurant and banquet facility.

Although JJC has one of the lowest tax rates in the state and has not had a tax increase since 1977, the Board of Trustees has operated with a balanced budget for the past twenty-seven years. With a projected $38.5 million budget for FY 2001, the college's financial position has remained sound largely because of significant economic and population growth in various parts of the district. In fact, JJC's master plan for the college district includes expansion of North Campus, renovation of City Center Campus, and new facilities on Main Campus to enhance both the academic program and student services. New campuses are also being considered to accommodate constituencies in the fastest growing areas of the district. In fact, the college's Institute of Economic Technology will soon open a satellite campus in Morris to better serve residents in the western region of the district.

As the college looks to the future, its facilities and programs will develop and evolve to equip students for the 21st century, providing them with the knowledge and skills to reach their individual goals. For example, one of the newest additions to the college program is the Cisco lab at North Campus, a lab-based certified program designed to prepare students for careers in the Internet/Web-related routing industry. Indeed, the curriculum will continue to expand and change, especially in the areas of science, technology, and occupational training. Whether classes are taken for university transfer, immediate employment, career advancement, personal enrichment, or simply for enjoyment, the determination to meet the diverse needs of District 525 students will propel the institution into the Global Age of the new millennium and its second century of serving the community as the people's college.

Joliet Junior College is a multicampus community college that has grown throughout the years to meet student needs.

One of three campuses today, JJC's Main Campus was opened in September 1969 on the west side of Joliet.

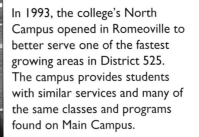

In 1993, the college's North Campus opened in Romeoville to better serve one of the fastest growing areas in District 525. The campus provides students with similar services and many of the same classes and programs found on Main Campus.

The college's City Center Campus is located at 214 North Ottawa Street in downtown Joliet. The facility is home base for the college's Institute of Economic Technology, Adult and Family Services Division, and the Renaissance Center with a full-service restaurant that provides practical experience for culinary arts students.

The Arthur G. and Vera C. Smith Business and Technology Building houses business, technical, and computer science programs on Main Campus. Opened in 1996, the 90,000 square-foot building includes a Conference Center, which is the setting for many training programs conducted by JJC's Institute of Economic Technology.

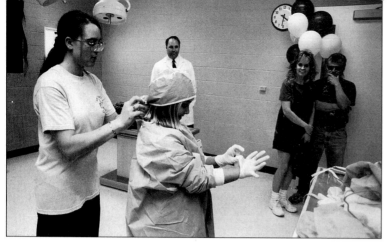

One of the newest programs at Joliet Junior College is the Veterinary Medical Technology program. The "Vet Tech" program is one of only two such programs in the state and is housed in a new building completed in 2000. During an Open House, the community was invited to visit the facility and learn about the program.

In class, students are taught how to examine animals and how to assist veterinarians in the treatment and care of animals.

With his family at his side, John H. Weitendorf, Jr. shares his thoughts and vision of how the John H. Weitendorf, Jr. Agricultural Education Center might be used to enhance JJC's Agricultural/Horticultural Sciences Department. Mr. Weitendorf, a 1942 JJC alumnus, donated a 30.7 acre parcel of land on Laraway Road for use as an off-campus site to serve the college community, especially students enrolled in agriculture, horticulture, and veterinary technology programs.

Each year nearly 15,000 people from numerous area companies and agencies work with the college's Institute of Economic Technology to improve work skills or participate in specialized job training. Computer & Network Services Manager Robert Johnson is seen here conducting an IET seminar.

A new addition on campus in the new millennium is the Cyber Cafe, where students socialize with friends, play games, or use the cafe's many computers to access the Internet.

JJC students use the latest technology to prepare their coursework. This high-tech student listens to tunes while completing a class assignment on his laptop computer in the busy college concourse. For a quieter setting, computer labs are available to students from early morning to late at night.

The new Student Center on Main Campus offers students a variety of programs and services including Holistic Wellness, Career Planning and Placement, and a Multicultural Transfer Center.

JJC students are provided an opportunity to participate in a Dialogue on Race, an all-campus forum held several times a year. Johnnie Johnson, Coordinator of the Joliet Area Math, Science and Computer Education Enrichment Program (JAMSCEEP), is pictured here facilitating student dialogue at the April 2000 program on techniques and strategies for becoming culturally diverse.

The Office of Student Services and Activities hosts Mainstreet, a popular recruiting/information fair that permits students to browse the wide assortment of clubs and activities available at the college.

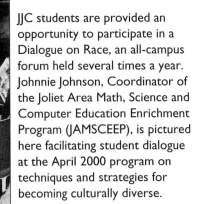

Joliet Junior College provides students firsthand experience with journalism through its student newspaper, *The Blazer*. Pictured here in April 2000 are faculty advisor Robert Marcink and student staff members working to meet a publication deadline.

Students find various ways to relax on campus between and after classes. Just outside the Fine Arts Theatre, some students gather for a game of cards while others explore their musical interests.

In 1998, a new Student Center and Cyber Cafe were opened on the college's Main Campus. This JJC student receives a helping hand – in the form of a chair – while studying at a table just outside the new center. Several locations like this are scattered across campus where students can enjoy coffee or cola while completing an assignment.

Comfortable chairs on campus invite students to chat, relax, or look over material for an upcoming class

The sun casts interesting shadows on the bridge that spans the small lake on Main Campus. Students and staff often cross the bridge several times a day to reach classrooms and buildings separated by water.

With the Vietnam Veteran's Memorial in the background, the bridge is a popular place for socializing and studying. Here students enjoy themselves while studying – their cards.

211

Joliet Junior College's Main Campus provides many quiet natural areas where students can retreat and relax before rejoining the swing and bustle of busy campus life.

Beginning with the first warm days of spring, students and staff enjoy meals and snacks on the cafeteria patio overlooking the lake.

The President's Cabinet at Joliet Junior College is pictured here in May 2000. **Front:** Dr. Denis Wright, Vice President for Academic Services; J. D. Ross, President; D. J. Wells, Community Relations Director. **Back:** John Byrnes, Human Resources Director; Tom Ryan, Vice President for Business and Financial Services; Andrew Mihelich, Associate Vice President, Extended Campuses.

Administrative Assistant Joan Tierney has the challenging task of organizing and coordinating the day-to-day operation of the President's office.

Vice President for Academic Services Denis Wright (under the centennial sign) is seen here in May 2000 conducting a bi-monthly meeting of department chairs.

Nelson Collins, Chair of the Mathematics Department, goes over paperwork with department secretary Patricia Shue.

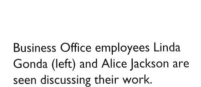

English/Foreign Languages Department Chair Patrick Asher discusses a memo with his secretary, Joan Pollack.

Business Office employees Linda Gonda (left) and Alice Jackson are seen discussing their work.

Members of the Executive Committee of the Joliet Junior College Foundation are pictured here in April 2000. **Front:** Walter Zaida, College President J. D. Ross, Robert Wysocki, Robert Biedron. **Back:** Dr. Peter Nichols, Richard DeGrush, William Kaplan, Joseph Burla.

Lead clerk Tawana Hughes takes a call in the Reprographics Office as she schedules work for the clerical pool.

Sandy Sotor of the Mail Center is seen making deliveries on Main Campus.

Tony Cota, Associate Vice President of Information Technology, charts the course of the college as it strives to keep pace with rapidly changing computer technology.

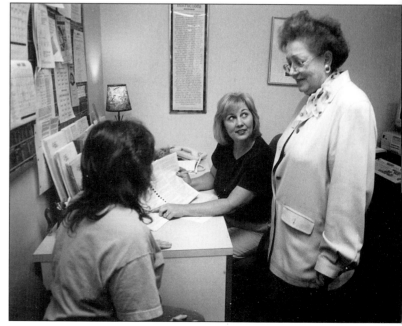

From computer labs to email services to the electronic backbone vital to the college, ITC employees like Dan Lantz (left) and Dave Johnson are responsible for maintaining and upgrading information technology.

Counselor Laura Conrad (center) and counseling department head Dr. Carolyn Engers (right) assist a student in planning her program.

The registration window on Main Campus is a busy place. However, today's students can also register from home by touch-tone phone. A system will soon be in place for online registration, a welcome alternative to standing in line at the registration window.

Jo Cirrencione of the Admissions Office is often the college's first point of contact with potential JJC students.

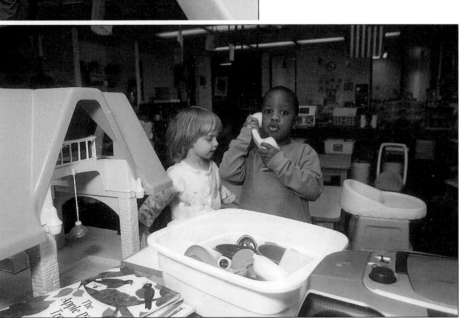

Joliet Junior College Bookstore Manager Michael Maier is pictured with Pam Campbell preparing shelves for the beginning of a new semester. The bookstore on Main Campus offers a complete line of college textbooks, school supplies, and miscellaneous merchandise.

For the convenience of students and staff members, Joliet Junior College provides a state-certified, licensed child care center on its Main Campus. Youngsters enrolled in the Early Childhood Center are exposed to a variety of enjoyable and educational experiences. The daily schedule includes story time, concept development, music appreciation, art activities, snacks, lunch, rest time, outdoor activities, and plenty of free time for play.

215

Students attending Youth College enjoy the engineering program developed by electronics engineering instructor John Koepke. In "Robolab," middle school-aged students design and build single-sensor robots to navigate a line pattern. Youth College is part of JJC's Lifelong Learning program and offers enrichment classes for young people from preschool through high school.

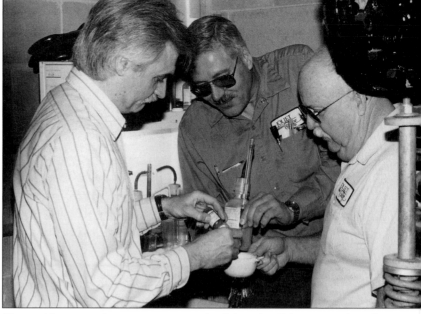

Pictured here running water tests on the Substation B heating and cooling system are head Energy Mechanic Rudy Wolf, Don Walker of Special Maintenance, and Gary Smock of General Maintenance.

Cashier Linda Browne in Food Services jokes with Scot Mangun of the Maintenance Department as she takes his money in the college cafeteria.

JJC's Culinary Arts Department has enjoyed considerable success in preparing students for the food services industry. Students are provided ample opportunity for hands-on experience in the Main Campus Cafeteria and at the Renaissance Center's full-service restaurant and banquet facility. Instructors often remind students that successful chefs make good "dough." With a student looking on, Certified Master Pastry Chef Albert Imming is seen making stollen, a Christmas bread of German origin containing fruit and nuts. Students often display their culinary creations in the college cafeteria

Chef Michael McGreal, Chair of the Culinary Arts Department, is seen kneeling in the foreground while working with students learning the art of sculpturing ice.

Ice sculptures created by culinary arts students often enhance the campus landscape, but they melt from the scene when warm weather arrives.

217

Joliet Junior College is a comprehensive community college offering higher education programs from accounting to word processing. The college offers pre-baccalaureate programs for students planning to transfer to a four-year university, occupational and technical education leading directly to employment, adult education and literacy programs, and support services to ensure student success. Automotive instructor John Rau and Pete Keifert, instructor in the Electrical/Electronic Automated Systems program, are seen providing students with individual hands-on learning experiences.

Joliet Junior College's highly regarded agriculture and horticulture programs prepare students for successful careers. From the mechanics of vintage tractors to computer and satellite-assisted site specific farming, instructors like Dave Cattron (right) provide learning experiences that give students marketable skills upon graduation.

JJC's Fine Arts Department offers students a full range of classes and activities, including graphic design, digital imaging, pottery, jewelry and metalsmithing, weaving, drawing, painting, fashion merchandising, interior design, music, and theatre. Students seen here are using computers to creatively capture, manipulate, and produce digital images.

218

Pottery instructor James Dugdale examines the wheel-thrown work of students in his class.

Instructor Beverly Decman (left) works with a student in a jewelry and metalsmithing class.

Painting instructor Joe Milosovich offers suggestions to a student in his class. Milosovich also serves as director of the Laura A. Sprague Art Gallery, which hosts art shows and provides students and local artists an opportunity to display their work.

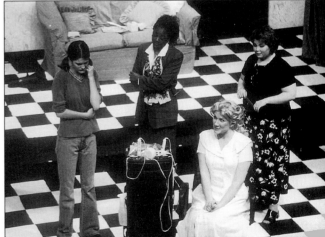

The college's Community Choir is pictured at one of its performances.

Students showcase their talent on stage and behind the lights by presenting a variety of plays and performances in the newly renovated Fine Arts Theatre on Main Campus.

Developing film and printing photographs in the college darkroom occupies much of O'Brien's time during a typical day.

Media Production Assistant Michael O'Brien serves as the college photographer and has shot most of the photographs in the Media Services collection. O'Brien is seen here shooting a picture of Lynn Orsini, supervising secretary in the Illinois Virtual Campus Support Center.

The library also provides students a quiet place to reflect and study.

Joliet Junior College boasts full-service Learning Resource Centers and libraries at its Main and North Campus sites. Although thousands of books and periodicals are available for checkout, other materials and information can also be accessed through interlibrary loan or online. Automated Services Librarian Barbara Wilson is pictured here assisting a student in searching one of JJC's automated data bases for books and articles on a term paper topic.

The Academic Skills Center offers students a variety of services, such as free peer tutoring, general academic assistance, and make-up, Constitution, and placement testing. Tutor Gene McClennahan is seen here providing assistance in American history.

Patrick McGuire, Project Achieve English/Writing Specialist, provides tutoring assistance and encouragement to a student in an English rhetoric class.

Ram Raghuraman, Chair of the Computer Information and Office Systems Department, is seen conducting a class in a computer lab at North Campus.

Edward Senu-Oke engages his political science class in a lively discussion of presidential politics and campaign strategies during the fall 2000 semester.

Dr. Tony Cuvalo is seen here teaching an honors course in the history of western civilization.

Jeanne Legan, who teaches education courses and supervises field experiences, meets with a student between classes.

Joliet Junior College students take classes from early morning until late at night. Flexible scheduling makes it easier for students juggling families and jobs to achieve their educational goals. Sometimes, however, pondering a test question never seems easy, day or night.

JJC nursing students in clinical lab are preparing medication for intramuscular injections. **L-R:** Stephanie Lemonta, Rita McKenzie, Sharon Kusreau, Lisa Hernandez.

Dr. Judy Kachel, Chair of the Nursing Education Department, supervises the administration of medication into the vastus lateralis muscle of pediatric models. **L-R:** Dr. Kachel, Erin Adams, Sharon Kusreau, Stephanie Lemonta, Rita McKenzie.

Students in instructor Ann Smith's anatomy and physiology class study various aspects of the human body by examining a cadaver. The course is designed primarily for students in medical and allied health fields.

Dr. Michael Lee chairs the Natural Sciences/Physical Education Department and also teaches a variety of biology courses. He is seen here working with students in the biology lab.

Cris Trillo instructs a foreign language class in one of the department's computer labs.

Roxanne Munch, English faculty and newly-elected department chair, is pictured here teaching a rhetoric class.

The teaching/learning process does not end when class is dismissed. Child development instructor Barbara Biles is seen here outside her office interacting with a student after class.

The application of technology to instruction has created facilities and staff positions virtually unknown a decade ago. Pictured here are Distance Education staff members in the Illinois Virtual Campus Support Center. **L-R:** Teri Dasbach, IVC Support Center secretary; Rebecca Sailor, Administrative Assistant, Distance Education Office; Lynn Orsini, IVC Support Center supervisory secretary.

JJC offers distance education classes in the interactive TV classroom pictured here. As a member of the South Metropolitan Regional Higher Education Consortium, the college transmits and receives distance education classes that are totally interactive, both audio and visual. Although students at remote sites are not physically present in the room with the instructor, they are able to fully participate in class sessions.

223

The JJC Alumni Association annually hosts a Spring Brunch where recipients of the Distinguished Alumni Achievement Award and the Susan H. Wood Hall of Fame Award are honored. At its most recent brunch in June 2000, Dr. Curtis J. Crawford and Dr. Robert E. Sterling were presented awards. Dr. Crawford, of the class of 1971 is seen here accepting the Distinguished Alumni Achievement Award. He is currently the Chairman, President, and Chief Executive Officer of ZiLOG, Inc. and past division president of Lucent Technologies.

Dr. Robert E. Sterling is pictured at the Alumni Brunch accepting the Susan H. Wood Hall of Fame Award. Sterling taught history at JJC for thirty-three years and chaired the Social and Behavioral Sciences Department for thirty years. He also served as the college's first Director of Distance Education.

JJC President J. D. Ross and Brother James Gaffney, President of Lewis University, are seen signing a dual admission agreement in January 2001. Joliet Junior College has agreements with several four-year institutions that guarantee dually enrolled students admission into the final two years of a B.A. or B.S. program.

Joliet Junior College holds its annual commencement exercises in mid-May. Attending the event are graduates and their families and friends, together with faculty, staff, college trustees, alumni, and other invited guests. Pictured here are horticulture instructor Roger Ross (left) and Dean of North Campus & Community Services Michael Townsend (right) assisting Counseling Department Chair Edward Johnson with his robe and hood prior to the ceremony on May 12, 2000.

Students in their caps and gowns are seen lining up for the processional.

Under the baton of Jerry Lewis, Chair of the Fine Arts Department, the Community Band provides music for the 2000 Commencement.

The stage party at the 2000 commencement included student trustee Rosa Salazar; college trustees Dick Dystrup, Elanor McGuan-Boza, and Robert J. Wunderlich; JJC President J. D. Ross; keynote speaker Dr. Wayne Watson, Chancellor of City Colleges of Chicago; Dr. Denis Wright, Vice President for Academic Services; Rev. Jason Zobel, Pastor of Shepherd of Peace Church, Braidwood; and Richard J. Koefoed, President of JJC Alumni Association.

Keynote speaker Dr. Wayne Watson, Chancellor of the City Colleges of Chicago, challenged graduates to set lofty goals and to reach for their dreams. Dr. Watson reminded those in caps and gowns that he was in their place in 1966 when he graduated from the college. "JJC gave me the foundation I needed," said Watson. "I am where I am today because of that Joliet Junior College foundation."

President J. D. Ross commended graduates for their academic achievement and conferred on them the degrees and certificates they had worked so hard to earn.

Beautiful Centennial Plaza was established to commemorate Joliet Junior College's centennial year, 2001. Students, alumni, faculty, staff, and friends of the college have purchased personalized plaza bricks that pave this historic area on Main Campus.

On February 1, 1987, during National Community College Month, JJC presented Centennial Awards to twenty-six children. The Centennial Scholars, who were all about three years old, received tuition scholarships of up to $1,800 to be used at JJC during the college's centennial celebration in 2001. Twenty-five children were chosen from the various communities in the college district, and one child was selected to represent alumni living outside the district. Pictured here with the pre-collegians are unidentified; Russ Corey, Director of Enrollment Management; Dr. James Lepanto, Vice President for Academic Affairs; Patricia Schneider, college trustee; Grant H. Brown, Jr., grandson of college founder; and unidentified.

One of the Centennial Scholars who is enrolled in JJC during the spring 2001 semester is Jessica Berkey, third from the left in the front row of the group photograph.

Dr. David Pierce, President and CEO, American Association of Community Colleges (retired), is seen congratulating JJC on pioneering the community college movement and reaching its historic centennial anniversary.

On January 13, 2001, Joliet Junior College kicked off its centennial year with a celebration on Main Campus. Dr. Hazel E. Loucks, Illinois Deputy Governor for Education & Workforce, was the keynote speaker for the event. Other special guests who offered remarks were John C. "Jack" McGuire, Illinois State Representative; Mike Sullivan, Immediate Past President, Illinois Community College Trustees Association; Jerry Weller, United States Congressman; Dr. Joe Cipfl, President and CEO, Illinois Community College Board; and Dr. David Pierce, President and CEO, American Association of Community Colleges (retired). Pictured here are Dr. David Pierce, John C. "Jack" McGuire, J. D. Ross (President of Joliet Junior College), Dr. Hazel E. Loucks, Mike Sullivan, and Dr. Joe Cipfl.

Cutting the centennial cake are J. D. Ross, President of Joliet Junior College; Dr. Hazel E. Loucks, Deputy Governor for Education & Workforce; and Eleanor McGuan-Boza, JJC Board of Trustees. Watching with approval and interest are Renee Kosel, Illinois State Representative; John C. "Jack" McGuire, Illinois State Representative; and Dr. Joe Cipfl, President and CEO, Illinois Community College Board.

227

Over the past one hundred years, numerous JJC graduates have made significant contributions to their chosen professions and society at large. Given the limitation of space and the availability of photographs, the people pictured here are merely representative of the many hundreds of graduates worthy of special recognition. The accomplishments of alumni reflect well on an educational institution, and JJC is extremely proud of its students and graduates.

Appearance **Before** Graduation	Achievement **After** Graduation	Appearance **Before** Graduation	Achievement **After** Graduation

James Agazzi, 1960

Art director and production designer for many films and TV programs such as *Hart to Hart, Moonlighting, Family Secrets,* and *Paper Dolls.*

Joan Hollister (Geissler), 1947

Superintendent of Union School District.

Dr. Katherine Dunham, 1928

Internationally known anthropologist, writer, composer, dancer, choreographer, and producer.

Dr. John C. Houbolt, 1938

NASA scientist responsible for conceptualizing and designing the lunar landing module(LEM).

William Glasscock, 1937

Joliet produce farmer and first president of the JJC Board of Trustees.

Dr. David Imig, 1959

Executive Director of the American Association of Colleges for Teacher Education.

Dr. Daniel Gutierrez, 1958

Physician of internal medicine with service as Chief of Staff of Silver Cross Hospital in Joliet and Director of the Will County Community Health Center.

Dr. Barbara Johnson (Smith), 1960

Assistant Professor of Food Science and Human Nutrition at Colorado State University.

Appearance
Before Graduation

Achievement **After** Graduation

Appearance
Before Graduation

Achievement **After** Graduation

NASA aeronautical engineer who designed the Mercury capsule and served as Rockwell International's chief project engineer for the Apollo Program.

Alan Kehlet, 1949

Award-winning author of more than eighty books for children and adults.

Phyllis Reynolds (Naylor), 1953

Professor of Physical Education and Education at the University of Southern California and author of a college textbook and numerous articles.

Dr. Eleanor Metheny, 1926

Illinois State Senator and United States Congressman.

George E. Sangmeister, 1951

Under the screen name Larry Parks starred as Al Jolson in *The Jolson Story*.

Klusman Parks, 1934

International authority on phosphorous chemistry with more than eighty patents and two books on the subject.

Dr. Arthur Toy, 1937

Chief Bankruptcy Judge of the United States Bankruptcy Court of the Northern District of Illinois.

Susan Pierson (Sonderby), 1967

Pioneer in Denver radio broadcasting with a telephone talk show and also a business entrepreneur; his generous donation to the college provided funds for modernizing and enhancing the planetarium, now known as the Herbert Trackman Planetarium.

Herbert Trackman, 1931

Dean of Joliet Junior College from 1947 to 1967 and first JJC President from 1967 to 1970.

Elmer W. Rowley, 1929

Chancellor of City Colleges of Chicago.

Dr. Wayne Watson, 1966

Chapter 1: The Founding and Formative Years, 1893 to 1919

1. The school was known as Joliet High School until 1899, when voters approved the creation of a township high school district. In April 1899, the school became known as Joliet Township High School. Today in 2001, there are two campuses in the high school district: Joliet Central is located in the original building, and Joliet West is located in a newer building on the west side of Joliet at Larkin and Glenwood Avenues.

2. Although he is often referred to as "Doctor" Brown, J. Stanley Brown did not have an earned doctorate. There are also some discrepancies in biographical sources regarding Brown's early years as an educator. The information presented here is taken from the *Genealogical and Biographical Record of Will County* (Chicago: Biographical Publishing Company, 1900), 601-603.

3. For an overview of Joliet's industrial and transportation history, see Robert E. Sterling, *Joliet Transportation and Industry: A Pictorial History* (St. Louis: G. Bradley Publishing, Inc.).

4. *First Report of Joliet Township High School* (Joliet, Ill.: Joliet News Printing Co., 1903), 30.

5. Susan H. Wood, *The People's Legacy: A History of Joliet Junior College from 1901 – 1984* (Joliet, Ill.: Joliet Junior College Foundation, 1987), 19.

6. *First Report of Joliet Township High School*, 30.

7. "Assistant Superintendent C. E. Spicer Taught First College Courses," *Joliet Township High School Bulletin* xi, no. 1 (1931): 7.

8. F. W. Kelsey, letter to J. Stanley Brown, 2 June 1896, quoted in Robert S. Smolich, "An Analysis of Influences Affecting the Origin and Early Development of Three Mid-Western Public Junior Colleges – Joliet, Goshen, and Crane," (Ed.D. diss., The University of Texas at Austin, 1967), 69. The original letter is missing from the files of Joliet Township High School.

9. Joseph H. Drake, letter to "My Dear Mr. Brown," 24 May 1898, quoted in Smolich, 72. The original letter is missing from the files of Joliet Township High School.

10. *First Report of Joliet Township High School*, 30.

11. Elizabeth Barns, audiotape, quoted in Smolich, 76.

12. J. Stanley Brown, "The Growth and Development of Junior Colleges in the United States," *National Conference of Junior Colleges, 1920* (Washington, D.C.: Department of Interior, Bureau of Education, Bulletin No. 19, Part I, 1922), 27.

13. Walter Crosby Eells, *The Junior College* (Cambridge, Mass.: The Riverside Press, 1931), 47.

14. William Rainey Harper, *The Trend in Higher Education* (Chicago: The University of Chicago Press, 1905), 378-79.

15. Henry P. Tappan, *University Education* (New York: G. P. Putnam, 1851), 44-45; William Watts Folwell, *University Addresses* (Minneapolis: H. W. Wilson Co., 1909), 37-38, 108-9.

16. "Minutes of the Board of Affiliation of the Academies and High Schools Affiliating or Co-operating with the University of Chicago," Board of Affiliation, The University of Chicago, 21 January 1899.

17. Dr. Grant Brown, letter to Susan H. Wood, 13 November 1975, quoted in Wood, 18-19.

18. Joseph H. Drake, letter to "My Dear Mr. Brown," 24 May 1898, quoted in Smolich, 71.

19. *First Report of Joliet Township High School*, 14-15.

20. *First Report of Joliet Township High School*, 18-19, 17, 27, 52.

21. *Ibid.*, 18-19, 55, 60, 8.

22. For a discussion of the conflicting views regarding the origin of Joliet Junior College, see Wood, 20-27.

23. Roosevelt Basler, "A Plan for Re-Designing the Curriculum of the Joliet Junior College," (Ed.D. diss., Teachers College, Columbia University, 1945), 20.

24. Monroe Stowe, "Report of a Survey of Junior Colleges of Detroit and Grand Rapids, Michigan, and Joliet, Illinois," *First Annual Meeting of American Association of Junior Colleges, 1921* (Washington: Department of Interior, Bureau of Education, Bulletin 19, Part II, 1922), 65.

25. *First Report of Joliet Township High School*, 30.

26. *Proceedings of the Board of Education*, 4 December 1900, 7 January 1901.

27. J. Stanley Brown, "The Growth and Development of Junior Colleges in the United States," 27.

28. *Proceedings of the Board of Education*, 3 September 1901.

29. *Proceedings of the Board of Education*, 3 September 1902, 3 December 1902.

30. "The High School of the Future," *The School Review* xi (January 1903): 1-3.

31. "The General Conference," *The School Review* xii (January 1904): 20-21.

32. *First Report of Joliet Township High School*, 76.

33. William S. Griffith, "Harper's Legacy to the Public Junior College," *Community College Frontiers* 4 (Spring 1976): 16.

34. Wood, 42.

35. *Ibid.*, 31, 41-43.

36. C. E. Spicer, letter to Lewis W. Smith, 16 January

1941, quoted in Lewis W. Smith, "Founding of Early Junior Colleges – President Harper's Influence," *The Junior College Journal* (May 1941): 518-19.

37. C. E. Spicer, letter to Lewis W. Smith, 19 October 1932, quoted in Roosevelt Basler, 25.

38. *Proceedings of the Board of Education*, 12 November 1912.

39. "The General Conference," 26.

40. "Editorial Notes," *The School Review* xiv (October 1906): 609.

41. I. D. Yaggy, letter to Elbert K. Fretwell, Jr., 5 July 1952, quoted in Elbert K. Fretwell, Jr., *Founding Public Junior Colleges* (New York: Columbia University Press, 1954), 15.

42. J. Stanley Brown, "Present Development of Secondary Schools According to the Proposed Plan," *The School Review* xii (June 1905): 15.

43. "Administration of the Junior College," *Joliet Township High School Bulletin* xi, no. 1 (March 1931): 7.

44. Thomas M. Deam, "Evolution of the Joliet Junior College," *The Junior College Journal* i (April 1931): 430.

45. "The Early Post-graduate School – A Junior College in Everything but Name," *Joliet Township High School Bulletin* xi, no. 1 (March 1931): 8.

46. *Jollier* (1907), 118-19.

47. *The J* (January 1917), 16.

48. *The J* (October 1916), 17.

49. *The J* (October 1916), 21.

50. *Proceedings of the Board of Education*, 21 April 1915; *The J* (October 1918), 28.

51. *Proceedings of the Board of Education*, 21 July 1916.

52. "Joliet Junior College," *Joliet Township High School Bulletin* xi, no. 1 (March 1931): 1.

53. "History of Teacher Training," *Joliet Township High School Bulletin* xi, no. 1 (March 1931): 2.

54. *The J* (October 1918), 28.

55. *Joliet Evening Herald-News*, 11 May 1919, 15 May 1919.

56. *Proceedings of the Board of Education*, 20 May 1919.

57. For a history of J. Stanley Brown's years at Northern Illinois Normal School, see Earl W. Hayter, *Education in Transition: The History of Northern Illinois University* (DeKalb, Ill.: Northern Illinois University Press, 1974), 181-208.

58. Wood, 81-82.

Chapter 2: Establishing a College Identity, 1919 to 1939

1. Susan H. Wood, *The People's Legacy: A History of Joliet Junior College from 1901 – 1984* (Joliet, Ill.: Joliet Junior College Foundation, 1987), 48.

2. *Ibid.*, 48-49.

3. *Joliet Junior College Bulletin, 1920*, 17-20.

4. *Joliet Township High School Bulletin* iii, no. 1 (November 1922): 5.

5. *Ibid.* i, no.1 (April 1921): 3; *Ibid.* viii, no. 2 (June 1928): 7; *Ibid.* iii, no.1 (November 1922): 5.

6. *The J* (May 1918), 27; *The J* (October 1918), 28.

7. *Joliet Junior College Bulletin, 1922*, 14.

8. *Joliet Township High School Bulletin* xi, no.1 (March 1931): 7.

9. *Ibid.*, 4.

10. Walter Crosby Eells, *The Junior College* (Cambridge, Mass.: The Riverside Press, 1931), 192.

11. *Joliet Township High School Bulletin* xi, no.1 (March 1931): 4-5.

12. *Ibid.* viii, no. 2 (June 1928): 6.

13. *Ibid.* viii, no. 1 (November 1927): 7.

14. *Ibid.* ii, no.1 (March 1922): 2.

15. *Ibid.*, 6.

16. *Proceedings of the Board of Education*, 15 November 1926.

17. *Joliet Township High School Bulletin* i, no. 1 (April 1921): 7.

18. *Joliet Township High School Year Book*, 1921, 79.

19. Report of the Executive Committee of the Student Council of Joliet Junior College, 1936-1937.

20. Minutes of Joliet Junior College Student Council, 4 March 1937.

21. *Joliet Township High School Bulletin* xi, no. 1 (March 1931): 8.

22. Wood, 57-58.

23. *Ibid.*, 60.

24. *Joliet Township High School Bulletin* xi, no. 1 (March 1931): 7.

25. *Ibid.*, 1.

26. Wood, 61-62.

27. *Ibid.*, 62-68.

28. *The Blazer*, 5 February 1932.

29. *Proceedings of the Board of Education*, 8 February 1932; *Ibid.*, 15 July 1933; Wood, 69.

30. *The Blazer*, 3 September 1932.

31. Wood, 69-70.

32. *The J* (1931), 168.

33. Wood, 74-75.

34. *Ibid.*, 76.

35. Robert Palinchak, *The Evolution of the Community College* (Metuchen, N.J.: The

Scarecrow Press, Inc., 1973), 88.

36. Wood, 77-79.
37. *Ibid.*, 80.
38. *Herald-News*, 9 June 1939, p. 1.

Chapter 3: Years of Challenge and Change, 1939 to 1967

1. *Proceedings of the Board of Education*, 21 August 1939.
2. *Ibid.*, 10 February 1942; 23 June 1942; 11 January 1943; 10 February 1943; 30 March 1943.
3. *Ibid.*, 26 February 1946; 22 May 1946; 12 June 1947; 30 July 1947.
4. *Ibid.*, 14 June 1960.
5. *Ibid.*, 11 March 1941.
6. *Ibid.*, 14 April 1942; 22 June 1943.
7. *Ibid.*, 27 August 1946; 8 October 1946.
8. *Ibid.*, 9 April 1946; 11 July 1946; John W. Gardner, *Excellence* (New York: Harper and Row, 1961), 86.
9. President's Commission on Higher Education, *Higher Education for American Democracy*, vol. 1, *Establishing the Goals* (New York: Harper Bros., 1947), 39, 67-69.
10. *The J.C. 1933* (college yearbook published internally), dedication page.
11. *Proceedings of the Board of Education*, 11 March 1947; 25 February 1947; 18 December 1947; 13 January 1948; 11 July 1944.
12. Susan H. Wood, *The People's Legacy: A History of Joliet Junior College from 1901 – 1984* (Joliet, Ill.: Joliet Junior College Foundation, 1987), 123-24.
13. *Proceedings of the Board of Education*, 9 January 1951; 10 February 1953; 13 October 1953; 13 December 1955.
14. *Ibid.*, 11 May 1943.
15. Coleman R. Griffith and Hortense Blackstone, *The Junior College in Illinois* (Urbana, Ill.: A Joint Publication of the Superintendent of Public Instruction of the State of Illinois and the University of Illinois Press, 1945), 244-47.
16. Wood, 109.
17. For a full discussion of the legislative history surrounding the junior college movement in Illinois, see Thomas Lewis Hardin, "A History of the Community Junior College in Illinois: 1901-1972," (Ph.D. diss., University of Illinois at Urbana-Champaign, 1975), 87-231; Gerald W. Smith, *Illinois Junior-Community College Development 1946-1980*, (Springfield, Ill.: Illinois Community College Board, 1980).
18. *Proceedings of the Board of Education*, 13 September 1955; 11 December 1956.
19. *Ibid.*, 14 October 1959; 15 December 1959.
20. *Ibid.*, 6 June 1961; 10 October 1961; 12 December 1961; 11 June 1963.

21. *Ibid.*, 28 August 1964; 6 October 1964.
22. *Ibid.*, 24 November 1964; 8 December 1964;10 August 1965.
23. *Ibid.*, 17 June 1965; 10 August 1965; 17 August 1965; 14 September 1965; 12 October 1965.
24. *Ibid.*, 20 September 1966.
25. *Ibid.*, 16 January 1939; 28 January 1947.
26. *Ibid.*, 12 April 1966; 10 May 1966; 25 May 1966; 14 June 1966; 11 October 1966; 24 January 1967; 21 February 1967.
27. Smith, 86-92.
28. *Proceedings of the Board of Education*, 12 October 1965; 14 December 1965; 19 April 1966; 10 November 1966; Wood, 113-18.
29. *Proceedings of the Board of Education*, 13 December 1966; 21 February 1967.
30. *The J. C. 1943* (college yearbook published internally), dedication page; *The 1949 Shield* (college yearbook published internally), 4.
31. Wood, 88-91, 99-100.
32. *The J. C. 1942* (college yearbook published internally), 69.
33. *Proceedings of the Board of Education*, 7 January 1942; *The J. C. 1942*, 71.
34. *The Blazer*, 16 October 1947.
35. *The Blazer*, 9 October 1959; 25 May 1964.
36. *The Blazer*, 7 March 1947; 10 April 1959.
37. *The Blazer*, 18 March 1960; 16 February 1962.
38. *The Blazer*, 15 November 1961; 16 February 1962.
39. *The Blazer*, 7 November 1952; 10 March 1953.
40. *The Blazer*, 25 February 1955; 26 May 1955.
41. *The Blazer*, 3 June 1967; 21 March 1958.
42. *The 1964 Shield* (college yearbook published internally), 29.
43. *The Blazer*, 19 November 1948.
44. *The Blazer*, 8 October 1948.
45. *The Blazer*, 16 February 1962.
46. *The Blazer*, 9 March 1966; 16 February 1962; 28 April 1967.
47. *The Blazer*, 14 November 1947.
48. *The Blazer*, 28 April 1967.
49. Louise H. Allen, "Fizz Wills of Joliet," *Community College Frontiers*, vol. 4, no. 3 (Spring 1976): 26-30.
50. *The Blazer*, 15 January 1960; 19 December 1958.
51. *Proceedings of the Board of Education*, 5 December 1938; 17 June 1940; 4 December 1945.
52. *Ibid.*, 16 January 1939; 9 March 1948.
53. *Ibid.*, 18 May 1953; 16 June 1958; 13 April 1948.
54. *Ibid.*, 23 January 1961; 20 February 1962; 14 September 1966; 13 March 1962.
55. *Ibid.*, 12 March 1963.
56. *Ibid.*, 12 April 1966; 10 May 1966; 25 May 1966; 14 June 1966.
57. *Ibid.*, 11 October 1966.
58. *Ibid.*, 24 January 1967; 21 February 1967; 11 April 1967.

Chapter 4: A New Home on Houbolt Road, 1967 to 2000

1. *Herald-News*, 25 March 1967; 16 April 1967.
2. Proceedings, District 525, *Minutes*, 12 June 1967; 10 July 1967; 14 August 1967.
3. For correspondence between President John Corradetti, AFT Local 604, JJC Council and College President Elmer W. Rowley regarding union recognition, see the correspondence files of the union. A few letters were also exchanged between the Union President and the Board of Trustees. For the formal action taken by the Board of Trustees, see Proceedings, *Minutes*, 29 April 1968.
4. Susan H. Wood, *The People's Legacy: A History of Joliet Junior College from 1901 – 1984* (Joliet, Ill.: Joliet Junior College Foundation, 1987), 144-45.
5. Proceedings, *Minutes*, 6 February 1968.
6. *Herald-News*, 31 March 1968; Proceedings, *Minutes*, 8 April 1968.
7. Proceedings, *Minutes*, 3 April 1968; *Herald-News*, 4 April 1968.
8. Proceedings, *Minutes*, 14 April 1969.
9. *Herald-News*, 25 July 1969.
10. *Ibid.*
11. *Ibid.*, 27 July 1969.
12. *Ibid.*, 6 August 1969; Proceedings, *Minutes*, 19 August 1969.
13. *Herald-News*, 23 September 1969, 28 September 1969.
14. Elmer W. Rowley, *The President's Report, 1969-1970.*
15. *Herald-News*, 19 September 1969.
16. *The Blazer*, 13 December 1993; *Herald-News*, 6 June 1994.
17. Wood, 157-59.
18. *Ibid.*, 161-62.
19. *Herald-News*, 16 November 1970; 28 January 1972; 22 October 1972; 13 August 1973; *The Blazer*, 28 January 1974; *Herald-News*, 18 August 1974.
20. Wood, 164-65.
21. *Ibid.*, 172-73.
22. *The Blazer*, 12 September 1975; 9 May 1980; 12 May 1992.
23. Wood, 185-86.
24. *Ibid.*, 188-90.
25. *Ibid.*, 174.
26. *Herald-News*, 19 April 1980; *The Blazer*, 11 September 1981; 30 October 1981.
27. *The Blazer*, 3 October 1994; 13 October 1999.
28. *Joliet Junior College 2000-2002 Student Handbook & Weekly Planner*, 31-36.
29. *The Blazer*, 16 October 1970.
30. *Alumni Action*, Fall 1977.
31. *Ibid.*
32. *The Blazer*, 19 October 1979.
33. *Herald-News*, 19 September 1969.
34. *Ibid.*
35. *Herald-News*, 14 March 1972.
36. *Ibid.*, 17 March 1972.
37. *The Blazer*, 12 March 1973; 26 February 1973.
38. *Ibid.*, 25 August 1978; 6 October 1978.
39. *Ibid.*, 4 May 1979; 13 December 1993.
40. *Herald-News*, 9 March 1974.

Chapter 5: Picture Us Now

1. Student data provided by JJC Admissions Office.
2. *Ibid.*
3. *The Blazer*, 6 December 2000.

Acknowledgements

Although an author alone is ultimately responsible for the substance and quality of his work, no one can write a book of this kind without the generous assistance of countless people. Attempting to acknowledge them in no way diminishes the contributions of those whose names have been inadvertently omitted. I am most grateful to my wife, Jo Ann, for once again sharing the journey of developing a book. Her encouragement, patience, suggestions, and proofreading skills were a blessing beyond measure. I am also deeply indebted to Patrick Asher, Patrick McGuire, Angela and Walter Zaida, Sharon Peck, and JJC President J. D. Ross for reading the manuscript and offering invaluable comments and suggestions. Without their generous assistance and attention to detail, the book would have many more rough edges. A special note of thanks goes to Rebecca Sailor for interviewing people and for gathering and organizing information. Her enthusiasm for the project, especially in the early months, was a great source of encouragement.

Special appreciation goes to the following people who contributed in other important ways: Cindy Jacobsen for writing caption material for chapter five; Dave Parker for providing photographs and caption material for sports; Teri Dasbach and Lynn Orsini for working on the index; Barbara Wilson for locating library material; Michael Mahoney for contributing several photographs to chapter one; and Liz Allen and Michael O'Brien for shooting pictures for chapter five.

Many other people and organizations provided photographs and information, and I am extremely grateful for their assistance. They include Frank Alberico, Virginia Allen, Gerald Anderson, Gil Bell, Darlene Boyle, David Cattron, Ted and Erma Chuk, Jo Cirrencione, Dr. James Clark, John Corradetti, Dorothy Crombie, Teri Cullen, Donald Ernst, Dr. James Ethridge, Mrs. William Glasscock, Shirley Hacker, Joan Hinch, Dale Hummel, Sunnie Hunter, Albert Imming, Johnnie Johnson, William Johnson, Joliet Area Historical Society, the *Herald-News*, the Jenkins family, Robert Jurgens, Dr. Judy Kachel, Wayne King, Matt Kochevar, Charles Kramer, Max Kuster, Sandy Lauer, Robert Marcink, Michael McGreal, James Morris, John Mraz, Janet Novotny, Linda Padilla, Dr. John Peterson, Virginia Piekarski, Henry Pillard, Linda Pollock, Virginia Richards, James Ridings, Richard Rivera, Willa Schroeder, Betty Schuck, Mary Schulte, James Shinn, Grady Shipp, Patricia Shue, Denise Sitar, Joyce Stejskal, Ray Strappazon, Joan Tierney, Tim Vanderwall, Don Walker, Arlene Walsh, Paul Washam, William Yarrow, and Emily Zabrocki.

Finally, heartfelt gratitude is extended to my mother, Dorothy; my son, Geoff; and my daughter-in-law, Kristina, for their encouraging and thoughtful phone calls. The answer is finally "yes" to their frequently asked question, "Is the book done yet?" It's done, and I'm pleased to acknowledge the assistance and support of those mentioned here and to express my warm appreciation. Thanks.

Bibliography

Allen, Louise H. "Fizz Wills of Joliet." *Community College Frontiers* iv (Spring 1976).

Alumni Action.

Basler, Roosevelt. "A Plan for Re-Designing the Curriculum of the Joliet Junior College." Ed.D. diss., Columbia University, 1945.

Brown, J. Stanley. "Present Development of Secondary Schools According to the Proposed Plan." *The School Review* xii (June 1905).

Deam, Thomas M. "Evolution of the Joliet Junior College." *The Junior College Journal* i (April 1931).

"Editorial Notes." *The School Review* xiv (October 1906).

Eells, Walter Crosby. *The Junior College.* Cambridge, Mass.: The Riverside Press, 1931.

First Report of Joliet Township High School. Joliet, Ill.: Joliet News Printing Co., 1903.

Folwell, William Watts. *University Addresses.* Minneapolis: H. W. Wilson Co., 1909.

Fretwell, Elbert K. Jr. *Founding Public Junior Colleges.* New York: Columbia University Press, 1954.

Genealogical and Biographical Record of Will County. Chicago: Biographical Publishing Company, 1900.

Griffith, Coleman R., and Hortense Blackstone. *The Junior College in Illinois.* Urbana, Ill.: A Joint Publication of the Superintendent of Public Instruction of the State of Illinois and the University of Illinois Press, 1945.

Griffith, William S. "Harper's Legacy to the Public Junior College " *Community College Frontiers* 4 (1976).

Hardin, Thomas Lewis. "A History of the Community Junior College in Illinois." Ph.D. diss., University of Illinois at Urbana-Champaign, 1975.

Harper, William Rainey. *The Trend in Higher Education.* Chicago: University of Chicago Press, 1905.

Hayter, Earl W. *Education in Transition: The History of Northern Illinois University.* DeKalb, Ill.: Northern Illinois University Press, 1974.

Joliet *Herald-News.*

Joliet Junior College Bulletin.

Joliet Junior College 2000-2002 Student Handbook & Weekly Planner.

Joliet Township High School Bulletin.

Jollier.

Minutes of the Board of Affiliation of the Academies and High Schools Affiliating or Co-operating with the University of Chicago. *Board of Affiliation.* University of Chicago, 1899.

National Conference of Junior Colleges, 1920. Washington, D.C.: Department of Interior, Bureau of Education, Bulletin No. 19.

Palinchak, Robert. *The Evolution of the Community College.* Metuchen, N.J.: The Scarecrow Press, Inc., 1973.

President's Commission on Higher Education. *Higher Education for American Democracy.* New York: Harper Bros., 1947.

Proceedings, District 525. *Minutes.*

Proceedings of the Board of Education, District 204.

Rowley, Elmer W. *The President's Report, 1969-1970.*

Smith, Gerald W. *Illinois Junior-Community College Development 1946-1980.* Springfield, Ill.: Illinois Community College Board, 1980.

Smith, Lewis W. "Founding of Early Junior Colleges – President Harper's Influence." *The Junior College Journal* (May 1941).

Smolich, Robert S. "An Analysis of Influences Affecting the Origin and Early Development of Three Mid-Western Public Junior Colleges – Joliet, Goshen, and Crane." Ed.D. diss., University of Texas at Austin, 1967.

Sterling, Robert E. *Joliet Transportation & Industry: A Pictorial History.* St. Louis: G. Bradley Publishing, Inc., 1997.

Stowe, Monroe. "Report of a Survey of Junior Colleges of Detroit and Grand Rapids, Michigan, and Joliet, Illinois." *First Annual Meeting of the American Association of Junior Colleges, 1921.* Washington, D.C.: Department of Interior, Bureau of Education, Bulletin 19, 1922.

Tappan, Henry P. *University Education.* New York: G. P. Putnam, 1851.

The Blazer.

"The General Conference." *The School Review* xii (January 1904).

"The High School of the Future." *The School Review* xi (January 1903).

The J.

The J.C.

Wood, Susan H. *The People's Legacy: A History of Joliet Junior College from 1901-1984.* Joliet, Ill.: Joliet Junior College Foundation, 1987.

Index